SHAKESPEARE'S PUBLIC

Queen Elizabeth I, the inspiration of at least one play. This carved and painted head was probably made in 1603 for the effigy carried on the Queen's coffin at her funeral. (The wig, ruff and collar are modern reconstructions, but the jewels in the hair and ears are actual Elizabethan specimens from the Cheapside Hoard.)

Shakespeare's Public

THE TOUCHSTONE OF HIS GENIUS

MARTIN HOLMES

John Murray

50 ALBEMARLE STREET

LONDON

© *Martin Holmes 1960*

Made and printed in Great Britain by
William Clowes and Sons, Limited, London and Beccles
and published by John Murray (Publishers) Ltd.

To the memory of my Mother
who first showed me
that people could read Shakespeare
for the pleasure of it

Contents

Illustrations

Queen Elizabeth I. This carved and painted head was probably made in 1603 for the effigy carried on the Queen's coffin at her funeral. (The wig, ruff and collar are modern reconstructions, but the jewels in the hair and ears are actual Elizabethan specimens from the Cheapside Hoard.) (By courtesy of the London Museum.) *Frontispiece*

Preface

THIS IS a book for Shakespearean playgoers of to-day, about Shakespearean playgoers of the poet's own time. Some of it is hard fact, some is necessarily conjecture, and I have tried to indicate, wherever possible, which is which, as an ounce of certainty is worth a hundredweight of suggestion. But a certain amount of suggestion is based on evidence, and the contemporary evidence, when available, is to be found in the various authorities cited in the text. The interested reader will find much that is relevant, and still more that is enjoyable, in all of them, but is particularly commended to the introductions to the First Folio edition of the plays and the special quarto edition of *Troilus and Cressida* (see *Appendixes*), for here Shakespeare's publishers are writing direct to Shakespeare's public, and it is interesting to see how much they have to tell us.

Turning to modern Shakespearean scholarship, I must at once express my indebtedness to the works of Dr John Masefield, Dr G. B. Harrison (whose conclusions I have generally followed in regard to the chronological order of the plays) and the late Sir Edmund Chambers, and even more emphatically to the personal kindness and encouragement of many Shakespearean scholars, actors and critics over many years. To name but a few, I would first thank Dr Harrison for inspiring this book by his approval of the general theme when it was tentatively put forward in a lecture to the London Society some twenty years ago. Since then, I have had cause to be deeply grateful for the helpful and illuminating conversation and publications of such authorities as Miss Dorothy Margaret Stuart, Miss Muriel St Clare Byrne, Mr Otto Sallmann, Mr Tom Heslewood, Mr George Skillan, Mr W. A. Darlington and Mr J. C. Trewin, and must at once express my gratitude to

xi

them for all the pleasure and information they have given me and exonerate them from responsibility for anything of which they may disapprove.

MARTIN HOLMES

Kensington, September 1959

APPROXIMATE ORDER OF THE PLAYS

and the suggested place of their production

HENRY VI, PART I	*1592*	Rose

TITUS ANDRONICUS		Rose
HENRY VI, PARTS II AND III		Theatre
RICHARD III		Theatre
LOVE'S LABOUR'S LOST	*all before 1594*	Private
THE TWO GENTLEMEN OF VERONA		Theatre
THE COMEDY OF ERRORS		Grays Inn
THE TAMING OF THE SHREW		Theatre

ROMEO AND JULIET		Theatre
A MIDSUMMER NIGHT'S DREAM		Private
RICHARD II	*between 1594 and 1597*	Theatre
KING JOHN		Theatre
THE MERCHANT OF VENICE		Theatre

HENRY IV, PARTS I AND II		Curtain
HENRY V		Curtain
MUCH ADO ABOUT NOTHING		Curtain
THE MERRY WIVES OF WINDSOR		Windsor
AS YOU LIKE IT		Globe
JULIUS CAESAR	*between 1597 and 1603*	Globe
TROILUS AND CRESSIDA		Blackfriars
HAMLET		Blackfriars
TWELFTH NIGHT		Globe
OTHELLO		Court (Westminster)

DEATH OF ELIZABETH I

MEASURE FOR MEASURE		Globe
ALL'S WELL THAT ENDS WELL		Globe
KING LEAR		Blackfriars
TIMON OF ATHENS	*between 1603 and 1608*	Globe
MACBETH		Globe
ANTONY AND CLEOPATRA		Globe
CORIOLANUS		Globe

PERICLES		Globe
CYMBELINE		Blackfriars
THE WINTER'S TALE	*all after 1608*	Globe
THE TEMPEST		Blackfriars

HENRY VIII	*1613*	Globe

Globe Theatre burned down during the performance

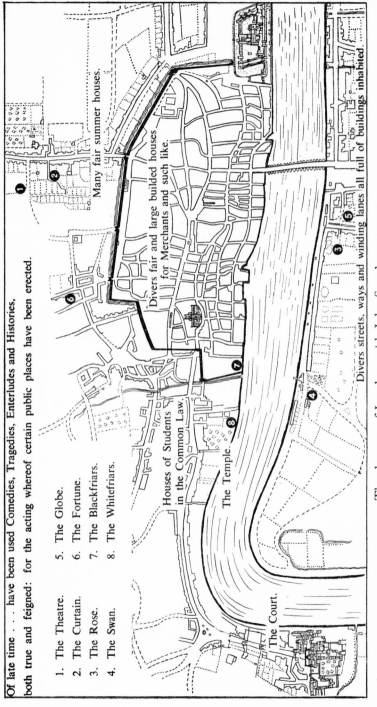

Of late time . . . have been used Comedies, Tragedies, Enterludes and Histories, both true and feigned: for the acting whereof certain public places have been erected.

1. The Theatre. 5. The Globe.
2. The Curtain. 6. The Fortune.
3. The Rose. 7. The Blackfriars.
4. The Swan. 8. The Whitefriars.

Many fair summer houses.

Divers fair and large builded houses for Merchants and such like.

Houses of Students in the Common Law.

The Temple.

The Court.

Divers streets, ways and winding lanes all full of buildings inhabited.

The theatres of London, with John Stow's comments on the districts in which they stood.

At the Rose

THE PLAYS of Shakespeare that have come down to us cover a stretch of roughly twenty years, but in that particular period, between 1592 and 1612, changes took place in London that signally affected the world of the theatre as they affected so much else. Some of the changes were social, some topographical, one was dynastic and all of them had their effect on the public that came to the theatre to be entertained, and consequently on the entertainment provided for that public. The fact that Shakespeare was writing masterpieces of English literature is something secondary to his main intention; from the outset of his literary career he seems to have been a stout pillar of that much-decried institution the Commercial Theatre, making it his business to provide his regular theatre-public—and anyone else who could be induced to come—with entertainment of a sort likely to make them come again.

The two main theatrical districts were Moorfields and Bank-side. Both lay outside the City boundaries, and consequently outside the jurisdiction of the City authorities (who disliked and discouraged public stage-performances inside London and hampered them to the best of their ability with troublesome restrictions), but they were not too far away to be easily accessible to the pleasure-seeking Londoner of the neighbourhood. Moorfields and Finsbury had the older theatrical tradition; plays had been performed by the parish-clerks of London at Clerkenwell and the Skinners' Well in the Middle Ages, and James Burbage had built the Theatre in the grounds of the dissolved Priory of Holywell somewhat further to the east of it, outside the postern of Moorgate, where the ground was still open and unbuilt-on because of its marshy quality. On the South Bank, on the other hand, bulls and bears had been baited since the establishment of Paris Garden in 1526, and the neighbourhood was notorious in addition for its taverns and for what Henry Chettle in 1592 roundly called 'dark dennes for adulterers, theeves, murderers, and every mischief worker'. There must have been a wide difference between the audiences of the two districts, and it is possible to trace a corresponding difference in the fare provided for them. Broadly speaking, the Theatre and the Curtain must always have had the more scholarly traditions, and would draw their audience, as we shall see, largely from the well-to-do merchant class, with a seasoning of young gentlemen from the Inns of Court, while the public south of the river was used to noise, bloodshed and excitement without much in the way of subtlety.

The theatres in both districts were of the same type architecturally, like the bull-ring and bear-garden from which they took their form. Tiers of covered galleries surrounded a central space open to the sky. The stage itself jutted out into this like a scaffold, and the part of the building immediately behind it was given up to the actors' dressing-rooms, property rooms and so on. A roof covered part of the stage, being supported in front by two pillars, and there was a gallery at the back that could be used for balconies, windows or as an upper stage when required. The whole building was capable of holding an audience of two or three thousand, standing in the central space at a penny a head, or sitting at a higher admission-fee in one or other of the covered galleries. The players themselves avoided the charge of being rogues and 'masterless men' by obtaining a licence from some person of importance, so that they were officially reckoned as members of his household. Their patron had no share in the theatre or in the takings, and correspondingly he paid them no wages, but they might be engaged on occasion to entertain him or his guests (for which they would be paid) and while they held his licence he was responsible to the authorities for their good behaviour and available for their support if they were wronged. Pettifogging officials and miscellaneous bullies would think twice before offending people who had the right to wear some great lord's livery, but players without a patron would have been fair game.

The first company that we can connect with Shakespeare was known as the Lord Strange's Men, and we know a certain amount about it from the diary and papers of Philip Henslowe, now preserved at Dulwich College. As Sir Walter Greg has shown in his valuable edition of the Diary, Henslowe himself was not primarily a man of the theatre. He was a dyer and moneylender who married his master's widow, bought property in South London, put money into theatres and plays as a commercial speculation and arranged a marriage for his stepdaughter with his leading tragedian, Edward Alleyn. His papers accordingly give us a valuable insight into the box-office side of the stage life of his day and show, as nothing else does, the tremendous number of plays in the repertory of the Lord Strange's Men and the very widely varying attraction they had for the public.

First in the list appears a play that has come down to us, Greene's *Friar Bacon and Friar Bungay*. It is a curious combination of pseudo-historical romance, magic and buffoonery, and we see that on Saturday the nineteenth of February 1591|2 it 'took' seventeen shillings and threepence. This is not a very high figure, particularly for a Saturday, but the takings for the next night rise to twenty-nine shillings for a mysterious 'mulomurco', which is one of a variety of spellings for 'Muly Mollocco' and has been conjecturally identified with Peele's play *The Battle of Alcazar*. After that come three lean nights, *Orlando*, *The Spanish Comedy of Don Horatio* and *Sir John Mandeville*, the last of which brings in only twelve and sixpence, and things pick up towards the end of the week with *Harry of Cornwall*—whoever he may have been—and two pounds ten for Marlowe's *Jew of Malta* on the Saturday. Here, as often in Marlowe, magnificence of poetic declamation and prodigality in the matter of bloodshed are of greater account than serious character-drawing or dramatic construction. The story is clearly told, crime succeeding crime in scenes of combined crudity and verbal splendour, till at last the wicked Jew, having caused the death of most of the other characters and betrayed Malta to the Turks, falls through an oubliette of his own contriving into a boiling cauldron, which does not prevent him from ending with a speech of fierce vituperation against Christians and Moslems alike. This play was a popular favourite and seems to have been kept continuously in the repertory. It was generally good for forty or fifty shillings, and seldom took less than thirty-five, so it is a useful indication of popular taste.

But in the next week, on Friday the third of March, appeared a play that surpassed it as a popular money-maker. It was called *Harry the Sixth*, and the takings that night amounted to three pounds sixteen and eightpence, the highest amount ever recorded in the diary for a single performance. It was repeated in four days' time, and again on the Saturday in the same week, and still drew good money, though not on quite such a scale. The Lord Strange's Men, and Mr Henslowe the manager, had found a box-office success.

Looking at the text of the *First Part of King Henry VI*—to give it the title it now bears—we may conjecture what were the particular qualities that endeared it to the audience of its day and location. It begins with a funeral procession and some sonorous and extravagant declamation in the manner of Marlowe, it shows fighting and quarrelling abroad and at home, it has at least two striking and noisy stage effects, and though like a good many others in the repertory it has no very coherent plot and no respect whatever for chronology, its qualities would make it exciting, in a succession of ways, to the contemporary Bankside mind.

At the outset that excitement is aroused by the purple patches at the funeral of Henry V. Soon the character of Talbot appears, to form the centre of several rousing episodes, some of them taken from history-books, others more probably from legend or imagination. The death of Salisbury when his observation-post in the suburbs of Orleans is shattered by the French cannon, the denunciation and degradation of Sir John Fastolfe for cowardice, the mysterious rise, career and downfall of the Maid of Orleans and the meeting and last fight of Talbot and his son are all expressively described in the works of Hall or Holinshed, and in their dramatic form follow very closely these historians' description. The scene where Talbot is nearly trapped by the Countess of Auvergne but calls his artillery to break down her gates at the sound of a horn is not traceable to history at all, but has its origin rather in the realms of knightly romance, and the famous scene of the plucking of the red and white roses in the Temple Gardens would appear to be based on oral tradition alone, if it is not a brilliant product of the author's imagination.

Of the various Elizabethan chroniclers, Edward Hall and Raphael Holinshed are outstanding for general readability and popularity. Where others such as Lanquet and Cooper had tried to give the history of the known world year by year from the time of the Creation, Hall concentrated on the period beginning with the rise of the House of Lancaster, and Holinshed, though covering a wider period of time, restricted his subject to the history of the British Isles. As a result, both writers were able to tell a story instead of compiling a summary of miscellaneous events, and in their pages we find a vast number of episodes that were well worth transferring to the stage. At the same time, in this particular play they are transferred haphazard as a collection of good scenes, without reference to their supposed historical order of occurrence. All that appeals to author and audience is theatrical effect. Nobody is expected to be critical, and as far as history is concerned the impression is that the audience did not know, and the author did not care, how widely the play departed from the ordinary record of events.

Turning again for a few moments to Henslowe's list of plays we may note one or two others of some significance. The 'Tragedy of the Guise' is the play by Marlowe better known as *The Massacre at Paris*, under which name it appears in later entries, and 'Jeronimo' is Kyd's *Spanish Tragedy*, a bloodthirsty tale of murder and revenge which had long been an immensely popular entertainment. Certain lines in it, notably Jeronimo's 'What outcries pluck me from my naked bed', are quoted, misquoted and parodied by Shakespeare and others to a degree that suggests they had become catch-phrases, even as was to happen to so many phrases of Shakespeare's in their turn.

Kyd, Peele, Greene and Marlowe, then, were among the authors most frequently played at the Rose, so it is quite natural that Shakespeare's first recorded play should have been a glorious hotch-potch of the styles of all of them—so much so, indeed, that many scholars have tried to assign different scenes in it to one or other of these authors. But there is no need to disintegrate it to that degree. The new author—presumably an actor here, as he certainly was later—had simply studied the normal theatre-going public, observed its likes and dislikes and set himself to provide it with the sort of fare he knew it would enjoy, and in so doing he naturally annoyed the normal purveyors of such material. Robert Greene's well-known diatribe against 'an upstart crow beautified with our feathers' has been taken as an indication that the author of the three parts of *King Henry VI* had actually appropriated lines written by Greene and his colleagues and passed them off as his own, but there is no need to stretch the metaphor so far. Aesop's crow borrowed odd feathers from a variety of other birds and appeared in a motley combination of all of them, and that is just what the upstart author is doing with his commercial success written now in the style of one best-seller, now of another. Paying no author the sincere flattery of consistent imitation, he uses the idiom of any that seems good to him, thereby proclaiming himself the imitator of all men and the disciple of none.

To a disappointed scholar, poor and on his death-bed, this combination of facility and success would be particularly galling, and would only too naturally inspire the very charges we find here, the scornful 'Johannes factotum', the parody of a pompous line from one of the successful plays (implying that the author's fault was writing his own bad lines, not borrowing other men's good ones) and the presumption that the new arrival must imagine himself as good as all his predecessors put together, and in fact 'the only Shake-scene in a country'. The charges were

6

unjust, and Henry Chettle, who had published them when acting in some sort as Greene's literary executor, subsequently admitted as much, so there is no need to consider the success of the play quite undeserved, or to compare it—necessarily to its dis-advantage—with the work Shakespeare wrote at a later period for other and more critical audiences. *The First Part of King Henry VI* may be considered very immature Shakespearean drama nowadays, but it was a typical and appropriate production for its time, for it was not only Shakespeare's style but the audience's taste that improved and developed in the course of the next twenty years.

The next identifiable Shakespeare play in Henslowe's repertory was an advance on *Henry VI* to the extent of possessing a plot. *Titus Andronicus* was no mere collection of odd dramatic scenes out of a history-book; it had a story to tell, and a glance at that story and its treatment may help us to see yet more clearly the audience for whose entertainment it was written. Once again the other plays in the repertory give us a clue. Mention has been made of Kyd's notoriously popular melodrama *The Spanish Tragedy*. Its theme is the persecution, near-madness and revenge of a deeply-wronged old man, and this theme, obviously successful in Kyd's play, has been 'lifted' bodily by the new author and served up in a different setting, with garnishings of Imperial Rome, a wicked blackamoor, a lascivious and beautiful barbarian queen and a wealth of lust, rape, murder, mutilation, adultery, canni-balism and revenge, largely taken out of Ovid, with blood in more generous allowance than Marlowe himself had given the public in *The Jew of Malta* or *The Massacre at Paris*.

To Mr Henslowe the play must have offered a story that had drawn good money before in another guise, and a part in which the great Mr Alleyn could be seen to good advantage. (Incident-ally, as we shall see, it may have given him the chance to make use of a piece of stage machinery constructed originally for *The Jew of Malta* but well worth using elsewhere whenever possible, like the pump and tubs of Mr Vincent Crummles.) To Alleyn himself it gave opportunities for declamation in the grand manner with the full sympathy of the audience. Shakespeare knew very well what a star tragedian could do with a part that suited him, even in those days. 'That will ask some tears in the true performing of it; if I do it, let the audience look to their eyes; I will move storms', says Bottom as he contemplates the opportunities of Pyramus. Even so may Alleyn have murmured appreciatively as he saw himself 'shaken with sorrows in ungrateful Rome'.

There remains the audience, on whose approval the success of the play would ultimately depend. An audience that is not dramatically sophisticated requires an appeal to the senses rather than to the intellect. It comes, in the first instance, to see and hear, and to exercise not its judgement but its emotions, and in consequence its interest is concentrated more on the known personalities of the players than on the idiosyncrasies of the characters they represent. Such audiences are by no means extinct to-day. They constitute a very large proportion of the film-going public, and the material devised for them is, in essentials, that provided in the old days on Bankside. The audience goes to see a favourite player, a certain amount of violent action or passion, and a degree of magnificence, or at least grandiosity, before coming out of the theatre into the ordinary world again.

In yet stronger degree can this be realized by anyone who has formed part of a Service audience at an entertainment given to the troops. To enjoy a skilled performance it is not always necessary to comprehend it, the senses themselves are fascinated by the sight and sound of an experienced performer doing something effectively and well, and the emotions come to the surface with unexpected ease. The tendency of military reciters of all ranks to declaim Kipling's 'Gunga Din' has been a matter for literary humour more than once in the past, but in practice the emotional effect of the poem when declaimed in the appropriate context, by a soldier to an audience of soldiers in the course of a highly-varied entertainment, can be overwhelming and apparently universal. Something of the same effect is gained by popular and sensational 'dramatic monologues' from less skilful pens than Kipling's, while on one occasion I have seen an Army audience roused to enthusiasm by a recitation that was in fact the closing scene of *Doctor Faustus*. No mention had been made of Marlowe, nor was any intimation given that the passage was a masterpiece of English literature; it was announced simply that 'Corporal D—— will now give you a monologue—Faust's last hour on earth before the Devil gets him.' Marlowe and the corporal achieved the rest between them.

This is the public, these the eager and unsophisticated auditors, for whom Henslowe provided entertainment, and for whom Marlowe, Greene and their followers wrote. It is not surprising that the emotions depicted in these early plays are simple to the point of crudity, and it may be worth while to see how Shakespeare has applied them to his purpose, and what particular stage devices he has found successful enough to be worth borrowing for use in *Titus Andronicus*.

Like Marlowe's *Tamburlaine the Great*, the play begins with recriminations between two characters of secondary importance. Saturninus and Bassianus are urging their rival claims to the Empire of Rome when they are told that the people have nominated a third candidate in the person of Titus Andronicus, whose virtues are announced with the news of his impending arrival victorious from the wars. All this makes a very good 'build-up' for the entry of a popular idol, who duly arrives in procession, followed by Tamora the captive queen of the Goths, with her three sons and Aaron the wicked Moor. A contemporary sketch preserved at Longleat (illustrated opposite p. 10) shows how the principals in this scene were dressed, with Titus in a more or less Roman cuirass, laurel wreath, spear, buskins and patriarchal beard, Tamora wearing a spiky crown and a robe with full brocaded or embroidered sleeves, Aaron an unmistakable negro, black-faced and curly-haired, in vaguely classical armour but with full white sleeves suggesting a bishop or a ballet-shirt, Tamora's two younger sons kneeling in reasonably good Roman cuirasses, and two small-part people, probably meant for Titus' sons Lucius and Mutius, in Elizabethan half-armour and round-hose. It would seem, accordingly, that the principal characters were 'costume' of some sort and the minor actors what they had or could get. Anyone with experience of repertory work will be familiar with both the principle and the practice.

Having made his entry, Titus has an impressive opening speech, and the bloodshed begins with a human sacrifice off-stage, the eldest son of Tamora being led out to be dismembered and immolated as an appeasement to the shades of the many sons of Titus who have perished in the war. Tamora's plea for her son's life is good declamatory matter in the heavy style appropriate to suppliant matrons on the romantic stage, and if the rest of the author's work were not so much better, and the rest of this particular play so much worse, its effective rhetoric might have kept it considerably longer on the boards. There are still actors, and there are still audiences, who find pleasure in the sonority of the passage that begins 'Victorious Titus, rue the tears I shed', and culminates in lines foreshadowing *Measure for Measure* and *The Merchant of Venice*:

> Wouldst thou draw near the nature of the gods?
> Draw near them then in being merciful;
> Sweet mercy is nobility's true badge:
> Thrice-noble Titus, spare my first-born son.

And here we see what is almost an innovation in the drama of the time—a decision, and an action, from which the whole lamentable tale arises. Titus rejects the plea, and by so doing brings down vengeance and calamity upon his head and his house. The early spectators, to whom the play came as a variation from an afternoon's bear-baiting, were given plenty of incident, some complication of plot and a wealth of quarrelling, trumpeting and oratory in a Rome such as no classical scholar ever knew. People break into Latin now and then, for no particular reason save that of showing that the author knew a Latin phrase that expressed what he wanted to say and that would be recognized and understood by his audience, for the few tags appear to be odd examples out of grammar-books, remembered by someone who had never got beyond a schoolboy's acquaintance with Rome and its

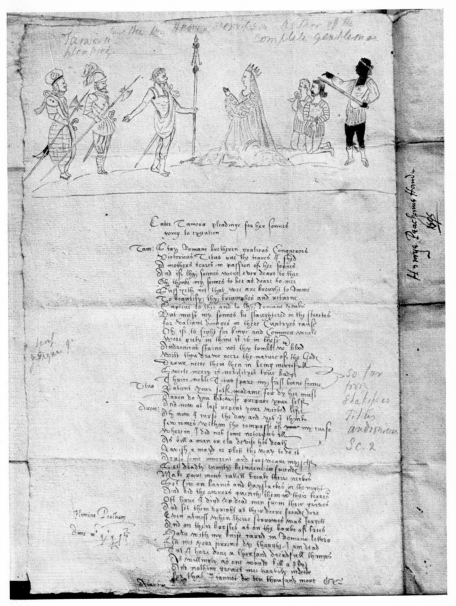

Titus and Tamora. Sketch by Henry Peacham, 1595, at the head of a scene ingeniously combining speeches from Acts I and V of *Titus Andronicus*.

language. He knew that Romans had tribunes, and that they had emperors, and that successful generals occasionally put on the white gown and presented themselves for election to some important office, but he did not know what that office was, and in guessing it to be the Imperial purple, he guessed wrong.

He was on safer ground in recalling that stern old Roman fathers could and did kill their sons for defying their authority, and in making his Roman patriarch do so in the very first scene, but the small Latin and less Greek with which Ben Jonson later credited him could not recognize the name Andronicus as a Greek one, with the stress upon its long third syllable, and though it should properly rhyme with 'as you like us', it has to be mispronounced throughout if it is not to play havoc with the scansion. Towards the end of his career we find him doing the very same thing in *Cymbeline*, scanning the name of Posthumus as if it were Postumius or Postummus, and in *Troilus and Cressida* his muddled mythology has confused Ariadne, whose silken clue guided Theseus through the labyrinth, with Arachne, the Lydian weaver whose skill rivalled that of Pallas Athene, so that he makes Troilus speak of 'Ariachne's broken woof'.

In fact, his general attitude at this stage is that of the schoolboy who has learnt a certain amount of Latin and retained some of it, read the usual school editions of classical authors and remembered a name or two, heard some stories from Roman mythology and history, chiefly out of Ovid's *Metamorphoses*, a popular schoolbook of which he scans the name wrongly, just as Gilbert and Sullivan did in the second act of *Princess Ida*, and has never got as far as learning what the Romans, as a people, actually did, or what part they played in the history of the world. That knowledge came to him in later years, from other sources, but by that time he had stopped playing the aggressive antiquarian, and his Brutus and Antony, and even Coriolanus, are humans first and Romans afterwards.

Meanwhile the play proceeds. At a hunting-party, Tamora's two sons murder Bassianus and ravish Titus' daughter Lavinia, depriving her of her tongue and hands to prevent her from accusing them. Aaron contrives a trap for Quintus and Martius Andronicus, who fall into a pit where the body of Bassianus has been thrown (possibly the Jew of Malta's trap-door and cauldron, which we know to have been listed in Henslowe's inventory of stage properties) and are condemned to death for his murder. At the suggestion of Aaron, Titus cuts off his own left hand to redeem his sons, but it is sent back to him in mockery with their severed heads. The old man feigns madness, urging his kinsmen to shoot arrows with messages of vain recrimination against the gods, and at last entertains Saturninus and Tamora to a horrible banquet at which he kills the dishonoured Lavinia, justifying the action by citing the story of Virginius, and then stabs Tamora herself, after revealing to her that the pie she has been eating is made of the dead bodies of her own children. Saturninus stabs him, and is in turn struck down by Lucius Andronicus, Titus' one surviving son, who is then hailed as emperor by the few people left alive, while Aaron is led out to a lingering death with a final Marlowe-like defiance on his lips.

There is a great deal in the play that is like Marlowe, and by no means Marlowe at his worst. Aaron's opening to the second act contains a passage that might well have been spoken by Tamburlaine himself, and it is clear that this was the sort of thing to go down well, if well delivered, with a simple and impressionable audience. The very bloodshed has a frank enthusiasm about it, as if it were devised to satisfy a natural appetite for thrills, and is very different from the far-fetched horrors devised in later years by Ford and Webster, at a time when dramatists were tormenting their imaginations to intrigue a blasé and ultra-sophisticated audience that had supped full with horrors and needed to season its palate with corruption. There is a wide gulf, even now, between the Demon Barber of Fleet Street and the subtleties of the *Grand Guignol*.

As has been said, much of the poetry is like Marlowe, but what is more significant is that some passages are unexpectedly like Shakespeare, and Shakespeare as we know him in his later days. Most of them are connected with the countryside. There is a passage introducing a royal hunting-party, and another depicting lovers listening to the distant clamour of hounds and horns duplicated by the echoes in a valley, that would be more readily remembered if the author had not written them again, quite differently and generally rather better, in another play. The hunting of Saturninus and Tamora has been surpassed, a few years later, by that of Theseus and Hippolyta, though we may question whether their decision to

> mark the musical confusion
> Of hounds and echo in conjunction

is really such an advance on the earlier

> whilst the babbling echo mocks the hounds
> Replying shrilly to the well-tun'd horns
> As if a double hunt were heard at once.

In the earlier play the country metaphors were instinctive, and probably went for nothing with the Londoners of the South Bank, which would make them all the more suitable for use again. The birds 'rising and cawing at the gun's report' of Puck's speech to Oberon have their earlier parallel in the lines by which Marcus Andronicus reassures the startled crowd in the last scene of the tragedy,

> You sad-fac'd men, people and sons of Rome,
> By uproar sever'd, like a flight of fowl
> Scatter'd by winds and high tempestuous gusts,

and these are by no means the only examples. If in the general scheme of the play there is much that looks back to *The Spanish Tragedy*, there is yet something in its imagery that looks forward to the very different public of *A Midsummer Night's Dream*.

II

At the Theatre

IN JUNE 1592 there was trouble on the South Bank. Some London apprentices, indignant at the imprisonment of a companion in the Marshalsea, had met ostensibly to see a play at the Rose, but had gone on from there to commit a breach of the peace by attempting to rescue the prisoner. One consequence of the affair was that the Privy Council, in the interests of order and good behaviour, had the theatres closed down till Michaelmas. It was not that the actors or the managements were concerned, or suspected of being concerned, in the attempt at prison-breaking, but one of the functions of the Council, when sitting in the Star Chamber, was to deal with cases of riot and sedition. Accordingly, places that could be used as rendezvous for turbulent conduct of this sort would be none the worse for a sharp lesson, to teach them to take better thought for what went on within their walls, and what sort of persons habitually frequented them. The average London citizen *in propria persona* liked the theatre as a source of entertainment; it was only when he was elevated to a responsible and official position, be it in his ward or on the Common Council or the Court of Aldermen, that he found himself considering it as a meeting-place for undesirable characters, and an establishment not to be encouraged within his own jurisdiction.

Accordingly, Henslowe's theatre closed its doors for a while, and Alleyn took his company on tour. We have no means of knowing what Shakespeare did with himself at this time, but by early September, when the dying Greene wrote his *Groat's Worth of Wit* and sneered at the 'Tyger's heart wrapped in a player's hide', the play containing the line he parodied must have been produced by some other management, presumably the Earl of

Pembroke's Servants, who had formed a company at about this time and are credited, on the title-page of the corrupt First Quarto of the *True Tragedie of Richard Duke of Yorke*, with the performance of the play.

It is really a vast ten-act play like *Tamburlaine*. Possibly it was originally called *The Contention betwixt the two famous Houses of Yorke and Lancaster*, but by the time of its publication in the Folio of 1623—the first collected edition of Shakespeare's dramatic works—it takes a supporting part as the Second and Third parts of *Henry VI*. It has no real connection with the First Part, which appears to have been loosely linked up with it at a later time by the writing in of an irrelevant courtship between Suffolk and Margaret of Anjou just when the play might be expected to come to an end. The real drama starts, effectively and spectacularly, with the introduction of Margaret as the bride of the unfortunate king whom she is to deceive, chide, patronize and hurry hither and thither in passionate championship not so much of his own cause as of their son's, until the defeat of Tewkesbury robs her of son and husband in tragical succession. A real *femme fatale* was a new thing in the Elizabethan theatre. Joan the Maid had been presented—quite unsuitably but with some success—as a beautiful but sinister enchantress, and now the author was giving some intelligent boy-player the chance to carry a much larger proportion of the play upon his shoulders. Margaret of Anjou could display beauty, wantonness, pride and sheer savagery in succession as the vast play went on, and the part must have been well worth playing in its own day, before the author had created Lady Macbeth and Cleopatra to eclipse it in infinitely greater dramas. In 1592 nobody had written anything like it, and it may well have stirred the interest of the citizen-audience that we can imagine frequenting the Theatre and the Curtain in the fields of Finsbury, near enough to the City for convenience of access, but far enough outside its boundaries to avoid embarrassment.

Of this audience we have an initial indication from a completely different source. In 1572, some four years before the building of the original Theatre in Shoreditch, Messrs Braun and Hogenberg brought out their *Civitates Orbis Terrarum*, a collection of maps or bird's-eye views of the principal cities of the world embellished with pictures of typical inhabitants in characteristic dress. The map of London is ascribed to Hoefnagel, and is a few years behind the times, as it shows St Paul's still carrying the tall central spire that had in fact been burned down in 1561 and never rebuilt, but what more closely concerns us is the group of figures at the foot of the design (see illustration facing p. 18). There is no suggestion of doublet and hose in these Elizabethan Londoners, nor of the farthingale and spreading ruff so readily associated with the Queen herself; the older man wears a belted, fur-trimmed gown, the younger a short cassock with sword and buckler at his side, while the women have decorous high-necked dresses trimmed or 'guarded' with velvet, the only sign of exaggeration being the older woman's long hanging over-sleeves, which are caught into a loop behind her. In other words, the inhabitants of London were tradesmen, not persons of fashion. The Court was not yet regularly established at Westminster, and it had not yet become desirable for the courtier to have a house in London as a matter of course. For him, it was enough to take lodgings there when called to Westminster by Court, legal or Parliamentary duties; for the rest, the only reason for living in London was that one worked or traded there. The West End audience, as such, did not exist, there was no purely residential quarter and as yet no leisured London population, and the London playgoer for whom Shakespeare usually wrote was not the gentleman of leisure seeking a sensation but the business man or law student seeking entertainment after a day's work in shop, counting-house or one of the Inns of Court.

Not that this meant he was an uneducated man. Since the Reformation, grammar-schools had been founded all over the country, to carry on the educational work formerly organized by the Church, and of these foundations London had an ample share. The London apprentice would have a good grounding in Latin— the ordinary conversations at school, as well as the actual classes, were carried on in that language—a nodding acquaintance with the chief classical authors, a certain amount of logic and rhetoric and possibly a little Greek, before leaving school and entering into indentures with a master. The curriculum of the schools of London, such as Westminster, Merchant Taylors', the Charter-house, Christ's Hospital and St Paul's, was intended as a 'sound commercial education' for the ordinary Londoner, and by no means reserved for the student who intended to pass on to one of the Universities and embrace the hard and unrewarding life of the professional scholar. The Renaissance had brought learning out into the ordinary life of the community, and it was no longer regarded as something fit only for the privileged circles of Church or Court but as a new, fascinating plaything to be enjoyed by all alike. Thomas Nicolls, who brought out the first English edition of Thucydides, was a London goldsmith. He translated not the original Greek but a French text based on a Latin version, just as in its turn North's famous *Lives of the Noble Grecians and Romans* was made from Amyot's French version of Plutarch's Greek.

Drama was represented by Plautus and Seneca, the latter being particularly esteemed, and at times regrettably imitated by persons who were seriously trying to bring tragedy 'after the high Roman fashion' to the London stage without fully realizing what it was. Where Plautus was a practical man of the theatre, making actable Latin comedies out of Greek originals, Seneca was a scholar and a philosopher, the son of a professional rhetorician, writing bad imitations of Greek plays not for performance but as examples of literary form. It is not impossible to write a fine dramatic piece without intending it to be acted—Milton did so in *Samson Agonistes*—but as a general rule the philosopher-turned-dramatist is a person to be avoided, and it is a matter for thankfulness that Shakespeare shows little or no trace of having been seriously conscious of Seneca at all. Quotations and misquotations from him turn up now and then, but they have the air of being stray phrases that had been 'learnt in the grammar long ago', and there is no sign of any attempt to imitate that grandiosity without grandeur that draws out long litigious complaints for page after page, where every possible argument is produced, paraded and discussed, passion gives place to peevishness and even Medea herself abandons the savagery of Isolde for the style and technique of Mr Serjeant Buzfuz.

To an audience that had read a little Seneca in its schooldays, and had not looked into the pages of Aeschylus to learn what ghosts, doom and tragedy could be when handled by a master, a play like *Henry VI* would come as a refreshing relief. This was life, not literature, though it had its moments of ear-filling rhetoric and passion. The scheming Beaufort, the cold ambitious York, Suffolk in his arrogance joining hands with them to pull down the Protector Gloucester and Jack Cade roaring his cheerful, ruffianly way through the suburbs to London Stone itself are not mere personifications of 'humours' or of mental or logical attitudes, they are human beings, expressing this or that natural passion in an exuberant but still natural way. There is a good deal of imitation Marlowe—the pirate captain who orders the death of Suffolk has his part written throughout in what Bottom would call Ercles' vein, and the Cade scenes, with their alternations of alarmed populace and triumphant invaders, are a ribald, unscrupulous, entertaining repetition of the rise and progress of Tamburlaine the Great—but it is all distributed more widely and more effectively among the cast than Marlowe himself appears to have distributed his 'mighty lines'. A good deal, as we shall see, may have been pruned away in first putting the play upon the stage, but even so, the cut-down acting version would give chances to a number of players rather than one star, and they and their audience would be correspondingly grateful.

For this clientèle, rather more orderly and sophisticated than the bear-garden public of Bankside, the drama of verbal splendour and frequent bloodshed has given place to something rather different—a play in which the splendour and the bloodshed are used to tell a chronicle-history. These playgoers went not only to hear poetry and to see violence but to watch the unfolding of a story vaguely known to them already. It is a different audience from the not-knowing, not-caring public at the Rose. It may not

Typical London citizens, from Hoefnagel's map.

know very much, but it cares to some extent, and the author has had to cater for it accordingly. These scenes admittedly fall short of the Henry IV sequence in history as in other things, but they have advanced beyond the crude string of anecdotes, unconnected by any real thread of story, that had gone to make up *Harry the Sixth* for Henslowe.

That the audience liked and supported these plays we may justifiably assume from Greene's resentment and his bitter perversion of the extravagant line 'O tiger's heart wrapped in a woman's hide' that is applied to Queen Margaret in the second one. Another piece of evidence pointing the same way is the existence of two plays, *The First Part of the Contention betwixt the two famous Houses of Yorke and Lancaster* and *The True Tragedie of Richard Duke of Yorke*, which were published in quarto in 1594 and 1595 and again in 1600 and 1619. They are both a great deal shorter than the corresponding plays in the Folio, and though there is a general correspondence of plot, and sometimes of text, there are also wild divergences, transferences, paraphrases and general vulgarizations, not to mention insertions and odd gags. Scholars have more or less abandoned the old idea that these were early plays which Shakespeare improved later on; they have little look of being the crude originals of the Folio text, and many signs of being corruptions from it. Who compiled them, and for what sort of audience, we may conjecture from an unexpected source.

In the summer of 1592, when the London theatres had been closed down and their companies disbanded or sent on tour, an English traveller named Fynes Moryson was travelling on the Continent and visited the Fair at Frankfurt-am-Main, where he found English actors performing to an appreciative audience that was largely ignorant of their language but was attracted by their actions and their unfamiliarity. His own words describe the entertainment graphically enough:

. . . So as I remember that when some of our cast dispised Stage players came out of England into Germany and played at Franckford in the tyme of the Mart, having nether a Complete number of Actours, nor any good Apparell, nor any ornament of the Stage, yet the Germans, not understanding a worde they sayde, both men and wemen, flocked wonderfully to see theire gesture and Action, rather than heare them, speaking English which they understoode not, and pronowncing peeces and Patches of English playes, which my selfe and some English men there present could not heare without great wearysomenes.

Elsewhere he mentions that he heard of them in the Low Countries, where they had been equally successful until the magistrates had to suppress them because 'many young virgines fell in love with some of the players, and followed them from Citty to Citty'.

For such an audience, either on the Continent or in the provinces, and by such a company, must the Shakespearean bad quartos have been compiled, and for the way of compilation, modern parallels can be found in the traditional practice of certain barn-storming companies within living memory, and even more recently in some of the entertainments provided by members of the Armed Forces for the diversion of their comrades. A music-hall sketch, say, has achieved a certain degree of success in the entertainment world, and it is thought a good idea to incorporate it, or a version of it, in a Service performance. One member of the company may have taken part in it in peacetime, or been 'in the bill' with it when performing in something else, others may have seen it once or twice, yet others may have heard it broadcast. Some may have been interested by it for its own sake, some may have but a hazy memory of it, having been more deeply intent, at that time, on other features of the programme, but between them all a script is evolved, a reconstruction based on recollection of actual lines and cues, memory of general situations and effective points, and a certain amount of sheer conjecture.

Even so, we may imagine, was a bad quarto text vamped up for performance by a company that had no copy of the original and no right to produce it. The same defects are common to both. The beginnings and ends of speeches are often well remembered when the matter in the middle has been forgotten and has to be reconstructed by guesswork. Telling lines and repartees are remembered and put in, but not always in the right place. Effective speeches that have come from other plays are inserted, either by a lapse of the compiler's memory or to save the trouble of writing original matter when something—not the right thing, but something appropriate—was ready to hand. The action is increased and vulgarized, the comedian insists on putting in jokes of his own, and while the compilation begins reasonably well it grows more heterogeneous and incoherent as rehearsal time grows shorter and memories are more wildly taxed. That is what still happens in practice, and the appearance of the *Contention* and the *True Tragedie* very strongly implies that they were put together in just such a manner for an audience that might or might not have heard of the original successful production and would not be too critical of the play presented to them. (Readers of Mark Twain will remember how Huckleberry Finn spent some time with a two-man company playing selections from Shakespeare on the same principle, and memorized a wonderful speech that is almost a whole bad quarto in itself.) Finally, when the tour was over, the book of the play could be disposed of to one of the less reputable publishers who would be glad to print and sell it as the 'authentic text' of a well-known and successful piece. These, surely, are the 'stolne and surreptitious copies' of which John Heminge and Henry Condell complained when they attempted, in the Folio of 1623, to produce a definitive edition of their old friend's work.

These texts have an added interest as indicating something of the cuts made in the original production. The preface to the first folio edition of Beaumont and Fletcher says, in quite straightforward language, that the plays were considerably cut down in performance, and that the fair copies obtained—often quite legitimately—from individual actors represented only the acting versions in which they were accustomed to appear. The Shakespearean bad quartos indicate some of the major omissions made for practical purposes at a time when Shakespeare was not the Swan of Avon and sacrosanct, but merely the author who wrote with incredible fluency and facility and needed drastic pruning if the play was to be got into the two hours normally allotted to a performance. Heminge and Condell pay tribute to the ease and rapidity with which he wrote, Ben Jonson went so far as to say roundly that now and then he needed suppressing, and heretical as it may seem to the modern reader there is every likelihood that he was treated in his own day as drastically as Mr Puff in *The Critic*. Mr Puff, it will be remembered, defiantly announced that he would 'print it, every word', and many eighteenth-century texts of plays indicate by the use of parentheses or inverted commas the passages usually omitted in representation. In the nineteenth century one need only compare the text of Tennyson's *Becket* or *Queen Mary* with the acting editions of the plays to see how much had to be done, in the way of compression and excision, to make them conform to the requirements of time and human endurance, and even nowadays it is not unknown for an author to write, and publish, lines of dialogue that he has never yet heard upon the stage. They may be entertaining in themselves, they may help to present a character more completely in the round, but if time is getting short, or the scene is getting slow, and they have no claim to be noticeably advancing the action, out they will come and never be missed. We may take it for a reasonable assumption, accordingly, that the Elizabethan playgoer saw rather less of a Shakespeare play than he or his son read when the text was at last available in a respectable edition, and that this is what was meant by the publisher's announcement, on the title-page of the 1604 quarto of *Hamlet*, that the play was 'Newly imprinted and enlarged to almost as much againe as it was.' The comparison is with the play as acted, rather than with the unauthorized quarto published piratically the year before.

Having briefly made the acquaintance of the citizen-audience that frequented the Theatre and the Curtain in Finsbury Fields, we may now look a little more closely at the actual neighbourhood of those theatres themselves. It has been described for us with most helpful wealth of detail by John Stow, whose *Survey of London* was first published in 1598 and is therefore a most useful authority for the conditions and topography of early Shakespearean London.

The City Wall and City Ditch had long lost their importance as practical defences, and while the Wall remained as a civic boundary, certain sections of the Ditch had been scientifically filled in and turned into market-gardens, while elsewhere it was being allowed gradually to silt up, and was increasingly used as a dump for miscellaneous rubbish. Not much had been done in the way of suburban building at this point; the ground was marshy and uncertain, and accordingly there was little except what we should now call some ribbon-development running northward along Bishopsgate Street Without the Walls. West of this there lay the open ground of Moorfields and Finsbury Fields, a great stretch of heath and marsh, accessible from London by way of the comparatively new-cut postern of Moorgate. In its day it had been a popular ground for archery-practice, by that time it was still used for musters and amateur military manœuvres generally, though diehards like William Harrison had long been lamenting that 'our strong shooting is decaied and laid in bedde'; and it was renowned as a pleasant walking-place on a summer evening for the London citizen and his wife when the shutters were up and there was time for a stroll and a meal before going to rest.

Recreation and refreshment could be obtained at one of the 'summer-houses' which were springing up in ever-increasing numbers on the drier ground near the city and earning the disapproval of old-fashioned people—such as Stow himself—who resented the over-running of the old open spaces by these new establishments of fantastic architecture and doubtful propriety. Bowling-alleys and skittle-alleys were generally attached to the summer-houses, and came in for more disapproval, just as the playhouses had done on Bankside, because of their tendency to attract undesirable people, not to mention the facilities they offered for miscellaneous betting and the waste of time and tempers generally. Further away scattered windmills stood here and there on mounds rising above the surface of the marsh. As the mounds themselves had originally been refuse-dumps, the foundations they provided were bulky rather than salubrious, but any kind of eminence, whatever its composition, came in useful to the opportunist who wanted to raise his mill-sails high enough to catch all the available wind. The mills were not necessarily for grinding corn, but may have been connected with the various experiments in pumping, drainage and irrigation by which the Moorfields area was being gradually rendered serviceable for cultivation, and ultimately for building.

Turning again to Stow, we find that the wards in this part of London consisted very largely of 'fair houses of merchants'—not the tenements of artisans and small tradesmen so much as the combined dwellings, warehouses and counting-houses of people of some consequence in the business world. These, as we have already seen, were men of standing and good general education, though without the specialization of the scholar or the fantastic and leisured ingenuity of the courtier-poet. In a few years' time, when it was beginning to be worth a playwright's while to write for the leisured playgoer and laugh at the citizen, Beaumont and Fletcher were to immortalize this type of spectator in *The Knight of the Burning Pestle*, and we can see from the honest grocer, with his talkative wife and stage-struck apprentice, the sort of person that must have made up many a Shakespearean audience in those first-built playhouses of London. The type belongs to no particular age; the Citizen's Wife of Beaumont and Fletcher's play has much in common with Mrs Primrose in *The Vicar of Wakefield*, and her genial, ready tongue is not stilled even yet, but may be heard to-day in queues, at jumble sales, and in train or omnibus, regaling total strangers with intimate, good-tempered discussion of her private concerns.

Communications were slow and uncertain. It was not possible in those days for a man in Finsbury to turn to his newspaper, or look at a poster on a hoarding, and learn as a matter of course what was being played that night on Bankside. Leaflets announcing special performances could be, and were, disseminated up and down the town—the Society of Antiquaries possesses one such handbill (illustrated opposite) advertising an elaborate

THE PLOT OF THE PLAY, CALLED
ENGLANDS JOY.

To be Playd at the Swan this 6. of Nouember. 1602.

IRST, there is induct by shew and in Action, the ciuill warres of England from *Edward* the third, to the end of Queene *Maries* raigne, with the ouerthrow of Vsurpation.

2 Secondly then the entrance of Englands Ioy by the Coronation of our Soueraigne Lady *Elizabeth*, her Throne attended with peace, Plenty, and ciuill Pollicy: A sacred Prelate standing at her right hand, betokening the Serenity of the Gospell: At her left hand Iustice: And at her feete Warre, with a Scarlet Roabe of peace vpon his Armour: A wreath of Bayes about his temples, and a braunch of Palme in his hand.

3 Thirdly is dragd in three Furies, presenting Dissention, Famine, and Bloudshed, which are throwne downe into hell.

4 Fourthly is exprest vnder the person of a Tyrant, the enuy of *Spayne*, who to shew his cruelty causeth his Souldiers dragge in a beautifull Lady, whome they mangle and wound, tearing her garments and Iewels from off her: And so Ieaue her bloudy, with her hayre about her shoulders, lying vpon the ground. To her come certaine Gentlemen, who seeing her pitious dispoylment, turne to the Throne of England, from whence one descendeth, taketh vp the Lady, wipeth her eyes, bindeth vp her woundes, giueth her treasure, and bringeth forth a band of Souldiers, who attend her forth: This Lady presenteth *Belgia*.

5 Fiftly, the Tyrant more enraged, taketh counsell, sends forth letters, priuie Spies, and secret vnderminers, taking their othes, and giuing them bagges of treasure. These signifie *Lopus*, and certaine Iesuites, who afterward, when the Tyrant lookes for an answere from them, are shewed to him in a glasse with halters about their neckes, which makes him mad with fury.

6 Sixtly, the Tyrant seeing all secret meanes to fayle him, intendeth open violence and inuasion by the hand of Warre, whereupon is set forth the battle at Sea in 88. with Englands victory.

7 Seuenthly, hee complotteth with the Irish rebelles, wherein is layd open the base ingratitude of *Tyrone*, the landing there of *Don Iohn de Aguila*, and their dissipation by the wisedome and valour of the Lord *Mountioy*.

8 Eightly, a great triumph is made with fighting of twelue Gentlemen at Barriers, and sundrie rewards sent from the Throne of England, to all sortes of well deseruers.

9 Lastly, the Nine Worthyes, with seuerall Coronets, present themselues before the Throne, which are put backe by certaine in the habite of Angels, who set vpon the Ladies head, which represents her Maiestie, an Emperiall Crowne, garnished with the *Sunne*, *Moone* and *Starres*: And so with Musicke both with voyce and Instruments shee is taken vp into Heauen, when presently appeares, a Throne of blessed Soules, and beneath vnder the Stage set forth with strange fireworkes, diuers blacke and damned Soules, wonderfully described in their seuerall torments.

An Elizabethan playbill.

pageant-play called *England's Joy*, that turned out to be a last-minute fiasco—but the average production was intended to attract and entertain a local audience, who could walk along to the theatre, read the bill stuck on the post outside (and still called a 'poster' to this day) and go in, if they liked the look of it, without any undue exertion.

The author who writes for a local audience finds himself, be it by instinct or design, making his meaning clear to that audience in the simplest and quickest way, often by local analogies and local jokes. Much of his work consists of building up a dramatic situation and preparing the minds of the spectators to understand its character and implications when it is set before them. Consciously or unconsciously he leads them to the goal by paths not entirely strange to them, and by so doing he concentrates their interest on that goal rather than dissipating it upon fascinating discussions by the way.

The Two Gentlemen of Verona may bid each other farewell in the ingenious and witty high-society style displayed to the fullest degree in *Love's Labour's Lost*, but after Valentine has taken boat from Verona to Milan—which he might well do at that time by canal—the audience is given a true Cockney comedian in the person of Launce, the 'clownish servant' to Proteus. With this character we leave Italy for the moment and come back in all essentials to London. Valentine's servant, Speed, is a story-book comedian, his wit is elaborate and artificial and is directed always at one or other of the characters in the play, but Launce addresses his first speech, and a good deal of his whole part, directly and unashamedly to the audience, claiming instinctive kinship with them and admitting them freely to his confidence, be it in the matter of his family leave-takings or the habits and character of his unforgettable dog. Accordingly, it is not surprising that at the end of his first scene he is given a command quite out of keeping with his character as a Veronese body-servant, but perfectly familiar to the London serving-man or apprentice accustomed to being sent on errands up and down the river. 'Thy master is shipped,' says Panthino, 'and thou art to post after with oars';

i.e. he is to take a boat and be rowed after Proteus to catch him up. Moreover, he is to bestir himself, or he will miss the tide.

This has no relation to any Italian inland waterway; it is purely a popular reference to a circumstance of London life. To anyone taking boat on the Thames—the broadest, cleanest and quickest highway of Tudor London—the state and direction of the tide had primarily to be considered, particularly if it was intended to go through the rapids of London Bridge to visit the seagoing craft anchored in the Pool. The close-set piers of the bridge had been grounded in days when the art of building a wide, shallow arch was still unknown, and the structure lay across the river like a great mill-dam pierced with a row of comparatively narrow sluices. Through each of these, accordingly, the river current went like a mill-race, and the passage could be safely negotiated only at certain positions of the tide. Some forty years before, indeed, the Queen had been in peril of her life there when, as the Lady Elizabeth, she was being sent by water to the Tower in her half-sister's reign, and her escort, in their anxiety to have her behind bars with the least possible delay, had run the risk of shooting the bridge when the safe period for doing so was already past. The London waterman of the sixteenth century had his points of resemblance to the London omnibus-conductor of the twentieth, particularly his reputation for versatility and repartee, and allusions to this section of riverside life would meet ready recognition and acceptance in any quarter of London and were by no means restricted to Bankside.

Many features of these early plays appear specially suitable to this type of comfortable middle-class audience. For one thing, the author reveals himself—unexpectedly for those days—as a stickler for the proprieties. Julia's action in dressing as a boy when travelling alone across country was in accordance with the principle and practice of the time, since in the circumstances a respectable woman would be expected to do everything in her power to conceal her sex rather than draw attention to it. When Silvia, later in the play, has to set out on a similar expedition, the author is faced with the problem of either repeating his effects or making his second heroine forfeit the sympathy of a proportion of the audience by conduct which the average citizen's wife would not consider respectable. He avoids the difficulty by providing her with a chaperon, and introducing Sir Eglamour, who on the death of his own betrothed has vowed eternal celibacy, and is therefore an unimpeachable escort for a young woman on her travels. Just so, in tales of romance, a virtuous but distressed damsel, if she had no other company, would travel attended by a hermit. Two examples from Ariosto's *Orlando Furioso* occur to the mind. Though the hermit who accompanied the Princess Angelica fell regrettably from grace when he tried to take uncanonical advantage of his position, the one who attended the ill-starred Isabella was true to the traditions of his office and his temporary employment when he fared so ill at the hands of Rodomont. Such a hermit also makes a momentary appearance in the text, though not on the stage, of *The Merchant of Venice*. Doctor Johnson, it is true, expressed his inability to see the reason for him, but he is there as the supposed travelling companion of Portia *in propria persona*, to maintain her position as a grave young matron on a pilgrimage, not a bold-faced hussy gadding about on her own as soon as her husband is out of the way, which is what would be said of a Portia known to be riding unattended from Belmont.

Eglamour proves but an inefficient escort for Silvia; we never see him again after they have set out, and we hear that he ran away when they were attacked by outlaws, but the important thing about him is the fact that he was considered necessary at all. His existence is corroborative evidence of a desire to conciliate the proprieties and avoid all suspicion of unpleasantness. Similarly the outlaws themselves are no sooner introduced than they are made to express their detestation of such 'vile base practices' as robbing 'silly women or poor passengers'; Valentine, when he becomes their head, explains that he has tried to reform them still further, and they are ultimately pardoned as easily, and on much the same considerations, as the more notorious Pirates of Penzance. Pleasantness, rather than reason or truth to nature, must be allowed to govern the last few scenes and send the audience away feeling satisfied, comfortable and ready to come again.

As with comedy, so with tragedy. The tale of Romeo and Juliet is one in which the conclusion is brought about by circumstances rather than by character, so that we can feel pity for the star-crossed lovers without the vague fears aroused in the later, darker tragedies by the revelation of unexpected depths and terrors in the human soul. Pity without fear, a good cry without any uncomfortable feelings that anything of the sort could happen to ourselves, or any doubts about our own ability to do better in the circumstances—these were, and are, the main requirements of 'comfortable tragedy' for middle-class family entertainment, be it on stage or screen. The play is filled with beauty of speech and thought, the protagonists have a simplicity about them that is compelling in itself, though it is further removed from nature than the only too life-like mind-changing of Proteus in the *Two Gentlemen*, and the story is discreetly removed from everyday life by being set in a foreign country, with its whole climax depending on a method of burial never employed in London but understood to be the regular practice in contemporary Italy. We may safely assume that Fynes Moryson was not the only Englishman to have observed and mentioned the custom of depositing the dead body uncoffined in the family vault. This curious habit might be one of the few things the general public knew about Italian domestic ceremonies, and in case it did *not* know, the author wrote a line or two for Friar Laurence to make it quite clear that the arrangements for Juliet's funeral were not designed specifically for dramatic effect but were the normal practice, carried out 'as the manner of our country is'.

The principal tragic figures being set at a safe distance both in place and time, the subordinate and comic characters can be treated in the opposite fashion and made mirrors—slightly distorting mirrors, it may be admitted—of the public of the day in general and the theatre-public in particular. Just the same thing is still done, and for the same sort of comfortable middle-class audience by the purveyors of musical romance and not-too-refined suburban pantomime. The serious characters are separated by time or place or both, while the comedians are unashamedly contemporary and generally plebeian. The father of the Sleeping Beauty may be called a king and allowed the eminence of a throne and crown, but he seldom finds much dignity in either, and is traditionally presented as a testy old gentleman perpetually caught at a disadvantage and bustling around in an atmosphere of chronic domestic difficulties under the critical observation of the Dame, who may be his Royal Consort or, as in Shakespeare's play, the Sleeping Beauty's nurse. We see him season after season, under various names and in various pantomimes, making his passionate but ineffectual attempts to assert himself, and we find him funny enough without the least attempt to relate him to nature; and Shakespeare's audience found him just as funny when he appeared before them, with the same sort of jokes and doing the same sort of business, under the name of Old Capulet. There is more of the peppery London merchant than the Veronese nobleman about him at his first appearance, when we see him clamouring to take part in a street fight and being told promptly by his wife that he is too old for it.

Half the joke here is that the old gentleman introduces himself by calling for an out-of-date weapon. It is true that in Continental armies there were still special bodies of heavy infantry, mostly Germans or Swiss, who were armed with the great two-hander nearly six feet long, but the ordinary English sword of the type, once popular with all who followed manly exercises, had fallen into disuse, and survived mainly in the conversation of old men who had been ready to swear by it when they were young. The new Italianate fence of rapier and dagger was coming in among fashionable people, the use of broadsword and buckler was still popular, though some were beginning to think it vulgar, and the long-sword had probably seen little exercise in London since the days of Wyatt's rebellion forty years before. The mercantile public of Finsbury was, broadly speaking, a sword-and-buckler public, or at least one well imbued with the sword-and-buckler tradition, and such a public would be the readiest to enjoy

Mercutio's genial disparagement of rapier-play and the punctilio of honourable quarrels, as expressed in his strictures on Tybalt and Benvolio respectively. Camden in his *Annals* and George Silver in his *Paradoxes of Defence* both express the popular view that this new fashion of thrusting with a rapier was unsatisfactory and unsporting, and it was with the ordinary Londoner, rather than the elegant courtier of Southampton's type, that these opinions would persist.

The opening of the play is in its way significant of the type. After the charming sonnet of the Prologue comes a passage of back-chat or cross-talk between two comedians. On its own merits it does not seem particularly inspiring or inspired. Knowing what we do of his other work, we feel entitled to expect something better than this from Shakespeare if he is indeed the Unique Literary Figure that we have always been instructed to revere. Actors and producers often take particular pains with this opening passage, and we dutifully laugh at it and say to ourselves that of course, in those crude times, audiences must have been very easily pleased, while a shorter passage of the same type between Peter and the musicians after Juliet's supposed death is almost always omitted.

But is there so much difference between those days and ours? Put either passage beside the actual text of a piece of cross-talk between two modern pantomime comedians, and there seems very little difference in quality or in kind. Our mistake has been that of thinking in terms of high comedy about something written for the methods of the variety stage. The two serving-men, one making truculent announcement of his character and intentions and the other genially ridiculing them with a string of bad and sometimes very vulgar puns, are by no means period pieces even yet. Our entertainment world still offers us, now and again, the other type of light cross-talk provided in this play in the shape of a quick thrust-and-parry of dialogue, brilliant and inane at once, between young men of fashion and leisure. It is not the heart and soul of the piece, as in *Love's Labour's Lost*; it is one of the many adornments of it, a passage of genial idiocy between cheerful young members of a Smart Set to which the audience made no pretence of belonging, but which it liked to contemplate now and then at a reasonable distance and not for too long at a time.

Low-comedy back-chat, high-comedy repartee, a general street fight suppressed by the authorities, a young man walking in a grove just outside the town, a garrulous old woman wordily re-calling just when and how she weaned her employer's little girl, a scholar gathering medicinal herbs in the early morning—all these would be pleasantly familiar to the particular middle-class com-mercial population that lived by London Wall and Bishopsgate and amused itself by going to the theatre. The very points and coincidences on which the action turns find their easiest accept-ance in a society that knew only too well how young men could get into trouble by starting a general brawl in the streets—the story of Evil May Day was not yet forgotten—or how the local authorities could take alarm in plague-time and clap somebody into quarantine on suspicion of infection. There had been bad outbreaks in 1592 and 1593, and plague, quarantine and street disturbances meant more to the London citizen than to the courtier of those times or the average audience of these.

Even when he is serious, Capulet is a London merchant rather than a Renaissance nobleman. Fathers could be disappointed in their children, and stunned and broken by bereavement, in the commercial world of London no less than in the Italian aristo-cracy, and the mourning figures at the end of the play bring the tragedy most clearly home to that particular type of spectator. The romantic characters are out of sight—a line in the Prince's part has given instruction for this—and it is the realistic figures who are left to mourn them. Managers catering for the romantic audience in later ages preferred to leave them out and end the play at Juliet's death, but it was not for the romantic-literary audience that Shakespeare wrote it. The true end, the end that the Elizabethan audience would want to see, is the effect of the tragedy on the stricken parents. It is for this that Friar Laurence has to recapitulate the whole story, so that we may see how they take it when the truth is made plain to them, and their final hand-clasp over the tomb is the forerunner of a similar tragic reconciliation, from another time and another country, when the two dominating characters of Ibsen's *John Gabriel Borkman*, the two old sisters who have been enemies for half their lives, join hands at last as 'two shadows over a dead man'.

III

Two Productions in High Society

THERE WAS yet another type of audience distinct from the well-read tradesmen of northern London and the sensation-seekers of Bankside. The nobles of Elizabeth's court, patrons of poets and artists and by no means inconsiderable poets and artists on their own account, amused themselves with entertainments written by their friends or *protégés* and performed either by their own regular companies of players or by artists hired for the occasion. A marriage, a christening, a visit from Elizabeth herself—any of these would involve a great deal of miscellaneous hospitality and entertainment, and the festivities would be arranged to please the eye, ear and intellect as well as the palate and the appetite.

On such an occasion the conditions in general, and the audience in particular, would differ very widely from those we have considered hitherto. It was a smaller audience than that at the Curtain or the Rose, it was much closer to the actors and quicker in the uptake, as it consisted largely of men and women with keen, practised agility of mind and the leisure to give it full play. The excitement of the unsophisticated, the interest of the careful business man, were here replaced by the appreciation and intelligence of the brilliant amateur, quick to applaud artistry and ingenuity of thought, phrase or setting. So clearly was this audience and its particular type of entertainment differentiated from the regular playgoing public of London that it had special playhouses built for it, small and well-appointed, with good scenic devices for spectacular presentation and companies and choirs of schoolboy actors ostensibly borne on some fashionable or ecclesiastical foundation. Like many small coterie-theatres and theatre-clubs of the present day, they catered not for the general public but for a small audience of specialists. The fare provided for these was assumed, as a matter of course, to be quite un-suitable for the commercial theatre and its more widely-assorted patrons, and it was many years before the salient features of the one were considered as being in any way applicable to the other. The public theatres were slow to adopt practices that had been associated with private performances only, and to credit their audiences with the capacity for enjoying beauty and ingenuity of words, action or staging as well as chronicles and sensational drama. For some time private and public theatres existed side by side, each catering for a different audience and appealing to different instincts.

The use of scenery is a case in point. The pageantry of the great private entertainments usually involved the introduction, and frequently the destruction, of some elaborate structure like a castle, a mountain or a grove, and the tradition was maintained in the masques written for performance at Court. Music, dancing, lighting and scene-painting were all called into service to produce stage pictures and transformations of great beauty and splendour, but it was not at first assumed that such development of the pictorial side would be at all appropriate to a common stage-play, so that we have to wait until the production of Davenant's *Siege of Rhodes* in 1656 to find 'the art of perspective in scenes' adver-tised as one of the attractions of a public entertainment,* although that art had been studied, practised and applied for more than half a century to a limited section of the drama.

It is for such an audience, then, that *Love's Labour's Lost* appears to have been designed. There is nothing striking or sen-sational about the plot; it is merely the story of three or four

---

* And even here we must remember that *The Siege of Rhodes* was being deliberately advertised as an opera, not a stage play, since plays were pro-hibited in Puritan London and Davenant was claiming to present something that was a different, and more refined, form of entertainment. At the Restora-tion, however, he did in fact present stage plays with the scenic adornments familiar to the masques and pageants of his youth.

wealthy young gentlemen who make a serious attempt to avoid the distractions of female society but find human nature and feminine attractiveness too strong for them. They woo in secret, and are ridiculed by one another when found out; they woo openly, and are ridiculed in turn by the ladies to whom they sue, and at the end they are dismissed on probation, to renew their suit in a year's time. The interest lies not in the events of the story, not even in the characters themselves, but in the brilliance of their conversation. The opening is again a good piece of imitation Marlowe—the first seven or eight lines might have been spoken by Tamburlaine to his lieutenants—but in a few moments we find that it is not being taken quite seriously. The King of Navarre, and his courtiers Longaville and Dumaine, are very much in earnest about their plan of academic self-seclusion and celibacy, but the frivolous Berowne does not approve of it as a principle or believe in it as a practice, and joins in the scheme under protest, maintaining that three years' residence and study is one thing, but self-mortification in the matter of food, sleep and society is very much another. His protests and the replies of the king and his companions are cast not in the blank verse that normally did duty for dramatic dialogue but in rhyme, and rhyme with a particular ingenuity and variation in its lyrical quality. For once in a way the playwright is deliberately and unashamedly writing poetry, to delight a poetry-loving audience. Sometimes a speech contains an entire sonnet, sometimes odd quatrains or couplets give the effect of sonnets begun and abandoned, sometimes the very metre changes and the conversation goes with the lightness of a dance. There is no parade of sincerity or depth of sentiment, the very motive of the Princess's visit to Navarre—a question concerning the surrender of Aquitaine and the payment or non-payment of a hundred thousand crowns—is politely hustled into the background as soon as it has served the purpose of bringing the characters together at all, and the play consists of a series of brilliant, almost lyrical conversations in which high-spirited young men laugh at each other or are laughed at by equally high-spirited young women, and join them at last in laughing at a comic countryman, a comic constable, a comic foreigner, a comic schoolmaster and a comic curate, with a page, a courtier and a 'day-woman' thrown in for good measure. The foreigner provides the occasion for some ingenious and not widely exaggerated travesties of consequential Euphuistic prose, full of points only to be taken by those fully familiar with the literary styles, disputes and gossip of the time; his very name, on the other hand, is a joke of the simplest and crudest form, more in the manner of Bankside than of the wit and ingenuity of the rest of the play. The great naval enterprise of Spain, with the threat it brought to the whole existence of Elizabeth and of England, was as fresh a memory in those days as the German 'lightning war' on London is in our own, and when Shakespeare wanted a foreigner for a figure of fun, he made him a Spaniard and called him Don Adriano de Armado, just as an author in the present century, with somewhat elementary humour, might create a comic German and christen him Herr Blitz. We can seldom take our perils seriously for long.

But this is one of the heavier jokes in the play. For the most part it is an exhibition of brilliant verbal pyrotechnics with a continuously lyrical quality. The lines cannot be resolutely bellowed to catch and keep the attention of people in the back benches of the pit, they must be thrown briskly and clearly to an intelligent and appreciative audience in the stalls—an audience quick to catch and appreciate literary and personal allusions at which we can only guess to-day, an audience that has come prepared to enjoy an exercise in elegant bubble-blowing and bubble-pricking, and that accounts itself something of a connoisseur in the fine art of fashionable repartee. It is not an audience of the Court as a whole—that, as we shall see, appears to have been rather a different thing, with a good deal less subtlety—it is an audience of the wits and poets of the Court and its outskirts, an audience of men who made a point of conducting their lives and, when necessary, their deaths with a degree of conscious elegance epitomized to us to-day in that scholar, poet and soldier who died at Arnhem nearly four centuries ago, and whom Richard Carew, when writing a note on English literature for the *Remaines* of his friend Camden, summarized as 'all in all for prose or verse . . . the miracle of our age, Sir Philip Sidney'. He died too soon to see what the drama was to become; in his own day it was in its child-hood, and he had little use for it as a literary form, but none the less it was to the friends who knew him, and carried on the tradition he had so brilliantly established, that a play like this must have been intended to appeal.

Another play, *A Midsummer Night's Dream*, is associated with a private function, possibly the wedding of William Stanley, Earl of Derby, early in 1595. The association is based on internal evidence, and carries a reasonable degree of conviction, but we may none the less do something to confirm it by comparing the special appeal of this play with that of its predecessors. There are differences in two kinds—in the style of the piece and in the resources required for its presentation. It has none of the solid family-entertainment quality of *Romeo and Juliet*, nor does it repeat, or try to repeat, the intellectual slickness, brilliance and word-jugglery of *Love's Labour's Lost*. Its tale of runaway lovers at cross-purposes in a moonlit wood has little to do with the playgoing shopkeeper of Finsbury, but is filled with the spirit of the countryside and directed at a country audience—which means, paradoxically enough, that it was intended for the court.

For the Tudor courtier was almost inevitably a countryman. Elizabeth herself had not yet established her court permanently at Whitehall, but moved about from one to another of the vast royal estates in the south and west of England, and the great men who made up her household were landed nobility with country estates of their own. Court society was county society, country-house society, riding-and-hunting society, at the court of England, and its ways of life and thought were very different from the polished urbanity of the court of France. The difference between the two had been strongly marked in the Middle Ages, as Dr Joan Evans has expressively demonstrated, and in the last decade of the sixteenth century the world of high society was not yet the

same as the world of polite letters. The two were overlapping
to an increasing degree, but the time had not come for them to
coincide.

It is to the country-house audience, then, that this play is
directed. There is nothing in it to bore or scare the country gentleman by a display of brilliance or brains; it opens instead with a
familiar sight, a great nobleman about to celebrate his own
wedding by lavish hospitality to his dependants and benign
administration of their affairs. Something of the sort was happening almost every summer up and down the country; something of
the sort was probably happening on the very occasion for which
this play was written and on which it was performed. The names
of Theseus and Hippolyta constitute a suitable concession to the
classics, but the man himself might well be the lord of an English
manor, bringing to it a hard-riding bride from the next county
and listening at the same time to the complaints of an elderly
tenant whose daughter rebels against the bridegroom her father
has found for her. The hunting scenes and metaphors that go for
so little in *Titus Andronicus* may be employed and elaborated here
to an audience trained and ready to appreciate them at their full
value, and the author employs them to good purpose, not to
accompany a lurid murder-story but to rouse the sleeping lovers
after a night of cross-purposes and herald the morning of a triple
wedding.

For such an audience, likewise, the comedians have to be quite
different—not comic Cockneys exchanging back-answers in a
Verona that has developed an unexpected affinity with Moorgate
and London Wall, but countrymen gravely exercised over the
problem of their contribution to the general entertainment. Such
a theme would be particularly apposite to an occasion which
represented the result of weeks of elaborate planning, preparation
and discussion, and many in the audience and behind the scenes
would have had their own recent experience of Quince's problems
—whether there is to be a play, what sort of a play, who is to
write it, who is to act it, how they are to get over some of the
difficulties of staging it in the Great Chamber and how to make

certain that nothing about the subject or the presentation is likely to give offence, not to mention the final crisis caused by the unaccountable disappearance of the leading man at rehearsal, until he turns up miraculously at the last possible moment without any comprehensible explanation. The very play that they perform is what people generally perform on such occasions—their own interpretation of the latest London success. It is hardly by pure coincidence that the theme, plot and construction of Quince's play correspond with those of *Romeo and Juliet*. Two 'star-cross'd lovers' born of contending families, a secret meeting wherein they pledge their mutual troth across a piece of scenery—a wall in the one play, a balcony in the other—a last meeting at a tomb, and the tragic misapprehension whereby the faithful lover 'kills himself most gallant for love' constitute a series of parallels too close to be accidental.

The cast of the play, likewise, indicates an occasion when good parts have to be provided for all the best actors of the company, with careful avoidance, whenever possible, of advancing anyone at the expense of anyone else. Both the boy-actresses are required, the small vivacious one and the taller one who plays serious, forsaken ladies, and as they are balanced one with another, so the 'juveniles' are balanced likewise. The serious old man, the comic old man and the man who plays bland or despotic princes are all given their chances, and even the minor actors who can do comparatively little are fitted in, with names and personalities of their own, by means of the theatrical performance that winds up the play. Most ingenious of all, there is a part specially written for the exuberant exhibitionist of the company, the man who is so energetic, so enthusiastic, so ingenious, so successful with audiences and withal such a thorn in the side of the producer because he is so full of ideas, variations and improvements to his own part that he makes it very difficult for anyone else to play with him, and yet is so pleasant and so unquestionably talented that it would be a thousand pities if he were left out or kept in the background. In this play there would be little or no opportunity for any player to feel that he had been slighted, kept down or deprived of his legitimate opportunity to distinguish himself before the Quality.

More than this, the cast is designed to include a whole extra company of a different sort. Some years before, John Lyly had run a season of select plays at a small private theatre in Blackfriars with a company of boys from the choirs of St Paul's and the Chapels Royal. It had ceased its activities before 1595, but the idea remained, and where there was any collection of boys living together under some sort of discipline, were they the pupils of a schoolmaster, the choirboys of a collegiate church or the pages and children of a nobleman's household, there was material for the rehearsal and performance of plays to small and specialized audiences. Now, at an occasion like Lord Derby's wedding, a number of such pages, choirboys and embryo players would be ready to hand, and sure enough we find them given their opportunity here. Instead of being set aside as a rival or alternative company to the players from London, they are given their chance to act with them, and yet to remain free from any risk of invidious comparison. Oberon, Titania and their attendant fairies have their own passions, encounters and emotions, which for the most part they take very seriously, but the passions and the players are such as may well be represented on a smaller scale than those of the Athenian mortals. Their scenes and speeches are so devised that they can be learned and rehearsed independently, and—with all respect to many famous Oberons and Titanias who have charmed us—they do not demand a very high standard of acting ability. If the audience can hear the actual words, whether of Titania, Oberon or the fairy whose brief scene with Puck prepares us for the entry of her mistress, the sheer beauty of the verse and imagery will do the rest. For character and dramatic tension we must look to the mortal lovers and the experienced actors who portray them. The two companies, adult professionals and child-amateurs, move through the intricacies of the plot without ever meeting save once, and even then the only 'common player' who has a love-passage with the children of the politer company plays the scene in a property donkey's head. Thus muzzled, he can take his part in a love-scene where his bare-faced presence might have seemed vaguely unsuitable.

It may be argued that the play has been performed again and again to ordinary 'commercial' audiences, without any of the special conditions just indicated, and has succeeded by virtue of its charm and natural qualities. That is so, but its acceptability to a general audience need not be an argument against its having been constructed for a particular one. Certain features—the country atmosphere, the even balancing of the parts, the intervention of an independent set of characters whose smallness is the matter of constant allusion in the text—are not what a manager catering for the London public of the fifteen-nineties would encourage, or even permit, his author to introduce into a play written specially for his management. In a new play for the Theatre or the Curtain they would all count as disadvantages, and potential causes either of loss of revenue or of actual increase in production-costs, so they would be discouraged at the outset. The saving clause is to be found on the title-page of the 1600 quarto, 'As it hath beene sundry times publickely acted, by the Right honourable, the Lord Chamberlaine his servants'. The very factors that would militate against the success or popularity of a new play become interesting and attractive in the revival of one known to have been originally produced in special circumstances. A similar state of things may be observed in the theatre of to-day when a play written for performance in a church is transferred, after the original production, to the ordinary stage. Mr Eliot's *Murder in the Cathedral* and the late Miss Sayers's *The Zeal of Thy House*, had they started from scratch in the West End, might have found it harder to win recognition in view of certain unconventionalities of form, thought and production which would have seemed unfamiliar and possibly unwelcome. As it was, the London audiences knew that the plays had been written for performance in the Cathedral Church of Canterbury, which easily accounted for anything that might otherwise appear incongruous.

And in the same way, it may be conjectured, did London

audiences first receive a play widely different from the usual material provided by the Chamberlain's Men in general, or William Shakespeare in particular. The comedy conceived, rehearsed and produced for a comparatively small audience proved itself capable of a far wider appeal and was consequently worth putting into the general repertory. With variations of treatment, it has remained there ever since.

IV

History and Business

LEAVING THE special requirements of the country and the court, we may return to the theatreland of Finsbury and its characteristic inhabitants. The citizen-audience appears still to have been the main support of the Theatre and its neighbour the Curtain, though there were occasional excursions elsewhere, as when *The Comedy of Errors* had been acted at Grays Inn as part of the Christmas festivities of 1594. The young gentlemen of the Inns of Court would appreciate a farcical comedy-romance written with some brilliance on the model of Plautus, while the plot and pace of the intrigue, the uproarious absurdity of the situations and cross-purposes and the juggler-like artistry of the dialogue would go to the hearts and ribs of the ordinary public, who would find matter enough to laugh at and passages of serious beauty to serve as a relief from laughter without any uneasy feeling that the author had written over their heads for more classically-educated people. Such people did come, unquestionably, and enjoyed themselves and came again, but they did not yet constitute the real theatre-going public for whom the players and the author exercised their talents.

By this time the story of the House of Lancaster has been taken to its logical end with the culminating play of *Richard III*. Once more we have a play which, while at its best in the place for which it was originally written, is able also to stand alone and command interest and admiration. The clarity and dramatic effect of Richard's courtship of Anne Neville over the body of the murdered king are incredibly enhanced when the play is seen immediately after the *Henry VI* cycle, just as the confrontation of Richard and Margaret takes on a deeper significance when we have seen that same Margaret commanding the butchery of Richard's father, and Edward, Clarence and Richard in their turn butchering Margaret's son. At the same time, the play itself is better written than its predecessors, and shows, in comparison with them, a great advance in Shakespeare's relations with his audience. Gone are the days when anything will do provided there is enough blood and oratory; we have progressed even beyond the stage of the untidy chronicle of miscellaneous battles, betrayals and enthronement. The author has gone almost exclusively to one book, and is sticking to it as if he knew the audience to be as deeply versed in it as himself. The new art of literature was flourishing, the presses were turning out ballads, news-pamphlets, volumes of satire, literary criticism or thinly-veiled personal abuse, all of them welcome to the keen, up-to-date reader; but apart from those productions and their purchasers there was a different variety of reading-matter directed at the steady man who liked his book to be serious without being controversial.

An indication of this taste had been given as far back as 1577, when Harrison's introduction to Holinshed had praised the practice of leaving serious works such as the Bible, Foxe's *Actes and Monuments* (better known as his *Book of Martyrs*) or some volumes of history on tables and window-seats in the royal palaces to pass the time for those in attendance. The example set on the Continent by Hartmann Schedel with his great *Nuremberg Chronicle* was finding its imitators in our own country. Lanquet and Cooper had tried to produce a general year-by-year history of the whole world from the time of the Creation, and the result contained a vast amount of miscellaneous information from various early historians, but its construction made it heavy and inconsequent. Others, however, were writing historical works that covered a narrower field and could be read for the pleasure and interest of the story they told. Polydore Vergil early in the century had written Latin histories of England that became available before long in an English version, as did the Latin life of Richard III attributed to Sir Thomas More and incorporated by Hall, Holinshed and Speed in their histories, not in any spirit of plagiarism but as the best possible account of the subject. Hall had produced his history of the Wars of the Roses, and his work, like that of Grafton, was welcomed and embodied later on— usually with careful acknowledgement—in the better-known chronicle of Holinshed. The very existence of such a number of English chronicles and translations indicates their popularity as general reading-matter. They are mentioned, as we have seen, among the furniture of palaces, they are cited, in the Induction to *The Taming of the Shrew*, by a drunken tinker while being thrown out of a pothouse, and they were well and widely known to the large London public that came in between.

Richard III is our first real evidence of this. Far more than any of the Henry VI plays does it coincide, both in the story and in its treatment, with Hall's narrative. Comparison between the history and the play shows that the latter is not, and does not pretend to be, an original dramatic work. It is the stage version of a well-known and popular book, and as such it is subject to certain peculiarities of construction. We all know how our attitude to the stage or film version of a novel is influenced by certain episodes in the original that have attracted our attention and interest. They may or may not play a part in the unfolding of the story, but even if they are less relevant to the stage or screen play we are quick to resent their omission if they are left out. Even so, the story of the rise and fall of Richard contains a multitude of small, expressive scenes which are effective in themselves yet not essential to the action. It is not easy at first to see just what they are doing there, until one looks into Hall or Holinshed and finds the answer. They are in the play because they are in the book, and in the book they are so striking and effective that to omit them from the stage version would cause instant dissatisfaction in anyone who knew and liked the ordinary story. The progress of the doomed Hastings to that last council at the Tower is full of such episodes. First comes the news of Stanley's dread that 'the boar had razed his helm', then the brief conversations with the pursuivant and the priest, in which Hastings and

Buckingham allude all too lightly to the imminent fate of the Queen's supporters, Rivers, Vaughan and Grey. The irony of the scenes is obvious in retrospect, when we see Hastings confronted with his own sudden arrest and condemnation, but it is apparent in the scenes themselves when they are played to an audience familiar not only with the general course of the story but with Hall's—or, we may say, Sir Thomas More's—individual presentation of it.

Indeed, this familiarity can sometimes make a point that the stage has no power to make. In the narrative we learn that when Hastings was arrested at the council-board Stanley dived under the table in alarm and was wounded in the head, as he did so, by one of Richard's men, but an attempt to reproduce this on the stage would be confusing and probably ludicrous. An old theatrical tradition, however, used to make Stanley sit rigid in his place for a moment, rising only after all the others, and in response to an ominous glance from Richard. This is as far as the stage can go in suggesting the fulfilment of Stanley's symbolic dream, but an audience that knew the story would feel that the danger was a real one, and that the white boar had come perilously near to Stanley's helm. Other details, such as the request for strawberries from Holborn, Richard's dressing himself and Buckingham hastily in old armour from the Tower to give the suggestion of a sudden alarm and emergency, and the Scrivener's comments on the indictment of Lord Hastings, a document which took eleven hours to copy out and yet was finished and available no more than five hours after the alarm and execution, are put in for the same reason. They are good points in the book, and will be remembered from the book, and must be reproduced accordingly.

There is a still more interesting example of the book's providing material for the play. In the Chronicle, just after the story of the fall of Hastings, there occurs a passage that makes a powerful impression on the reader, though it has very little relevance to the story as it has been seen to unfold. It is a brief account of the career, character and appearance of Jane Shore, a London goldsmith's wife who had been mistress to Edward IV and to Hastings in turn, and was still living when More's account was first written, though her beauty and prosperity were things of the past, and she was no more than a withered, wrinkled remnant, begging 'of many at this day living, that at this day had begged if she had not been'. The whole passage is an impressive commentary and object-lesson on the vanity of earthly things, and once again those who had read it in the book would welcome its inclusion in the play.

The actual inclusion, however, might be difficult. Jane Shore herself was not thought to have had anything much to do with the actual course of circumstances, and the days of her degradation and beggary came long after the period of the play. It was better to keep her off stage, as a mere subject for jokes against Hastings and the King, and make use of the situation and the moral by applying them to someone else. There was another character, after all, whom the chronicles no longer mentioned but who had dominated the two preceding plays and might well be brought on, in the light of this suggestion, to mark the contrast between her present state and the old days of her beauty and her power. The audience that had read the story of Jane Shore's degradation would experience almost the same emotions by contemplating Queen Margaret's, and by comparing her two tremendous scenes with the above-cited passage in the history books we may conjecture a little more clearly what the spectators were most probably prepared to see.

Not, it would seem, an old woman, as she is usually played now. The old woman's part in this play is the Duchess of York, mother to Edward, Clarence and Richard. She is over eighty, and says so, and in many speeches she lays emphasis on her seniority to the king and the dukes, while her very curses are those of one who feels herself on the threshold of the grave. Margaret, by contrast, is never referred to as old. She is called 'withered', and 'wrinkled', it is true, but the terms are used always in association with the suggestion that she is a witch. Half the point of the reference is that sorrow and banishment have destroyed her

beauty and wrinkled her before her time. To those who had seen
the other plays of the cycle she must still be just recognizable as
the Margaret who had come to England as a bride with no dower
but ill-luck, who had played her almost lyrical farewell scene with
Suffolk her lover, and who had savagely baited and insulted the
captive York before having him beheaded. And, whether or not
they had seen the Margaret of the early plays, that was the
Margaret of the book, and the account of Shore's wife showed
how Margaret could be presented again in one last terrible
manifestation.

> Thus say they that knew hir in hir youth. Albeit some that now see
> hir (for yet she liveth) deme her never to have been wel visaged,
> whose judgment seemeth me somewhat like as though men should
> gesse the beautie of one long before departed, by hir scalpe taken
> out of the charnell house; for now is she old, leane, withered, and
> dryed up, nothing left but riveld skinne and hard bone.

There is 'good theatre' in that, and no one could better
exemplify it than the leading lady of the Henry VI plays, who
had rather faded out of the story unless the author could find
some good pretext for bringing her back again. And, as we can
see, he found one.

With the battle of Bosworth, and the arrival of the first Tudor
to lead England back to peace and prosperity, he had got as near
to the events of his own time as it was wise to go. If his public
wanted still more dramatized Hall, he would have to turn back
to the beginning of the book, and that, it would seem, is exactly
what he did. Hall's Chronicle, though purporting to deal only
with the houses of Lancaster and York, contains in its introductory material an account of the fall of Richard II, and the
accession of Henry of Lancaster to the throne. Using this as a
general outline, with corroborative detail gathered in from Holinshed and perhaps from Froissart, he produced another stage
version of a well-known story.

This time his patrons were given a special blend for their
money. Not only was it a good dose of Hall and Holinshed, it was

Hall and Holinshed presented in the manner of Marlowe. The author of *Edward II* had been stabbed in a tavern-brawl in 1593; two or three years after his death it would be about time for people to be overlooking the more scandalous tales about him and expressing their regret that there was no one who could write a play like that nowadays. It would be the moment, accordingly, for the former 'Johannes fac-totum' of the Rose, the player who had written imitation Marlowe for Alleyn on the other side of the river, to turn his hand to a purely poetic play on a Hall-and-Holinshed theme, particularly as the one that lay readiest to his hand was the one that provided the best chance for challenging comparison with his model. Accordingly the playgoers were confronted with something more lyrical and poetic than the Henry VI series, and at the same time better constructed than Marlowe's *Edward II*. The story familiar to readers of the book had been given a touch here, a new angle there, and was presented with heightened dramatic effect as a contrast of two temperaments —a contrast appreciated and pointed out by the principal character in the great scene—mentioned by Froissart and Hall but not by Holinshed—of Richard's physical surrender of the crown of England.

The modern reader or playgoer cannot but be hampered to some extent by unfamiliarity with the main historical facts, or rather with the version of them that the author and his audience took for granted. Hardly has the play begun before we hear Bolingbroke accusing Mowbray to his face of having murdered the Duke of Gloucester, and we have no hint how we are to take the accusation. The Elizabethan historians and their readers took it as common knowledge that Gloucester had been murdered with Mowbray's connivance *and on the king's instructions*. For them the opening of the play had far more tension than for those who saw in it a mere slanging-match between two unfamiliar historical figures, since they were in a position to appreciate Richard's own state of anxiety. Bolingbroke is coming to lay an official accusation against Mowbray; King Richard has every reason to know the justice of the charge, and what he wants to know, and asks

Bolingbroke's father in the opening lines, is the motive that has inspired the accusation, whether it is no more than personal dislike or whether something of the truth may have leaked out. That being taken for granted, there is a wealth of irony in the question

> Tell me, moreover, hast thou sounded him
> If he appeal the duke of ancient malice
> Or worthily, as a good subject should,
> On some known ground of treachery in him?

In the same way, Mowbray's own refutation of the charge contains a striking *double entendre*, when he denies the killing but blames himself for 'neglecting his sworn duty in that case'. On the face of it, he is lamenting his negligent guard of the nobleman whom, as Captain of Calais, he had a duty to protect, while to the king it is a word of regret that he had entrusted the murder to others instead of committing it himself. The emotions on the surface are only secondary to the fears and apprehensions that lie at the heart of the protagonist, and this must have been so obvious to the theatre-audiences of 1595 that the author felt no need to remind them of the point. An obscure remark by John of Gaunt in the second scene (which is not infrequently omitted from modern productions) alludes to the task of correction lying in 'those hands that made the fault', but even then it makes no specific mention of the king, easy as it would have been to do so.

Consequently, an audience without the Elizabethans' firm acceptance of Richard's guilt and Mowbray's knowledge of it will miss the underlying tension when the accusation is about to be tried by combat in the lists at Coventry. Richard knows that if Heaven *does* defend the right, Mowbray will be vanquished and will be compelled to make full confession, and he has no means of telling how much a vanquished and repentant Mowbray may see fit to confess. Mowbray's own speech before the king, therefore, has a double meaning. Outwardly a formal protestation of loyalty, it is in fact, for Richard and for the audience who know the story, a reassurance that whatever the issue of the combat Mowbray will not betray his king. In the light of that, Richard's weakness appears still more culpable when he fights shy of the test by throwing down his wardstaff at the last moment, and basely deserts his 'loyal, just and upright gentleman' by banishing him for life. Moreover, he extracts an oath from appellant and defendant alike that they will never meet or communicate with each other in banishment. The man who has nearly found out the truth must be prevented from all further communication with the one who knows it, and while the first may safely be allowed to return in a few years' time when it has all blown over, the other must never come home again. Yet, as it proves, it is Bolingbroke whose return from exile means dethronement and death for King Richard, and the more dangerous Mowbray loyally takes his secret and his master's to a Venetian grave.

All these points would present themselves almost automatically to a London playgoer who knew his Hall or Holinshed, but later audiences—and, for that matter, performers, producers and annotators of the play—often come to it without that necessary foreknowledge of the king's position that gives the poetry its proper backbone of tense drama. We go to *Richard II* nowadays for its poetry and character-drawing, not for the dramatic excitement that made it acceptable to the specially-primed audience for which it was written. We cut out, and do not miss, the scenes relating to Aumerle's conspiracy against the new King Henry, as they contribute little but doggerel to the dialogue and we are not interested in their contribution to the plot. Readers of the history would require some suggestion of a plot against King Henry in Richard's cause, if only to see in action what was well known in the story—the fact that a Richard kept in captivity, so long as he lived, must be a potential danger to England's throne and an unexceptionable excuse for conspiracy against the king.

Indeed, they knew it only too well, for not ten years had gone by since that very state of things had last been seen in England. Many who saw the players enact the plotting and pardon of Aumerle might also have stood in the crowd to see in all reality the ghastly end of a plotter who had *not* been pardoned, when Babington and his confederates were hanged, disembowelled and cut into quarters for conspiracy against their Sovereign in the cause—and, it was said, with the knowledge—of the captive Queen of Scots. And even as Piers of Exton had ridden to Pontefract to make all safe by killing Richard in his prison, so Mr Secretary Davison and the Council had sent off a Royal warrant without instructions, and a once-crowned head had fallen beneath the axe at Fotheringhay. London had every reason to know the significance of those last scenes, of Exton's action, be it to save his king or to curry favour with him, and that same king's horror-struck repudiation of the deed: and historian and playwright alike, while expressing and compelling sympathy for Richard, had contrived at the same time to explain and practically to justify the conduct of his supplanter.

Too much so, indeed, for some people's peace of mind. There were those—and Elizabeth herself was one of them—who saw in the story a dangerous reminder that a king of England had been deposed before now, not as a matter of sheer conspiracy and treason, like Marlowe's Edward II, by a rebellious nobleman who came to a bad end in the last act, but on positively humdrum, self-righteous grounds of public policy, just as in fact another king of England was to lose both crown and life two generations later. This was not the author's intention. The middle-class public brought up on Hall and Holinshed looked on all these historical plays in the light of the principle repeated and expounded throughout Hall's work from its very first sentence; namely, the misery and desperation to which a country can be reduced by civil quarrels. The whole story of the Wars of the Roses was treated by Hall, and by Shakespeare after him, as an awful warning against such internal dissension; events of the previous reign had reminded the Londoner how near at hand was the possibility that such days might precipitately return, and the keynote of the City pageants at Elizabeth's own coronation had been that of rejoicing at a reign that promised to unite contending parties, as her grandfather's had done, and keep England supreme abroad, peaceful and prosperous at home.

To the ordinary London citizen, this play was a stage version of a well-known story about the evils of civil strife, but other spectators, not primed with one or two popular history-books but consciously proud of their open, enquiring minds, might get unsuitable ideas from it. Even in our own days, *Richard II* has been billed at one time for a 'grand patriotic night' by a touring company in the North of England, and at another, by some earnest Londoners, as a 'study of decadent monarchy in the cruellest days of England's history'. There were, and are, many different ideas to be found in it, and the Elizabethan authorities decided that some of them were best left alone. When the text was published the deposition scene was discreetly left out; but even so the story of Bolingbroke's removal of Richard and assumption of his throne by general consent suggested an unwise parallel to the doings of the popular, turbulent Earl of Essex. In 1597 Dr John Hayward rather unwisely wrote, and still more unwisely dedicated to Essex, a history of Richard's fall and Bolingbroke's accession as Henry IV. There was trouble all round. Hayward was sent to the Tower and interrogated by a Committee of the Privy Council, and the chaplain to the Bishop of London, who had licensed the publication, was taken to task for it and had to admit that he had recommended the grant of a licence without actually reading the book.

Worse was to follow before many months were out. Two days before the abortive rising in 1601 which cost Essex his life, some of his friends made a special request to the Lord Chamberlain's Men (who were playing at the Globe Theatre by that time) for a production of the play. It seems to have been fresh enough in the repertory for such a revival to be possible, but the actors were reluctant to perform it, claiming that it was out of date and would no longer draw an audience. Indeed, it was only in consideration of an extra payment of forty shillings to offset their losses that they eventually put it on at all. Their hesitation may be attributed partly to knowledge that the subject was a dangerous one since the publication of Hayward's book, if not before, but some of it may be taken at its face value as evidence that audiences and their tastes were changing, and that there was no longer a public—if ever there had been one on the South Bank—for a purely poetic chronicle-play with no humorous characters, no prose and hardly any fighting. A new planet had come into the heavens and eclipsed the sun of Richard, and it was not the usurper Bolingbroke but one of his subordinates—the vast, genial, discreditable bulk of Sir John Falstaff. Small wonder that there would be little point in the revival of an earlier play without him, and that the eccentric noblemen who wanted such a thing were obliged to 'guarantee the house' by a cash payment before it was worth anyone's while to produce it.

Meanwhile, up in Finsbury, *Richard II* had probably been followed by *King John*, an attempt to bring an old play up to date. The earlier *Troublesome Reign of King John* contains practically the same characters as Shakespeare's play, but devotes much more time and energy to ridiculing the Church of Rome. Pope-baiting had been typical in the years leading up to the attempted Spanish invasion, but the public had lost interest in it since then, and the King John play had to be rewritten if it were to be kept in the repertory at all. Comparison of the two texts indicates that Shakespeare found it easiest in the long run to rewrite all the dialogue throughout while keeping the characters (he adds only one of his own, and gives him four words to speak) and a good many of the main situations. John's story was to be found in Holinshed but not in Hall, and people's ideas about him were very vague. There was an idea that he defied the Pope and was rather unscrupulous, but then one might say as much of the Queen's own father, not yet fifty years in his grave. He might even be the victim of Popery and disloyalty—one Elizabethan black-letter ballad uncompromisingly calls him 'good King John' —but there were other stories about him, and he seemed to have behaved very badly to his nephew Arthur of Brittany. In other words, there was no fixed King John legend in men's minds, and the author was free to play about with chronology as much as he liked.

He took full advantage of his freedom, as the author of the earlier play had done before him, and ended on the familiar note of England's invincibility as long as she can keep free from internal warfare—the note sounded throughout by Hall. It is interesting to see, as one goes through the historical plays, that while they owe much to Holinshed in the way of detail it is the earlier chronicler who has given them their general form and outlook. Men might be reading Holinshed in middle age, and appreciating the references to him in the theatre, but it was from Hall that they had first learned in their youth the significance of the Wars of the Roses and the rise, triumph and decline of the House of York.

Before writing any more historical plays, apparently, Shakespeare turned to a theme more closely connected with the life and interests of his particular audience. We have seen that the London citizen in general, and the Finsbury resident in particular, was a business man. Now, when he has got into his stride, the author finds himself able to forsake his warring kings for a while and write a play about business men, fashioning it from an ingenious foreign story that happens to have a business background. The introduction and development in later years of a leisured London population has meant that we regard *The Merchant of Venice* from a standpoint diametrically opposite to that of the commercially-minded Tudor Londoner. For us, the story of Shylock and the bond is the unnatural one, and Bassanio's wooing of Portia we take as the real, comprehensible part that shows us men and women—or, more particularly, one woman—whom we know and understand and welcome to our hearts. But the playgoers who went to the Theatre and the Curtain, the dwellers in those 'fair houses of merchants' that Stow has recorded for us, were of the same type and status as Antonio and his circle, and the house-party at Belmont represented their pleasant conjectures about life as it might possibly be lived by ladies and gentlemen of a fashionable world that as yet had nothing to do with London. The play was written for an audience of Antonios and Salanios, not for the Portias, Bassanios and Gratianos who now occupy the stalls.

It is a problem-play, and its problem is a business one. The change from business-audience to social-audience has meant that the companions of Antonio at the outset are conventionally played, nowadays, as young men of fashion who have little in common with Antonio and little knowledge of what he is talking about. Present them on the other hand as Antonio's contemporaries and business associates, and his position is established far more clearly, and in far less time. The speeches beginning 'Your mind is tossing on the ocean', and 'Believe me, sir, had I such venture forth', coming from young men of fashion who could never conceivably organize anything of the sort, are brilliant pieces of Shakespearean verse and nothing more—a consolation prize given to a couple of young men who are not quite good enough to be cast for Gratiano and Lorenzo. On the lips of two serious, responsible fellow-merchants the passage is not only as delightful poetry as before but an integral part of the drama, since it shows us what Antonio's ventures look like to the ordinary mercantile world of which he is a part. The opinions of two young men-about-town on such a point are worth little or nothing; the opinions of two other merchants of Antonio's type are clear enough indication that he is running a serious risk by hazarding so much of his fortune in these experiments overseas. It is the first faint warning that he is tempting Providence and that his affairs may possibly go wrong. And, sure enough, in due course they do go wrong, and in the very way foreshadowed by these opening apprehensions.

Fynes Moryson, the traveller who was so thoroughly bored by the bad acting of the English players at Frankfurt, spent some time in Venice in the course of his travels, and his account gives an expressive picture of that great city as it was known to Shakespeare's contemporaries. The London merchant knew more about Venice than the Venetian usually knew about London. Whereas the Londoner often went abroad in the interests of commerce, the Venetian, in his central position, was content to let commerce come to him from the various quarters of the Adriatic and the Mediterranean. Quite a number of London merchants would have seen, and even more would have heard of, the inexorable custom by which the Venetian gentleman, be he courtier, scholar or merchant prince, went decorously gowned, close-buttoned to the neck and wrists, when in the precincts of Venice, revealing the bravery of his doublet and hose only when on the mainland or when visiting his mistress at night, within doors. Most of these gowns were black, though Senators, Knights and Doctors wore them of scarlet. In a theatre where scenery was restricted to stage furniture and not much of it at that, the appearance of the first group of characters in an individual style of dress would do much to establish the location of the play and the general opening situation. The argument that it would cause confusion by making all the men look alike might be applied with as much or as little relevance to the evening dress worn by the actors in the first act of *Dear Brutus* or *Dangerous Corner*. The more a costume follows simple conventional lines, the more emphasis does it give to the individuality of a player's face, movement and expression, in which his true character resides.

The business conversation is broken up by the breezy arrival of Bassanio and his companions. The spectator was being given a change from the familiar topics of the opening, set in a world he knew quite well, to a glimpse of something different, the fascinating unrealities of an imaginary smart set, all brilliant conversation, insolvency and charm. It is a world to which Antonio's colleagues do not belong, and they quickly make their excuses and are gone. Bassanio has come to borrow money, and his companions, having seen him to the threshold of the attempt, tactfully withdraw in a whirl of genial absurdity after arranging to meet him at dinner, when they will be able to learn how he has got on. The action is being taken a step further, and the young nobleman and the Merchant of Venice have the stage to themselves for an important scene.

Critics in our own century have been inclined either to censure Bassanio or to find excuses for him. Audiences find less occasion for criticism and the original audience saw none at all. Because Shakespeare is Literature, and a National Institution, we are tempted to take all his characters somewhat too seriously, and to consider Bassanio a scheming hypocrite because he wants to

Nobilis Anglus   Nobilis matrona in Anglia

Fæmina Londinensis ornatus.   Ciuis Londinensis honesta vestitu

Two styles of audience. Courtiers (above) and citizens
(below), from Abraham de Bruyn.

dress in a style he cannot afford, so as to make a good impression on an heiress. He has been called a cad and a fortune-hunter for expressing sentiments, and formulating designs, which we should admit without question had his creator been not Shakespeare but Dr P. G. Wodehouse. The young man with a big heart, big ideas and a still bigger overdraft, 'touching' a friend for a loan so that he may equip himself for a house-party where there is a girl who combines all lovable qualities with a satisfactory fortune, was as good entertainment then as he is now, and represented, then as now, a mode of life that the audience liked to contemplate and did not pretend to share, let alone set it up as a serious code of conduct. The type is as old as Menander, and yet remains perennially young.

Comparison of this play with *King John*, too, may help to indicate how Bassanio's part was played. In a stock company or repertory company, as the Elizabethan companies were, there must necessarily be a certain amount of casting to type, and an author writing for such a company must necessarily take into consideration the appearance and abilities of the principal players. In regard to the principals there is a very close and significant correspondence. King John himself, compound as he is of majesty and malignity, is obviously marked out for Shylock, as Hubert de Burgh is for Antonio, while Bassanio would almost certainly have been played by the Bastard Faulconbridge. His conclusions about self-seeking and 'commodity' in the earlier play are made in the cheerful spirit of the Englishman who would make the most outrageous parade of self-interest rather than lie under the awful imputation of patriotism, loyalty or affection, and utter the most hard-headed and cynical sentiments to distract attention from the nature of his actions. The actor who had made a successful appearance in such a character would be expected by his public to give them something more of the same sort in his next part, and that, with a love-interest added, is exactly what the part of Bassanio enables him to do. Connect the lines of the scene with the good looks and good humour of an audience's ideal Fine Young Gentleman of Fashion, and the result is something that is none the less likeable for being popular with the public.

From the business man's point of view, the scene progresses naturally enough. Antonio is not in a position to lend his friend any money direct—and we have quite clearly seen why not—but he is prepared to stand security for him if Bassanio can raise the actual cash from anyone else on the strength of Antonio's credit. It is, in fact, the common and tempting operation of backing a bill for a friend, a practice against which we are all warned almost automatically when we attain any sort of control over our own finances. Bassanio goes off to seek his money and Antonio, deeply committed already, has committed himself a little deeper still.

As an antidote to this realism we are transported suddenly to the world of fancy. In Portia's home at Belmont, she and Nerissa talk in elegant, literary prose such as nobody outside John Lyly's plays would use for ordinary conversation. It is reminiscent of the talk of the goddesses in his *Endymion*, and it serves very well to suggest the language of High Society. We have only to look at some of Pinero's dialogue to find a nineteenth-century dramatist doing much the same thing for exactly the same reason, and some may be prepared to trace the practice and the principle later still. Shakespeare is merciful, however, and after a few sentences in this idiom to 'place' his people socially, he lets Portia become a human being, with a series of personal remarks about her various wooers. It was a line that had gone down well in the *Two Gentlemen*, and it was quite worth doing again.

At the end of the scene, we are given an extra pointer to Bassanio's character. We have seen him for ourselves, and heard him make his cheerfully depreciatory remarks about his own habits, motives and past conduct; now it is time to see what his own set think of him. Two words of Nerissa's give us the clue. To her he is 'a scholar and a soldier', and it is perhaps important that he has made no parade of being either. Comic scholars and comic soldiers, and those who aped their qualities, were among the regular character parts of the Tudor stage and all its successors and Shakespeare has given us good measure in both kinds, but here he reminds us that a man can be a scholar without being a pedant and a soldier without being a braggart, and could combine the two to form the ideal Elizabethan gentleman. But neither scholarship nor soldiering is traditionally the ideal way to make money, and in a few minutes we see Bassanio doing his best to borrow some, from an important character who has not been mentioned before. Instead of the black gown and small round cap of the Venetian merchant, we are confronted with the gaberdine and yellow cap of the Venetian Jew.

And here, once again, comes a great difference between the audiences of the sixteenth century and those of the twentieth. To us the Jew may be estimable, humorous, enviable, pitiable, contemptible or detestable, according to our personal, racial or political inclinations, but whatever else he is, he will not be unfamiliar. We are used to plays about Jews, jokes about Jews, newspaper rumours about Jews, fashionable photographs of successful Jews and the sight of miscellaneous Jews in all walks of our ordinary life, but the Londoner who first saw Shylock had very few examples for comparison. Half a century was yet to go by before the Jewish race, banished from England in the Middle Ages, would return at the command of Cromwell. Broadly speaking, therefore, the Elizabethan playgoer had only two Jews in his mind's eye—one in fiction, the other in fact. He had probably applauded Alleyn as the villainous plotter and poisoner in Marlowe's play, and he might even have stood in the crowd and seen the execution of old Doctor Lopez, a Portuguese Jew by race though not by religion, who had been convicted of accepting a bribe to poison the Queen. His defence, that he had intended to take the money but not to commit the murder, is probably a perfectly truthful one, but it did not save him from the scaffold, and there was something of the true Jew-of-Malta touch about the rumour that he had been arranging to put poison on the pommel of the royal saddle and on the arms of a State chair. It was a real-life mixture of Marlowe's Barabbas in *The Jew of Malta* with the poisoned gloves in his *Massacre at Paris*, and established the Jew as someone who might be legitimately considered capable of any enormity. There was no serious anti-Semitism in it; on the contrary, it was because the race had become unfamiliar and exotic that it was possible to believe anything of it without any particular ill-feeling, just as there was no racial prejudice behind the fashion for scientific and sinister Chinese villains in early twentieth-century fiction. Even the name was not one calculated to raise prejudice against its bearer. If it suggested anything Jewish to the man-in-the-street, it was the name of Shiloh, the sanctuary of Jehovah. In the English Bible of 1586 this word had been spelt *Silo*, but the 1594 text had restored the aspirates at beginning and end, so that the latest version bore a close resemblance to the name of Shakespeare's Hebrew villain. Incidentally, the Hebrew word *shalach*, 'cormorant', has also been put forward, but would seem less likely to occur to the mind either of the average London playgoer or of the author himself.

The commercial part of the story runs clearly and naturally. Shylock in turn has his doubts about the wisdom of Antonio's many ventures, and consequently about the wisdom of doing business with him. The two men meet, and dislike each other as much in person as they have done on principle in the past. Shylock explains to the audience, as clearly and crudely as could Richard of Gloucester himself, his opinion of Antonio's character and business habits, and Antonio makes it quite clear to Shylock that only Bassanio's urgent need has compelled him to a practice that he dislikes and ordinarily avoids. Shylock, however, is enjoying himself, and in a way that the commercial world will appreciate in detail. He does not admit the possibility of raising the whole sum himself—it is natural to him not to reveal how much capital he can muster when required—but he thinks his friend Tubal will be able to accommodate him; he chuckles over a long, complicated and not particularly edifying Old Testament story about one smart Jew getting the better of another, and cites it in justification of usury, and when Antonio tries to bring the conversation strictly back to business the Jew twits the Christian with his change of views in coming to do business with him at all. Antonio wishes it to be clearly understood that he has not changed his opinion of usurers, and that though on this occasion he has been compelled to break his usual custom, it is not to be taken as evidence of a change of heart or as a forerunner of further business deals. Shylock's answer is an exasperating plea for friendship, followed by an almost embarrassing renunciation of his own practice of interest. To do business with Antonio alone, he will lend him the money with 'no doit of usance', and no security but the purely formal one—quite unprofitable, as he himself points out—of a pound of Antonio's flesh. He does not insist on it, he puts it forward merely as a jocular suggestion of something that would never be worth claiming, and it is Antonio who agrees to it in spite of Bassanio's protest.

Another short scene in Belmont, and we are ready for the low relief. Shakespearean scholars, producers and actors have tried, with more zeal than conviction, to persuade us that Lancelot Gobbo's lines are funny in themselves, and part of the Shakespeare tradition, but the real secret is surely that Lancelot is, and must be, funny in *him*self, quite independently of his patter. The merchant in the audience has just been given the beginning of a strong and potentially interesting story about problems of commerce, the merchant's wife has enjoyed a charming scene or two in High Life, with a romantic Prince of Morocco speaking fine poetry, now it is the turn of the groundlings—the occupants of the standing-room or promenade area in the uncovered centre of the theatre—to be given what *they* like, and what they like is the Clown.

Lancelot Gobbo must have been played by Kempe or some equally popular idol, whose reputation and appearance would assure him a welcome before he did so much as open his mouth. At once he comes down to the audience, like that other Launce in the *Two Gentlemen of Verona*, with a long and confidential explanation of his present uncertainty and the trouble he is having with his conscience. Hard on that comes a little back-chat and buffoonery with his doddering old father, who serves as foil to him in exactly the sort of conversation we are accustomed to hear, in later entertainments, from the Clown and Pantaloon.

The actual name Gobbo has been connected with particular places, and even family names, both in Italy and in England, but there is no need to assume that Shakespeare was so precise, or expected his audience to be so. The word was, and is, straightforward Italian for a hump or hunchback, and would be an obviously appropriate name for a bent old man in a play about Italy. When we find the word used in later years to denote the round-shouldered Robert Cecil, it is in this anatomical sense and without any sign of Shakespearean cross-reference.

A cantankerous old gentleman with a beard and a worldly-wise young gentleman with an appetite make a good comedy couple in any period, and there is no need to give them a pedantically-serious pedigree back to the *Commedia dell' Arte* or anywhere else. They turn up wherever there is a public for them, and that is in almost any period of civilization. The traditional starveling, out-at-elbows Lancelot of many productions is quite possibly a mistake based on Lancelot's own claim that he never gets enough to eat. A fat Lancelot Gobbo, as Sir John Gielgud's production showed us before the war, is a great deal funnier. 'Do I *look* like a cudgel or a hovel-post?' he asks indignantly when revealing himself to his father, and this, rather than his own assertion that he is 'famished', suggests that what the original public saw was, if not a fat clown, at least a well-nourished one. The hunger of starvation is not a matter for laughter, the continual hunger of gluttony is, and always has been, and once again we find in the scene a particular application to its original audience. If there was one type of boy above all others whose chronic announcement was that he was starved by his master and was going to run away, it was the London merchant's apprentice. In popular imagination it was almost expected of him, just as the merchant's official opinion of his apprentice, as a convention, was that he was idle, greedy and unintelligent, and sure enough, 'a huge feeder, snail-slow in profit' is Shylock's own description of Lancelot.

There are times when convention finds a readier welcome than originality, and even so, when the Fat Boy of Venice appeared to voice the eternal complaint of the traditional London apprentice it was an audience of apprentices and their masters that got the highest degree of pleasure out of it, since those with the fullest knowledge of the real thing could best appreciate the caricature. Incidentally, it is worth noticing, in Lancelot's later scene with Lorenzo and Jessica at Belmont, how continually his mind runs to the thought of food. The actor may have made a speciality, indeed, of this kind of conventional gluttony, and have played the clown who was so particular, in an earlier play, to secure good finger-licking cooks for Capulet's banquet, or to get one of his fellows to save him a piece of marchpane.

Jessica, the Jew's daughter, is nowadays more hardly judged than the playwright seems to have intended. To a less sophisticated audience she was the Fair Heathen, the daughter of the Sinister Oriental, whose function was to run away with a Christian lover in the best fairy-tale style, taking a certain amount of her father's treasure with her. So, accordingly, she does. Lorenzo and Gratiano arrange the elopement, while Antonio's business friends lend a somewhat grudging support. Antonio himself seems to have no knowledge of what is going on under cover of an evening's masqueing-party, and soon we hear that he has seen Bassanio off on his way to Belmont and that there are disturbing rumours about his fortunes on the sea.

In the meantime two of Portia's noble wooers are seen choosing their caskets, and choosing wrong. If Shylock in this play is the Wicked Oriental, the Prince of Morocco is his antithesis the Noble Savage. He speaks poetry that recalls the more lyrical moods of Tamburlaine, he bases his choice on a compliment to Portia, and he is a good loser. The Prince of Aragon, by contrast, is sententious, priggish and rather precious (another version of the traditional Spanish melancholy that we have seen in *Love's Labour's Lost*) and we welcome his discomfiture, followed as it is by the news of Bassanio's arrival.

The opening of Act III is customarily taken lightly and fast, if only because the serious discussion of Antonio's ventures is all too heavy for the young men of fashion whom Salanio and Salarino generally try to depict. Accordingly, their opening of the scene is apt to sound laboured and unreal, and their baiting of the bereaved Shylock particularly distasteful. When we consider it in the light of the late sixteenth century, however, with merchants of London in the audience observing merchants of Venice on the stage, it takes on rather a different aspect. Instead of two flighty young men conveying information to the audience in a rather obvious and unplausible way, we see two business men talking 'shop' in a perfectly natural manner about a friend, and their words to Shylock seem less gratuitously insulting simply because they all three belong to the same world of commerce (however much they would resent admitting it). The Venetians are not going out of their way to mock at an old man in trouble; indeed, it is interesting to see how ready they are to speak Shylock fair as soon as they recollect that he is Antonio's creditor. When they are gone, Tubal has his own turn at tormenting Shylock even when giving him news, as tales of Antonio's ill-luck and Jessica's prodigality come turn and turn about. Finally, after another interlude of sheer lyrical beauty at Belmont, in which Bassanio wins his lady and his fortune, we are confronted with the real problem of the story as it would present itself to the Londoner of Shakespeare's day.

Antonio's ships have not come home, his bond is forfeit and there is no escape. Commentators in modern times have often declared that such a bond would be annulled in almost any court as 'contrary to public policy', and that Antonio is in no real danger of his life, but they have not realized that Salarino has been before them, with his assurance that the Duke 'will never grant this forfeiture to hold', and has been answered completely by Antonio. If he keeps his pledge, he makes sacrifice of his life, but if he does not, and repudiates the bond, he makes sacrifice of his integrity and commercial standing. His credit and reputation go by the board, and if the Duke's court upholds or enforces that repudiation, the credit and reputation of Venice go down likewise. There is no future among honest men for the merchant, or the firm, or the nation, that declares a promise may be made and value taken for it without any intention of its being fulfilled. If Antonio breaks his word, and the authority of Venice helps him to break it, he is 'finished' as completely as if he had died under Shylock's knife, and he and Shylock both know it. That is the problem as it would present itself to the contemporary playgoer —not, perhaps, to the original Italian reader of the story in the source-book, *Il Pecorone*, but certainly to the Londoner for whose benefit Shakespeare had turned it into a topical problem-play.

Once in court, the matter is made clearer still. The Jew has the Christian merchant and all the administration of Venice in a cleft stick, and the Duke's only course is to pay Shylock the compliment of assuming that he is going to show his magnanimity at the last moment by renouncing his claim and perhaps even writing off some of the original debt. The suggestion falls absolutely flat. Shylock points out that he is asking for no more than the price that Antonio, by a duly executed instrument, has agreed to give. This is quite unanswerable, and the Duke has no answer. Instead of further argument he is prepared to dismiss the court until he has had the benefit of a professional jurist on the legal problem, and there in due course is the cue for Portia to arrive, in the long gown of a Venetian gentleman, but in scarlet, as befits a Doctor of Laws, instead of the merchants' black.

Her first view coincides with that of the Duke. If Antonio admits the bond—why, then, the Jew will have to be merciful. There is nothing else for it. Bassanio's offer to pay the money is of no avail if Shylock does not choose to accept it, and any 'wresting of the law' is not to be thought of. If he demands what lawyers still call 'specific performance' of his client's pledge, he is entitled to have it, and the Court will support him. It is to be noted that these pronouncements come, not from an advocate retained on behalf of Antonio, but from an independent legal authority acting as arbitrator and adviser to the Duke. It is in this capacity that Portia points out to Shylock that mercy, though by no means compulsory, is sometimes preferable to exact justice, and then gives him the chance, first of taking three times the original loan, and then of providing a surgeon to prevent Antonio from bleeding to death. He refuses the money and unwittingly seals his own doom by dismissing the other suggestion with the query: 'Is it so nominated in the bond?' His claim is for specific performance of the agreement and he flatly refuses to admit any variation or addition in the cause of common humanity or common sense. Accordingly, the sentence is pronounced of what the law allows and what in consequence the court awards. Shylock is told to take his due and, as an afterthought, is warned what will happen if he does anything—such as shedding blood—not specified in the agreement. The effect is not that of the Savoy operas, by which a Koko or Iolanthe can evade impending fate by the re-inter-pretation or actual re-drafting of an Act of Parliament. On the contrary, it is sternly logical. Shylock, not Portia, has claimed that blood is not nominated in the bond and has ob-jected to its being allowed for. Shylock, not Portia, has urged the doctrine of specific performance till it becomes intolerable; all she has done is to take it logically still further till it becomes absurd.

Shylock's response is, first incredulity, then a brisk attempt to close with Bassanio's earlier offer of threefold restitution, then a claim for the original principal; and finally he decides to cut his losses and 'stay no longer question'. But now for the first time he is charged roundly with plotting against Antonio's life and con-fronted with the penalty for his own malice. Half his property is forfeit to his victim, half to the Venetian State, and his very life is at the Duke's mercy. Commentators who have charged the Christians with harshness at this point to a fallen enemy would appear to have missed the significance of what follows. The Duke grants Shylock his life at once and intimates that the State's claim to half his goods may be reduced, on submission, to a fine. Antonio in his turn renounces his absolute claim to the other half, undertaking only to have the use of it in Shylock's life-time and to settle it on Lorenzo at his death if Shylock will do the same with the half which the Duke's generosity has left to him. The final point—his compulsory conversion to Christianity —would seem the best possible thing that could be done for him, from the point of view not only of the Court of Venice but of the original spectators and, quite possibly, of the author himself.

To the Elizabethan mind, a man who had received Christian baptism, however reluctantly, must stand a better chance of salvation than one who had lived and died in a false faith. It was in just such a spirit that Elizabeth's commissioners had denied Mary, Queen of Scots, the services of her own priest when she mounted the scaffold in the great hall at Fotheringhay. The Dean of Peterborough—father of Shakespeare's successor and possible collaborator John Fletcher—was in attendance to give any spiritual help that might be asked for, but the commissioners were not willing to imperil their victim's slender chances of salvation by letting her go to her death new-fortified by the rites of Rome. Even so, Shylock is to be brought, albeit by force, within the pale of Christianity, so that the play may have a happy ending and even the Sinister Oriental be given an ultimate chance of Heaven.

The trial scene, therefore, ends on a rising note of relief and happiness. Gratiano's observations throughout have been those of a ribald chorus, and a recent production has shown that they are much funnier and less malicious when delivered as *obiter dicta* from a balcony—as if the irrepressible Gratiano, having no business in the body of the Court, had got himself into the front row of the public gallery—than when they are uttered face to face with the plaintiff. A short informal scene brings us into the mood of high comedy again, and the play ends with a last act of poetry and romantic beauty in which exquisite verse-speaking in a static situation, with distant music, no tension and next to no movement, takes the place of the excitement and suspense of the professional problem just worked out in the Duke's court. Antonio's fallen fortunes are set up again by an outrageously crude announcement, which even the author will not attempt to justify, that three of his ships have come home safely after all,

Bassanio and Gratiano have had their legs pulled by their wives, Lancelot Gobbo has made one final, fleeting appearance apparently imitating a post-horn, and they all go in to live happily ever after, while the London merchant and his wife, and Ralph the apprentice to boot, can go home to London over Finsbury fields after an evening's entertainment that has had something in it for all of them.

V

History and Prince Hal

THE TWO plays about Henry IV show a great advance from
the earlier histories, even from those of only a few years back,
such as *Richard II* and *King John*. The technique of *The Merchant
of Venice* has been applied to a historical subject, and has been
once more successful. For the well-read merchant there is the
serious, straightforward story of the king who had put down
Richard II and uneasily occupied his throne. For his wife there is
the passionate, romantic figure of Hotspur, with his wealth of
energy, his impatience, his delightful lady and his unexpected
repertory of local allusions, and opposed to him the corresponding figure of the Prince, who gets on so badly with his father until
he saves his life in battle, and who has such reprehensibly funny
adventures in the meantime. And, for the apprentice and the
groundlings originally, but since then for all the Shakespeare-
going world, there is Falstaff.

By comparison with the preceding play we can even guess at
some of the casting. The 'heavy man', who gave his name to the
last piece and spoke the opening lines, does just the same here,
except that from a Merchant of Venice he has become a King of
England. The popular, impulsive, impecunious Bassanio reappears, in another version of the same character, as Prince Hal,
and the versatile Gratiano is permitted to show off his brilliance
in a stronger part than before, as Hotspur. It is the regular patron
of his local theatre who gets to know the character and capacities
of most of the principal players and to expect—even to demand—
a particular kind of performance from each; and it is just this sort
of regular patron that local managements and authors like to
encourage in his habits by providing entertainment in accordance

with expectation. We may not see at first glance where the villain is to come in, until we try the experiment of mentally casting our scheming King John and Shylock for the part of Worcester, when he suddenly falls into place. It is Worcester who is roundly accused of putting rebellious ideas into Hotspur's head, Worcester who is sent out of the council-chamber before Hotspur's scene with the king, but lies in wait for him afterwards and works his temperament to fever-heat, and Worcester, last of all, who precipitates the battle and Hotspur's death—and incidentally his own—by suppressing the king's offer of terms in their last interview. The tendency nowadays is to underplay him and to give greater emphasis to the much smaller part of Northumberland, but it may be questioned whether the dramatic quality of the play has not suffered by this practice.

Another member of the company may have acquitted himself well in *The Merchant of Venice* and earned a better part in the succeeding play. Lancelot Gobbo the clown has a technique of coming down stage and giving the audience his views in an intimate and conversational commentary. We have seen that this technique works best with a player who is acceptable to his audience from the very first moment, and we have had reason to conjecture that Lancelot was intended to be fat. If we look in *Henry IV* for a fat man with a popular and engaging personality and a habit of making long prose speeches in which he takes the audience into his discreditable confidence, it is not long before we find one, and those who saw the late Sir George Robey in the part will remember how the author's lines fell into place as the true patter of the variety artist. Indeed, the actor was thought by those not familiar with the text to be interpolating matter of his own into the part, such was the deceptive ease with which he uttered, in the orthodox Robey manner, the lines that Shakespeare had written for the same sort of comedian more than three hundred years before.

The fat old sinner started life under the name of Sir John Oldcastle. There is a pun about it in one place and an indication of it, in the early texts, in another. After a complaint had been made, apparently, by the Lord Cobham of the day about the scandalous misrepresentation of an early Lollard martyr, the name was changed to that of the runaway knight who had been denounced and degraded for cowardice in *King Henry VI*. Modern texts of this play give him the historical name of Sir John Fastolfe, but the First Folio editors, and presumably the author as well, called him Falstaff, and Falstaff was the name accorded to the fat comedian of *King Henry IV* when Oldcastle was barred. There may even have been an idea that he should go through all the appropriate plays and show the cowardly knight in characteristic early adventures before his disgrace by Talbot; but, as we shall see, the fortunes of the players and the composition of the company seem to have inclined his fate another way.

By this time the company must have firmly established itself in the consciousness of the neighbourhood and worked up a regular connection with a local audience. Gratiano-turned-Hotspur is particularly well equipped with remarks that have a special significance for the local family party amusing itself after business hours. In the scene at Bangor, where the rebel leaders are the guests of Owen Glendower, he shows a lively impatience with the impressive and mystical Welsh chieftain, whom he regards as rather a boring old gentleman and possibly a humbug to boot, and expresses himself in terms especially significant to the neighbourhood of Guildhall, Moorfields and London Wall. He decries poetry by saying he would

> rather hear a brazen canstick turn'd
> Or a dry wheel grate on the axle-tree,

and though the comparison would seem a natural one to any audience it would gain force and effect in a locality not far from the notorious nuisance of Lothbury, where the metal-turners worked at their lathes in the open air, turning brazen candlesticks and other domestic objects, and the resultant sounds were worth Stow's while to mention with dislike in his *Survey*. The two nastiest local noises were probably turners' lathes and miscellaneous wheels that needed oiling, and the latter, at any rate, were comparatively recent innovations in London streets. The day of the pack-horse and the hand-barrow was just closing, four-wheeled vehicles were just lately permitted to lumber along streets never designed for them, and the London traffic problem, with its combination of discomfort to the ear and danger to the person, had come into its own. Stow notes it with gloomy disapproval, and his remark that 'the world runs on wheels' appears to have been a catch-phrase of the time, cropping up some years later as part of a very vulgar song in *The Knight of the Burning Pestle*.

Hardly has Hotspur brought in these local allusions than he is venturing on ground still nearer to the Theatre and the Curtain. Rather than endure Owen Glendower's conversation, even over a good meal 'in any summer-house in Christendom', he himself would gladly feed on 'cheese and garlic in a windmill'. We have already seen how the old open spaces of Moorfields were being encroached upon, so that the Londoner in search of refreshment before or after the play could in fact choose between country fare in the old-fashioned establishments and the new delights available in the fantastic towered and pinnacled buildings that were springing up in ever-increasing numbers, to the disgust of old-fashioned people like Stubbes, whose *Anatomy of Abuses* shows that he thought them flashy in design and sinful in association. It was the contrast between farmhouse tea and road-house *thé dansant* as we may imagine it to-day, with an appeal to the nose thrown in, as there was a common belief that the windmills of the neighbourhood were reared on ancient dunghills. The combination of cheese, garlic and a windmill suggests an atmosphere that some people might consider difficult to enjoy, and intensifies Hotspur's point in preferring it to the company of Glendower.

Most audacious of all, perhaps, is Hotspur's allusion to citizens' wives a little later in the same scene, when he is rallying Lady Percy on her refined taste in expletives. She is swearing 'like a comfit-maker's wife', and 'as if she had never walked further than Finsbury'. It is significant that all these local allusions are given to one actor, and we can see the point still more clearly if we concede that he was the high-comedy man who played parts like

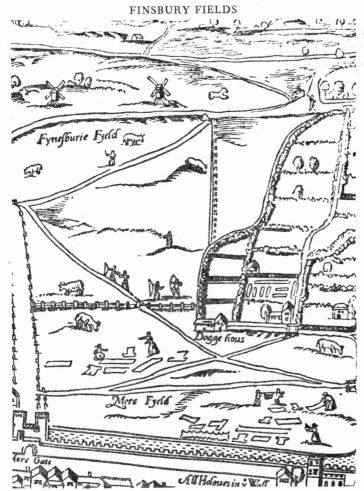

Moorfields, with windmills, archers, drying grounds
and two men carrying a washing basket on a staff.
From Agas' map of London.

Gratiano and could bring out his accusations while cocking a
lively eye at the typical 'velvet-guards and Sunday-citizens' who
had come over Finsbury Fields to hear him.

Having got his effect in this scene the author wisely leaves
local allusions alone for the rest of the play. Hotspur has played
enough comedy for the evening, and must now be shown rushing

to his tragic end, till at last he is face to face with the Prince of Wales who has been contrasted with him, in action and report, through all that has gone before.

The treatment of Hal himself, in the meantime, has shown some consideration for the nature and feelings of the comfortable burgess-and-family audience. Like his counterpart Bassanio he has been somewhat misjudged by readers and spectators of a more critical and sophisticated type, who have seen in his first great monologue a considered statement of policy by an astute and rather unlikeable young man. That is what it would be if it were to them that it had been directed, but it was not. We have just been introduced to the king's son and a selection of his not very reputable companions, arranging the preliminaries of what sounds very like a crime and is at best a heavy-handed practical joke. It is important that the audience should be told, at the first opportunity, what sort of a young man Hal really is, and left in no doubt about his ability to distinguish right from wrong. In an earlier play, Richard of Gloucester had taken the audience into his confidence by announcing that he was going to be a villain. Here the prince does the same with a contrary announcement, a mixture of apology and excuse for behaviour that the spectators have just seen and cannot be expected to approve whole-heartedly. We have not yet come to an audience that revels in the study and analysis of men's motives; Master Citizen and his wife are expecting to see a tale out of history, and they like to be told at once how they are to regard the principal young man, without wasting time wondering whether he is meant to be a hero or the reverse, or trying to fit his character to the hero-king of Hall and Holinshed. *The Knight of the Burning Pestle* shows us such a couple giving applause and sympathy to the comic lover in mistake for the hero and misunderstanding the greater part of the play in consequence, and it is such a misunderstanding on the part of just such an audience that the speech is designed to prevent.

There is a reminder of this warning a little later on, when Falstaff and the prince in succession give their impressions of King Henry lecturing his son. Falstaff's version begins with a little

Marlovian blank verse in the style of Alleyn on the South Bank, then he lapses into prose, and the measured antitheses of Lyly—much the sort of thing that had served Portia for smart conversation on her first entry in the last play—with a dash of the Puritan preacher groaning windily in the pulpit, 'Shall the blessed sun of heaven prove a micher and eat blackberries? A question not to be asked.' When in his turn he plays the prince, he expands gloriously on the excellent character of Sir John Falstaff as a companion for royalty. 'Banish plump Jack,' he cries, 'and banish all the world.' The answer comes in four words, and he does not heed them. 'I do, I will,' says Hal, and the audience may see what Falstaff does not—that he means it. It is very different from the eloquent indelicacies about Falstaff's figure that have gone before it; it is the first warning of something that will have to happen one day and will not be denied.

But before then there is much to show us. The interview that we have seen in mockery takes place in earnest, and the spectators are given a chance to see how far the prince's frivolities have estranged him from his father. In a world of masters, journeymen and apprentices, the relation between a young man and his father or his master was a thing well known and appreciated in all its possibilities. Both parties could watch with interest and sympathy, as they beheld this play, the older man's sad resignation and disillusionment and the younger one's asseverations of reform. Most men in the audience would feel that they had played something like that scene, in one capacity or the other, in real life, and all alike would notice and welcome the prince's efforts at self-discipline, the modesty and courtesy of his request to meet Hotspur in single combat and the moment when he rescues his father from the hand of Douglas and 'redeems his lost opinion'. The fight with Hotspur gives the actor an opportunity for a display of swordsmanship, but for Hal, as a character, the most dramatic moment he has in the battle is his re-entry just as Douglas is about to strike down the king. A nick-of-time rescue, in armour or out of it, is always good theatre, and this situation is additionally heightened by the relations between father and son. The spectators have seen and regretted their difficulties, and the elder Henry's only too natural mistrust of the younger, so it is with peculiar satisfaction that they see that mistrust dispelled by a heroic and spectacular rescue.

Unsophisticated audiences still cheer and applaud the arrival of the United States Marines at the right moment in a certain type of motion picture, and in the same way, and the same spirit, I have seen an older generation in a country market-hall welcome the arrival of a barn-storming gentleman who appeared suddenly beside the much-wronged heroine, announced himself as 'Loo-tenant Markham of His Majesty's Ship *Magnificent!*' and knocked everybody down. Hal's redemption of his honour is even more important than his conquest of Hotspur, though even in the latter he is given more than one chance to show his knightly courtesy. Then the battle is won, the family differences are settled and the family audience can pick up its gear and go comfortably home with a feeling that all has ended pretty well as it should.

The play was published as an independent quarto in 1598, and this fact would seem to have established the text beyond possi-bility of serious alteration. The sequel fared rather differently. Our earliest text of the Second Part is a quarto published in 1600, and it may well be that by the time this came out, the play had undergone a revision entailed by a change of locality and con-sequently a change of audience, who demanded rather different matter for their diversion.

For some time the players had been having trouble with Giles Alleyn their ground landlord, and had had to leave the Theatre and give their performances at the Curtain, a neighbouring play-house on a plot of ground which took its name from some for-gotten curtain-wall or outwork of the City and is still com-memorated in Shoreditch by the name of Curtain Road. At Christmas-time in 1598 things came to a head, and in the last few days of that year some of the company, with one Peter Street, a builder, mustered at the Theatre with swords and carpenters' tools and proceeded to demolish the building. A timber-framed house is not difficult to dismember; as the planks and beams came down they were loaded into carts and taken through London to the riverside, whence they were ferried over to Southwark, to a new plot of land which the Chamberlain's Men had procured in readiness. On this new ground, and with the help of the old timbers, there arose a building which was to be associated with Shakespeare's name and to see the performance of most of his later works, its very last production being the latest of them all. Finsbury and the Theatre had given place to Bankside and the Globe.

The Chamberlain's Men had taken their playhouse with them piecemeal, but they could not take their audience in the same way. Some loyal patrons of the company might make the journey now and then, but from the point of view of the citizen and his family there was all the difference in the world between walking out of the City into Finsbury Fields in search of entertainment and walking right *across* the City, crossing the Bridge or being ferried over the Thames, to go to an unfamiliar playhouse in a not very respectable neighbourhood. The company must not count on the support of the audience for which it had catered hitherto, and must rearrange its plays and its general atmosphere accordingly.

In some ways the new audience was rather more keenly intelligent than the last one. It represented, not the regular residents of the neighbourhood, but the personnel and patrons of the local taverns and houses of entertainment or ill-fame. The average playgoer on the South Bank was not the London tradesman taking his wife to the local theatre, but the man-about-town seeking such recreation as a prelude, a sequel or an alternative to other forms of self-indulgence. Here was something a great deal more like the intellectual audience of *Love's Labour's Lost*, or the country-house audience of *A Midsummer Night's Dream*, with much more acute perceptions than the Finsbury public and at the same time with little or none of its sound middle-class morality.

The two parts of *Henry IV*, then, reflect the tastes of two different audiences. We have no means of knowing what text was originally written for the Second Part at the Curtain; by the time the 1600 edition was printed it was being played at the Globe, and the printed text, cuts and all, reflects the South Bank version. Gone are all things like the Moorfields jokes and the criticism of the inn at Rochester 'from a sanitary and social point of view'. Falstaff's own house of call has changed its nature, and instead of being administered by a vintner with a hen-like wife and a comic drawer named Francis it is now something more like a thieves' kitchen, where swords might be drawn and a brawler 'quoited downstairs like a shove-groat shilling', and where Pistol and Doll Tearsheet—and possibly the Hostess—beat a man to death among them. The jokes are often subtler, and usually lower, than those in the First Part, and there seems much less assumption that the audience knew its Hall and Holinshed, the play being opened this time by an explanatory prologue put into the mouth of Rumour, and the historical matter occupying a far smaller proportion of the whole than in the earlier piece. Indeed, the printing of the 1600 quarto indicates that one of King Henry's few scenes, the one containing his famous commentary on sleep, was very nearly omitted from the printed text, which is a strong suggestion that it had been cut in the actual performance.

Yet there are local jests of a sort, and they are found, as before, in the lines of the flamboyant actor who likes playing slightly exaggerated character-parts or, as the Elizabethans were learning to call them, 'humours'. As Gratiano his line had been florid comedy, as Hotspur it had been an excitable romanticism that came very near ranting, now it appears as ranting pure and simple, for Hotspur is dead, his interpreter has to have a part, and a good one, and accordingly Falstaff's company is enriched by the presence of a junior officer, Falstaff's ensign or 'ancient', who goes bellowing round the place like a parody of a blood-and-thunder tragedian and interlards his speech with misquotations from plays in which Alleyn and his colleagues were still appearing upstream at the Rose. A player of the type required for Gratiano and Hotspur would enjoy himself thoroughly, and give enjoyment to his audience, with an outrageous imitation of Alleyn himself in situations in which no London actor-manager would wish to be exhibited, fighting in a pot-house with a lady of the town, playing courier and hanger-on to Sir John Falstaff, loudly glorying in the prospect of prosperity at a corrupt court, swaggering over a country justice who is too drunk to give much account of himself, and finally being haled away to the lock-up, mouthing his version of 'Se Fortuna mi tormenta, la Speranza mi contenta'*, a stock cutler's motto off a sword-blade. The fortunes and misfortunes of Pistol must have been still funnier when they could be associated by implication with the old lion still roaring his way through Kyd and Marlowe a little further along Bankside.

The straightforward historical scenes would need little alteration and presumably stand very much as they did in the original North Bank version of the play, so it is worth while, perhaps, to give them rather more detailed consideration. Prince Hal has been separated from Falstaff by his father's order, and Sir John is now serving under the less congenial John of Lancaster. The king no longer suspects his son of possible conspiracy or rebellion but he is not unjustifiably apprehensive about the use Hal will make of the kingly power when he comes to it, and his apprehensions are shared by his younger sons and the nobility of the kingdom. Falstaff typifies the raffish, unscrupulous world that may so easily invade the Court, and over against him is set the representative of law and order in the person of the Lord Chief Justice. The arrangement of construction by which these two characters are contrasted has been obscured, in the version we know, by the Falstaff scenes that may have been written in specifically for Bankside, but if we remove the trimmings and elaborations that would appeal to a 'smart' audience familiar alike with town taverns and country justices we are left with a different sort of play, but still a coherent and perhaps a more significant one. Hal is presented like a character in a Morality, or like Doctor Faustus himself, standing between two main figures, who represent Justice and Iniquity. The Lord Chief Justice is introduced into each of the earlier Falstaff scenes, the two have conversations with their own companions and with each other, but (if we accept the Doll Tearsheet scene as a Bankside interpolation) neither of

* If Fate use me ill, Hope cheereth me still.

them exchanges a word with the Prince until he has assumed the crown.

The famous story of Hal's taking the actual diadem from his father's pillow is the only part of the Hall-and-Holinshed story that is particularly good theatre, and the author has accordingly made it the occasion of a 'strong' scene between the two, corresponding yet contrasting with their earlier interview in the First Part. After that, the new king is confronted with the sudden realization that he has succeeded not only to the crown but to the terrible isolation of kingship. His own brothers look at him apprehensively, the Lord Chief Justice answers him respectfully and firmly but without hope. Neither his dead father nor his living kinsfolk can show any confidence in him to use his power aright now that he has come to it, and if he is to choose righteousness and reject iniquity he must do it on his own initiative, without even the encouragement of popular expectation. He chooses aright in confirming (quite unhistorically) the Lord Chief Justice in his office and submitting to his 'well-practised wise directions'.

As if that were not enough, we must see him faced with another thing that his father had prophesied. The news of his accession is hailed with enthusiasm by the 'apes of idleness' who look forward to a reign of license and frivolity. No sooner has Falstaff heard the news than he is shouting for his horse, promising honour and office to his friends, and bucketing off to London, uttering a gibe at the Lord Chief Justice as he does so, and proposing to requisition what horses he pleases on the way, since he is sure that henceforth 'the laws of England are at his commandment'. Hardly has Henry come forth from the solemn sacrament of his consecration than this fat shadow of his past rises to confront him, attended by the unspeakable Pistol and a complete stranger, apparently senile, whom they must have picked up somewhere in the country. He tries to ignore him, and leave the Lord Chief Justice to deal with him, but Falstaff will not be ignored. He hails the king again with uproarious, embarrassing familiarity, and it is only too evident that he looks forward to just the sort of reign that the dying Henry IV had so sadly foreseen. Hal is finding his father's anxiety justified in the most painful, public and humiliating way, and there is only one thing to be done about it. The amendment which he promised to his father and reiterated to the Lord Chief Justice must be repeated to the other persons whom it most nearly concerns, and that will be the hardest of all. There is no place for half-measures, the break must be instant, unquestionable and complete. Falstaff must not be given so much as a chance to laugh himself back into favour and forgiveness with a witty reply, and accordingly he speaks to hit and to hurt as only an intimate friend can hurt, because from such a friend nothing less will be enough.

Hal has been condemned both for his action and his words by people not only of sentiment but of sensibility, and Falstaff has been correspondingly exalted, but the London citizen and his wife would regard the matter differently. The hereditary principle applied to shopkeepers in England as well as to princes, and this involved not only the difficulty of training-up young men, whether sons or apprentices, to be worthy successors to their elders, but the grim possibility of failure. Dekker and Marston in *Eastward Ho*, and Hogarth, for the matter of that, in his *Industry and Idleness* series a hundred and fifty years later, showed what could happen when a young London apprentice fell among bad companions, and they made no attempt to hide their knowledge that, however comical the process, the end was black tragedy and degradation. They were realists, and it is only the romanticist who can wholeheartedly welcome and applaud a Falstaff or a Macheath. People who know the character in real life, and what he stands for, cannot always escape his charm when he is present, but they cannot pretend that he is a good influence or a good friend, or deny a feeling of relief at the certainty that Falstaff is no longer to be a companion to the king. It was for people like these, and not for the country-gentry of the court or the bull-baiting public of the South Bank, that Shakespeare wrote this tale of a young man coming into his inheritance.

VI

Soldier-Heroes

BY THIS time there was another element in the London public. In 1596 Essex and the Lord Admiral had made their famous raid upon Cadiz, and in the next year he and Ralegh had sailed to the Azores, done some service there and come home blaming each other for having hampered the success of the venture. From the ordinary Londoner's point of view there were all sorts of men who had come back from these expeditions and were now seeking other work, or drinking in the taverns, playing the old soldier to anyone who would listen to them, with their stories of action against Spain, jealousy amongst captains, and their personal reminiscences (quite possibly apocryphal) of that popular figure 'the General'—the Earl of Essex, whose views, temperament and long square-cut beard were freely imitated by those who hoped thereby to imitate his wide popularity. The young man back from the wars, and the old soldier with a mouthful of military terms and 'a beard of the General's cut', as Shakespeare himself puts it, were such topical figures that it is not surprising to find them appearing, under various names, on the London stage by 1598 as legitimate subjects for general interest, admiration or ridicule as the case may be.

Shakespeare was not the only person to produce them. A new writer at the Curtain—sponsored, says a late and dubious tradition, by Shakespeare himself—was a young man named Jonson, who had had a classical education at Westminster before being apprenticed to a bricklayer, serving in the army abroad and finally taking to literature. He had written some tragedies that had been played on the South Bank (though he seems to have been ashamed of them later on and left them out of his collected works) and had had a share in a scurrilous comedy called *The Isle of Dogs*, which got him into prison for a time. He aimed at being a satirist in the classical manner, and his first Curtain play was a comedy set in Florence and ridiculing various types, temperaments or, as he and his audience called them, humours.* We are fortunate in having two versions of this play, the first one, produced at the Curtain in 1598, and a later revision carried out at a date not yet fully established, but obviously for a different audience, which is invited to laugh at the middle-class public of the Shoreditch neighbourhood and the shifts and shortcomings of the Curtain, which Jonson now thought to be safely behind him. *Every Man in his Humour* is what its name implies, a collection of stock characters, each of them brilliantly exemplifying some particular temperament. There is the young poet, his old father (a part Shakespeare is said on no good authority to have played), the town simpleton, the country simpleton (who has the rude remarks about North London citizens in the rewritten version), the jealous husband, the Justice and the Swaggering Captain, a gentleman as old as Plautus, Terence and Menander, but always new, because the thing itself is always with us, rich in joyous absurdities that rival the extravagances of fiction. Wild moustachios, tavern causeries and tall stories of the late campaign are not yet entirely unfamiliar or extinct, and Jonson's severe and seedy Captain Bobadil, caricature as he is, would seem to have been a caricature of something known to very many Londoners in the years following the Cadiz Venture and the Islands Voyage.

Bobadil and his circle had given the local audience a chance of laughing at the absurdities of the military man at the end of a campaign, and it may well be by something more than chance that Shakespeare in the same season gave them its antithesis, a

---

* The word literally means *liquids*, and was used to denote the various fluid contents of the human body, which were supposed to influence or determine the temperament, as exemplified by the use of the words sanguine, choleric, lymphatic or melancholic, as applied to different types of temperament. It was soon used haphazard, often with little or nothing of its original application to the vascular system.

play with a military hero. We have seen how the effect of *The Merchant of Venice* has changed with the advent of a more or less leisured theatre-going public, and there are various indications that exactly the same thing has happened with *Much Ado About Nothing*, which was produced by the same company and with very much the same cast. The young man in semi-dependent relation to an older one reappears as Claudio the Florentine, an officer in the service of the Prince of Aragon, the flamboyant young man tones down the extravagances of Pistol to the high-comedy part of Benedick, the serious old man is translated from the office of Lord Chief Justice of England to that of Governor of Messina, the Clown and Pantaloon have parts as municipal officials (where they would be welcomed by a citizen-public that had little to learn about the things that could happen in local administration) and once again there is a tremendously effective part written for the Villain.

We do not always realize this when we read the play, or even when we see some productions of it, because we tacitly identify our own social status with that of the characters, censure Claudio for behaving in a way that would be highly reprehensible in good society—our good society, that is, not Claudio's—and take refuge in the thought that what we really come to enjoy is not the story but the brilliant conversational exchanges, and gradual *rapprochement*, of Beatrice and Benedick. The Beatrice and Benedick type of audience, as soon as it took to theatre-going, welcomed these two delightful creatures to its heart, but to the original public for which the play was written they would have appeared, not as the principal characters, but as the light comedians, a Gratiano and Nerissa transported from Venice to Sicily and providing relief from the main tension of the plot.

It was a plot that an Elizabethan middle-class audience could take quite seriously, particularly if the characters were given the necessary separation from the spectators, not in point of time, as in the author's last plays, but of space. They are not 'history people' this time, but they are foreigners, and Spaniards and

Italians at that, and that is enough to explain any slight uncon-ventionality of situation or behaviour.

Let us look at it, for a few moments, with the eyes of the Elizabethan citizen. The play starts with the news that an action of some sort has been successfully concluded, wherein one Claudio has distinguished himself and earned the notice and favour of the Prince of Aragon. The Prince and Claudio (and incidentally Benedick) come to spend a month as the guests of the Governor of Messina, and Claudio tells his patron of his love for Hero, the Governor's daughter. He had been attracted before the campaign; now that he is back again, he has time to think seriously about it. The Prince instantly offers to make the necessary arrangements with Leonato, Hero's father, and to do some of Claudio's love-making for him in that night's masque-rade. All this would be reasonably topical in 1598. Many a young man back from Cadiz or the Islands would have been arranging to marry and settle down if he could find an attractive wife whose parents would accept him as a suitor, and it would be all the more helpful to him if one of his commanders should show him so much favour as to interest himself in the match and take part in the preliminary discussions and negotiations. It was by no means unusual for an older friend to do such an office; Shakespeare did much the same thing himself a few years later when his landlord's daughter married her father's apprentice. The only thing that disturbs Claudio a little is his patron's readiness to get on with the affair at once, regardless of the fact that the bridegroom is only just making sure that he knows his own mind.

A few minutes more, and we learn something else about the campaign, for the author brings forward the conquered enemy. This is Don John of Aragon, the Prince's half-brother, who has rebelled against him and been defeated—largely through Claudio's valour—and is now in Don Pedro's train, forgiven and at liberty, something less than a brother and something more than a prisoner, in his own bitter words 'trusted—with a muzzle—and en-franchised—with a clog', like a savage beast not actually in captivity but kept muzzled and hobbled none the less. Here is a new part for the man who specialized in dangerous malignity, and for whom accordingly the author had devised parts like Worcester, Shylock and King John. Spanish gravity and reserve, summarized by the Englishman as 'melancholy', was a known national characteristic. We can see it frowning in many a dark, thin-legged portrait, like that of a real Don John of Aragon whom Rolam de Mois had painted thirty years before (illustration facing p. 90). Shakespeare had made fun of it on the first entry of his fantastical Spaniard in *Love's Labour's Lost*, and now he was depicting it again in a different light, as the savage, dangerous, malevolent thing that a selfish man's melancholy can be. Don John envies and dislikes the Prince, and sullenly hates Claudio, so that he welcomes even the slightest chance of making mischief between them. A well-meaning hint—dropped to Claudio in pretended error—that the Prince is getting too deeply interested in Leonato's daughter, an untrue statement, made not by Don John himself but by one of his gentlemen, that he intends not only to woo the girl but actually to marry her, and the mischief is set on foot. There is no quarrel because it is not Claudio but the blunt yet tactful Benedick who taxes Don Pedro to his face, so the matter is cleared up at once, leaving no trace behind but one, and that one easily overlooked by those who regard Claudio as a subsidiary character and not as a principal. The effect on him is one simpler yet subtler than Don John's intention, and yet perfectly natural to an audience that knew a good deal about young men just emerging *ex statu pupillari*. He has been led for a moment into the mistake of doubting and doing less than justice to his Prince and patron, he has been proved wrong, and his natural reaction would be a determination *never* to make that mistake again. Next time he will know better, and will rely blindly and implicitly on the judgement of the Prince he serves.

And so it falls out. The Prince, Don John and Claudio are shown together in a brief scene which is all the more effective for its absence of emphasis. Don John opens the matter, not with a direct accusation to Claudio but with a word of regretful warning to the Prince that he should have seen fit to spend time and attention on a young person who does not seem to deserve them. He is not insistent; if they care to come with him that evening they may see the evidence and draw their own conclusions. If they do not believe what they see, they can always keep silence about the whole matter. His only concern is to ensure that they go into this marriage with their eyes open. Perhaps—a wonderful stroke of sardonic impudence—Claudio will think better of him in future after this good turn. It is Claudio and the Prince who burst out with an extravagant undertaking to disgrace the bride publicly if they see anything to prove her guilt. The promise is easily made, as easily as Antonio's was to Shylock, and for the same reason, the absolute faith that there will be, *can* be, no possible occasion for its fulfilment. Don John discreetly restrains them, begging them to wait for the evidence of their own eyes before they decide, and ends the scene with an assurance that they will think of the marriage as a 'plague right well prevented'.

At this point the audience has its attention diverted to the Clown and Pantaloon. The main situation is in an excellent state of tension, and can safely be left there for a few minutes while the stage is held by a couple of popular comedians and their supporters the Watch. Once again we are faced with scenes and jokes that were originally popular because they came so near to familiar experience. When the play was written, the official guardians of the peace in each ward were still the citizens themselves, serving turn and turn about as watchmen, personally or by deputy. The City Letter-books at Guildhall contain the instructions framed in the Middle Ages and still largely current in Shakespeare's day. The ordinary Londoner in the audience would have enough knowledge and experience of watch-duties and responsibilities to relish the glorious inefficiency of Messrs Dogberry and Verges, his wife would have had excitement and entertainment enough in following to its present stage the story of a plot against the good name of a bride and the happiness of a nice young couple, and for the apprentice there was the personality of the individual comedian. The Quarto and Folio texts both show us that Dogberry was played by the ever-popular Will Kempe, and Verges by one Cowley, of whom we know nothing else, though we may conjecture from the similarity of the parts that he regularly acted as foil to Kempe—Pantaloon, in fact, to his Clown—and played senile old men like Shallow and Old Gobbo.

This time the comedians, unlike the Gobbos, have a real share in the plot. Their watchmen are mounted with a degree of ceremony, adjuration and uncomprehending instruction that looks backwards to the mediaeval ordinances and forwards to a solemn and unintelligent lance-corporal reading the official 'instructions to sentry' to the present writer on guard duty in 1939. After the exhortations and explanations, Dogberry and Verges retire, and the Watch decide to sit down quietly and avoid incidents of any kind until it is time to dismiss, but before they know where they are they are actually doing what they are there to do and arresting a drunken malefactor in the street. Don John's plot is nearly foiled at its very start, but the truth fails to come out because Dogberry is too stupid to carry out his duties as a constable and Leonato too fussily self-important to attend to his duties as a magistrate. He is not a figure of fun like old Capulet, but he is busy, and rather too ready to show it, and to hurry off to his daughter's wedding, delegating his responsibilities to the incompetent Dogberry without a second thought. His neglect of official duty, natural as it might be, is uncompromisingly shown to us as responsible for the catastrophe of the next scene, and once again it was not the courtier but the well-to-do burgher who would most readily recognize the implications of the position, and for whom it would most clearly have a meaning and a moral. It was an episode to draw the attention not of doublet and hose but of furred gown, flat cap and chain, and reminds us that when this play was written the company had not yet removed to Bankside.

At the church, Leonato is just the same. He opens the scene by telling the friar what to do, he tries to make Claudio's responses for him because he is sure he knows what they will be, or ought to be, and he tries to explain away Claudio's first accusation of

Spanish dignity. Don Juan Alonso de Aragón, eldest son of Don Martín de Aragón y de Guerra, Conde de Rivagorza, Maestrante de Calatravas, Duque de Villahermosa, by Rolam de Mois.

his bride rather than to contradict it. Step by step he is convinced against his will. He turns to the Prince, and the Prince answers him. He turns to Hero, and her denial sounds like a weak falsehood in the face of three eye-witnesses. Don Pedro and Don John are regretfully certain, Claudio is heartbroken and disillusioned, and his very grief confirms to Leonato's mind the incredible circumstances. His character and characteristics never alter, he is just as ready to exceed in frenzy as he was in self-confidence, but he is allowed to express himself meanwhile, when lamenting the destruction and degradation of something beloved, in words that are to find their echo in later years on the lips of an Othello or an Antony.

Claudio, in this scene particularly, is only too often underestimated and underplayed because the spectators are waiting for Beatrice and Benedick, and are consciously or unconsciously impatient with the story of the play for keeping them from its most brilliant dialogue. The Curtain audience knew the feelings a father might have about his daughter and a young soldier about his bride more intimately than they knew or cared about the habits and conversation of the nobility. To them the story was the natural, familiar, interesting part, and it was broken up in the usual manner by scenes of a different kind, to give the necessary relief and variety. With the development of the 'picture-stage' in the eighteenth and nineteenth centuries, dramatists very frequently employed this device in what were called 'carpenters' scenes', wherein two characters exchanged a great deal of lively or passionate conversation before a painted front-cloth, while the stage carpenters were setting the next really important scene behind it. Sometimes it takes the form of a scene between a pair of comic lovers; sometimes, as in *The Rivals*, between lovers of passionate seriousness, but long before such scenes were used to cover a scene-change they were employed to give the audience a change of emotion, so that from the tension and excitement of a strong scene in the main play it could turn for a few moments to the contemplation of a couple of brilliant cross-talkers, as it would to an acrobatic turn, a ballet interlude, or anything of the sort that was at once intricate, artificial and reasonably irrelevant, as a relief from the naturalism of the simpler emotions.

Something of this we have seen already in the Belmont scenes of *The Merchant of Venice* and in certain passages of *Romeo and Juliet*. This time, however, Shakespeare's supporting characters have taken the bit between their teeth and run away with the play. When it was played at Court only fourteen years after it was written it abandoned its original title, to be called instead by the names of the two chief characters, and it seems that by 1614 these were not Claudio, Leonato, Don Pedro or the ill-used Hero but Beatrice and Benedick, as they have been ever since. The difference to-day, however, is that once we equate ourselves with these two we find it hard to take the rest of the drama seriously; while Shakespeare's audience found Beatrice and her sparring-partner a pair of delightful though impossible people, and considered the play itself as serious as a later generation considered Sardou. Indeed, the central situation is worth comparing with the great scene in *Diplomacy* (to give the name under which Sardou's *Dora* has usually been played in this country), in which a young man is brought, by the representations of two obviously honest and well-meaning friends, to the terrible realization that his newly-married bride is a treacherous adventuress. In Sardou's play as in Shakespeare's the weight of the scene lies in the fact that most of the people concerned are passionately reluctant to believe what the evidence appears to suggest to them till by an attempt at clear-headed logic and analysis they are convinced against their will.

Claudio has certainly seen a man at Hero's window, he has seen Hero's garments, and naturally thinks he has seen Hero wearing them, the man has himself confessed to the encounter, but there may still be some explanation that Hero can give. Instead, to Claudio's dismay, she flatly denies having spoken to anyone at all, and that, at any rate, he is sure he knows to be untrue. If she lies to him—and it seems self-evident that she must be lying—the only possible reason is that she has something to conceal, and the impossible, incredible accusation has been confirmed. His superior officers have seen the evidence, and accepted it without question, and he can only suppose that his hasty choice of a bride has been as ill-founded as his own second thoughts had vaguely hinted that it might be. All this is perfectly natural, moving drama, to the people for whom it was written. The world of rank and fashion may wear its infidelities with a difference, but to the sound, well-meaning, middle-class public at the Curtain it is only too clear that such things may happen in Messina, just as they sometimes did in a London war-time betrothal, based on mutual attraction rather than close acquaintance.

Even the deceit itself is made plausible for us if we have the mind to listen and the wit to understand. It does not take two minutes of Margaret's conversation to show us not only that she is in charge of Hero's wardrobe but that she is just the sort of genial, foolish creature who could be persuaded to try on one of her mistress' dresses and exhibit herself, thus attired, to the admiration of a plausible young man outside the window, and would think it the cream of the jest to have him call her by her mistress' name. The trouble is that nowadays we pay Margaret very little attention because we are waiting for Beatrice, and we miss, in consequence, 'some necessary question of the play'.

There is another Clown and Pantaloon scene, ushered in with the remark 'O, a stool and a cushion for the sexton'—an innocent one enough to modern ears, but to the Elizabethans a parody of the line 'Bring a chair and a cushion for the King', that begins the culmination of the ever-popular *Spanish Tragedy*. Don John's villainy is at last revealed to a sensible person—the sexton—and we hear that Don John himself is 'secretly stolen away' from Messina. Benedick justifies himself in the eyes of the audience by at last taking a part in the main action and confronting the Prince, his patron, and Claudio, his best friend. They make every effort to laugh with him or at him, but this time the comedian will not be drawn into merriment. Taking Claudio aside he challenges him to a duel, on pain of being proclaimed a coward. The Prince sees which way the wind is blowing, and tries to laugh matters off by talking about Beatrice and her views on Benedick. His station makes him a person who cannot be challenged, and consequently should not in fairness be insulted; but Benedick's leave-taking, in scrupulously courteous terms, comes as near to insult and challenge as the circumstances permit, and would warm the hearts of the Finsbury audience, for of all the champions of an ill-used heroine the comic 'swell', when he seriously takes her part, seems to rouse our readiest admiration.

Hard on the heels of this comes the discovery of the plot, and it is a small but significant point that after the initial shock Claudio's first thought is for Hero, his only consolation the knowledge that she was, and always had been, as true and honourable as he had first thought her, and that his scorn and disappointment can be kept for himself indeed but never in the slightest degree for her. His penance is performed at the family tomb, and the first few lines of the next scene are a clear indication to the audience *not* to take the view of him that audiences and critics take as a matter of course to-day. He has rejected the bride in the church, and in the church he has done penance for it. He has refused to marry Leonato's daughter, and must atone for that slight, and show how completely unjustified were his grounds for it, by 'doing the right thing' and marrying into Leonato's family. He does so unquestioningly, and finds at the end that he has gained the bride he thought he had lost for ever. His happiness is saved from cloying by the swiftly-following betrothal of Benedick and Beatrice, their discovery that they have been tricked into love-making, and the further discovery, proclaimed for them by Claudio and Hero, that the love-making has developed into genuine love. Don John's arrest is briefly announced, and summarily dismissed, for it is Claudio who has undergone the greatest degree of emotional strain and variation, and who seems to have been meant, originally, to be the central figure in the play.

As we have seen, he meant more to the Curtain audience than he does nowadays in the average stage production, but in another play, written in the spring of 1599, the young officer-hero still holds his own as he did when it was first produced. Prince Hal had been seen in *Henry IV* serving his unruly apprenticeship to the Crown. Now it was time for a play about him as king, or at least about the side of him best known to the public, namely his conquest of France and marriage with the King of France's daughter. As before, the author takes his general form and ideas from Hall and goes to Holinshed for corroborative details. Hall came from a strict hot-gospeller family of the days of Henry VIII and the Dissolution of the Monasteries, and his attitude to the opening of the whole campaign is one that Holinshed does not follow, whereas Shakespeare does. The project against France is represented as something deliberately introduced by a shrewd cleric in order to take the king's mind off a bill which might, if it became law, have a disastrous effect on ecclesiastical revenues. Incidentally, the archbishop gives another pointer to the spectators on the way they are to regard the king, even as Hal himself had given them a hint in an earlier play. He is a hero now, not merely a joyous and irresponsible young man, and that point must be driven home at the earliest possible opportunity. Accordingly, it is made the second subject of the prelates' conversation. The Curtain public was not interested in subtlety; it liked to be told where it stood and how it was expected to behave. The first few lines indicate what is on the minds of the bishop and archbishop, the rest of the scene shows what sort of a person the king is, and how the bishops regard him, and now that the audience have been told what the main situation is, and what they are expected to think of the principal character, they are ready for the main action of the drama to begin.

It has long been a convention to sneer at Henry as an aggressor and a hypocrite in this play, just as it was to accuse him of duplicity and callousness in the earlier two. Hall certainly did not share this view, nor, it would seem, did Shakespeare. Actor-managers have involuntarily contributed to it now and then by surrounding themselves with the splendour and man-power that they feel to be their due, instead of ranging it all on the side of France. Shakespeare's Henry does not necessarily make his first appearance at the head of a council consisting of everybody of note who is to appear later in the play, though editors and producers appear to take this for granted. As far as the text goes, he is attended, urged and advised only by the two prelates and by his uncle Exeter, with additional comments by Westmorland, and that urging and advice is couched in a form particularly acceptable to people who had had what passed in Elizabethan days for a good normal education.

The curriculum for this, it must be remembered, included logic and rhetoric, and as a result the ordinary educated man was readier than his modern successor to appreciate the technique of advocacy—or casuistry—as a fine art. The archbishop has announced in the first few minutes of the play that he hopes to incline Henry to take an interest in 'the crown and seat of France'. In due course he must make that pronouncement good, and a public that has some knowledge of rhetoric and some experience of litigation (one of the chief interests of the average London business man of that day) will be interested and expectant to see how he does it. His great speech, given at equal length in the pages of Hall and Holinshed, is regarded as tedious to-day because the modern audience is looking for drama and does not find it here. To the Elizabethan, on the other hand, it came as an elaborate and successful performance of something that was considered a desirable art, and studied by most men as a matter of course. The logical pursuit of the discourse piles up fact on fact in the orthodox way, first by proving the irrelevance of any appeal to the Salic Law, then by demonstrating its disregard at will by the French themselves, so that its technique as well as its matter could arouse and hold the interest of people who knew something about the rules and practice of argument.

After argument comes another branch of rhetoric, namely exhortation. The king put to his archbishop a brief, searching question that has the whole of the matter in it, 'May I with right and conscience make this claim?', and the answer comes direct, sonorous and uncompromising, with a quotation from the Pentateuch to back it. Then Canterbury, Ely, Exeter and Westmorland in succession urge the young Henry to follow the noble example of his ancestors, and their lines are a good example of the inspiring, declamatory speech that was part of the repertory of the trained rhetorician. Finally, in the passage about the honey-bees we are given a demonstration of the much-lauded practice of analogy or comparison. The trained speaker was expected to be able to draw close and ingenious comparisons between the subject of his discussion and some analogous state of things in the animal world, the Solar System or some other organization of animate or inanimate nature. It was a commonplace of the schools, of the law-courts and of the pulpit-oratory which the citizen regularly experienced on Sundays, and a combination of training and experience had necessarily made him something of a judge in matters of eloquence. Canterbury's scene, to an Elizabethan with that training and experience, was an exhibition of the three main devisions of oratory by a skilled performer, and could be enjoyed as a 'solo turn' for its own sake, quite independently of its bearing on the play.

The cast shows one or two variations from what we have seen hitherto. King Henry and Pistol are still parts for the hero and the flamboyant man, and the 'heavy man' possibly opened the play as Canterbury and came on again as the king of France. The villain seems to have turned to a new role, for there are odd suggestions of Don John's melancholy in a new comic character, Corporal Nym. His conversation at his first appearance is an unexpectedly close imitation of Don John's opening remarks about his temperament and position, and he goes on with a phrase or two in a style reminiscent of Jeronimo in the latest version of *The Spanish Tragedy*. Certain additions to the old play had got into print by 1602, so that in 1599, when *Henry V* was written, they would be very new indeed in the spoken text, and very fit matter for allusion or imitation, particularly if (as is now usually accepted) they came from the pen of Ben Jonson, who had so recently been displaying his humours at the Curtain before going over to a rival management. 'Well, Heaven is Heaven still', says the bereaved father in one of these interpolated passages, 'and there is Nemesis, and Furies, and things called whips, and they sometimes do meet with murderers', and Nym comments on the loss of his betrothed lady in just that style of sinister allusion, always falling short of a direct threat. In a few moments he is using the word that had an unmistakably Jonsonian significance for the audience at that particular theatre. 'Humour' had become a popular catchword, not entirely confined to its physiological sense but used loosely to denote a mood, an idiosyncrasy or an obsession. *Every Man in his Humour* had just lately served to keep the word, and the thing, fresh in the minds of playgoers at the Curtain. Its author had followed up the success of his play by fighting and killing an actor of the Admiral's Company in Hoxton Fields, and had gone to prison again in consequence. When he came out he seems to have joined the other company instead of writing any more plays for the Chamberlain's Men, so that from the viewpoint of the players and patrons of the Curtain, imitations of him might be considered fair game. Much of Nym's part seems out of date and not very funny nowadays, very largely because it had a wealth of topical meaning for a public that had laughed at *Every Man in his Humour*, applauded the revised version of *The Spanish Tragedy*, and watched the subtle machinations of Don John in *Much Ado*.

The conspiracy of Cambridge, Scroop and Grey is introduced rather abruptly and dealt with rather summarily in the next scene. It is difficult for an audience nowadays to get up very much excitement about a plot by three minor characters whom it has not seen before and will not see again, and whose attempt does not affect, in any degree, the action of the play or the fortunes of the principal character. The Londoners who saw the play at the Curtain were in a different position. They were more familiar with the story, and a good many of them would be familiar with the particular version of it which the players had adapted for their entertainment. The conspiracy was part of that story, and accordingly its introduction was not only accepted but expected. It had happened in real life, it was mentioned as having happened in the book, and it must be seen to happen likewise in the play. Those who knew their history or their *Henry VI* would appreciate a remark made by the Earl of Cambridge when he hints that he was not seduced by 'the gold of France', but had intended the king's death for a different reason, for he was the father of that Richard Plantagenet who was to dethrone Henry's son and set up the house of York in the place of that of Lancaster. It may be said, in effect, that the suppression of the conspiracy in *Henry V* deferred the Wars of the Roses for a generation.

Moreover, spectators living under a sovereign whose life had been attempted as often as Elizabeth's had been could be relied upon to bristle with loyal indignation at the sight of traitors putting a king of England in similar peril. They knew very well what that meant, and that there could be only one punishment for it. Ingeniously enough, the author makes the three conspirators forfeit our sympathy by urging the king to punish a drunken and disrespectful subject when he himself is giving orders to have the man released. Like Shylock they urge the stricter enforcement of the law, and like him again they provide arguments for their own downfall. The scene has given rise in more recent times to criticisms of the author and the principal character, but it was written for an audience that knew the facts and felt the implications rather more fully than do those who condemn it to-day.

After that, there is plenty to please the returned soldier and the stay-at-home civilian alike. The parts of the campaign that Shakespeare has treated in detail are those that can be most easily represented on the stage and that are more or less the same in all ages. Agincourt itself turned on a massed charge of cavalry in armour against dismounted troops supported by archers, and was correspondingly impossible to stage, so that the author most ingeniously avoided any attempt to do so. The earlier engagement at Harfleur, however, was a very different matter. It was an assault with scaling-ladders on a fortified position after a preliminary bombardment and the explosion of a mine. This was alike much easier to suggest and much more closely allied to the sort of warfare that the ex-soldiers in the audience really knew. A good many of them must have taken part in just such an assault themselves at one time or another, and they would all be reasonably well versed in the theory of such operations. Henry's famous speech of exhortation was not necessarily the highlight of the scene; more likely it was one of the various contributory features to a great spectacular effect with the storming of Harfleur amid explosions off-stage. It is a speech of preparation, gradually keying up the minds of the hearers to a high degree of tension before the release of the actual onset, and leading up to the climax of explosions, alarums and the assault upon the walls.

The necessary relief is provided at this point by the sight of the comedians and their attitude to the heroic charge. The pace of the scenes would be accelerated by the fact that there was no break for scene-changing, and the groups of characters succeeded each other on the bare stage. In such conditions it is easier to understand the acrimonious conversations of the Scottish, Welsh and Irish engineer officers as taking place at the base while the attack on the breach is still in progress. Popular traditions and popular prints indicated the main differences of dress among the various nations, one generally-accepted article of belief (not entirely without foundation) being that the wilder types of Irish soldiery wore neither shoes nor stockings. Irishmen were especially topical in the spring of 1599, when *Henry V* was first played, as it was against troops of this kind that the Englishman's idol, the Earl of Essex, was even then supposed to be campaigning in the cause of England and the Queen, and it is a loyal Irish officer who has a sudden quarrel with the pedantic Fluellen and bursts out into disappointed indignation at the news that the town is about to capitulate, thus depriving him of his hope of blowing it sky-high by some further advanced mining. Then in a few lines we are with Henry again, dictating his terms to the governor of the town, with a stern warning of the unavoidable carnage that must follow if they are refused, and the scene ends with the peaceful entry of his army into Harfleur. The three scenes—or two scenes and an interlude—are all intimately connected, and constitute the story of one military operation.

There is not much in this play for the boy-actresses to do.

Accordingly, the boy who played heroines has been given repeated appearances in his own sex, as Falstaff's boy, now serving Messrs Pistol, Nym and Bardolph and commenting with entertaining freedom on their various shortcomings. (His character-sketch of Nym is a perfect indictment of the solemn pretentiousness that sometimes passed for melancholy.) At last he is allowed to get into petticoats and do one of his regular female impersonations as the Princess of France having a comic English lesson culminating in some very low French puns before he goes back to doublet and hose for his part in the battle.

The action of Agincourt cannot be presented adequately on the stage, and Shakespeare does not try to re-create, or even to describe, the great charge of the French cavalry that was its most famous feature. All the same, the audience must be shown the hero achieving his immortal victory, and the author has a difficult task before him if he is not to spoil everything by repeating his effects. Henry has just been seen leading his troops into battle at the taking of a town, so he cannot have another exhortation-speech. It is not long since the public saw him rescuing his father at Shrewsbury and killing Hotspur in single combat, so personal feats of valour in the field are ruled out likewise. Instead, we are given something that must have been quite unexpected, and have come as a novelty to the original audience—a view of the man's mind, and something of the burden of his responsibilities. 'Alas, poor Harry of England,' says the Constable to Orleans on the night before the battle, 'He longs not for the dawning as we do.' The French are seen drinking and dicing, waiting impatiently for the morning, and taking victory for granted, but the state of the English camp is described in a prologue by the Chorus before any of it is presented in action. A famous descriptive passage brings before us the armies lying almost in earshot of each other in the dark, and the varied noises of camp and countryside that mark the passing of the night, but all leads up to the description of the king going his rounds among the camp-fires, watching, listening, inspecting, speaking a word or two here and there and reassuring the men under him by the very fact that he can appreciate and share their plight and yet remain undaunted by it.

Then, having claimed our admiration for the king's conduct, the author has to justify his claim by showing him in action. In rapid succession we see him discussing the position frankly yet lightly with his brothers, and moving off, in Sir Thomas Erpingham's cloak, to hear his own praises sung enthusiastically by Pistol of all people, to overhear Fluellen's insistence on the proper observance of security regulations, and to take his part in a camp-fire discussion about the day's prospects and the king's responsibility. Here he involves himself in an argument with a grumbling old soldier, adroitly turning the talk so that in a few minutes the man who had firmly expected never to see the end of the day has forgotten his pessimism and is making arrangements to find him and fight him over their private disagreement when the battle is over. Finally he is left alone, reflecting on the terrifying burden of his responsibility, and for the first time in the play showing the audience the real thoughts that he shows only to his God, until his nobles and kinsmen come to look for him and he turns to his work again.

We never see the field itself, only its outskirts—a far safer plan when playing with limited resources and before an audience that might be only too well equipped for criticism. An axiom among soldiers in every age is that the real prizes of battle invariably fall to the wrong people, and Shakespeare has taken the opportunity to illustrate it. History, in those days and in these, relates that the French at Agincourt were hampered by their heavy armour, and there may well be some suggestion of this in the ease with which Pistol and the boy between them capture a French gentleman worth two hundred crowns. The Dauphin and his officers try vainly to reorganize their shattered ranks, Henry receives news of the death of the Duke of York, and the sudden alarm that necessitates the killing of the prisoners; Fluellen and Gower show what it was that moved him to anger—the massacre of the camp-followers, Pistol's delightful boy among them—and the French herald comes with a request for leave to gather the dead and make the formal admission 'The day is yours.' We have seen not the hand-to-hand progress of the action but the succession of intense feelings aroused by it, and can turn, as Henry does, to a genial practical joke by way of relief, and enjoy the sight of the grumbler Williams hitting the peppery Fluellen in pursuance of last night's quarrel, and being finally rewarded with a glove-full of money from the king.

Little is left now but the reading of the casualty-lists and the solemn thanksgiving for the victory. This last, though stigmatized as 'nauseating' by a modern critic, would have a special significance to the English theatre-goer of 1599. Not only was it an integral part of the story, but it was a part that could be fully appreciated at that time, for only a matter of months before the play was performed to a London audience, Philip of Spain had died in the Escorial, and a great shadow seemed to be lifted from the world. More than forty years before he had been King-Consort of England, his portrait had appeared beside Queen Mary's on the coinage and the Great Seal, in his time he had paid unsuccessful suit to Elizabeth herself, and after his disappointment there he had been for most Englishmen the Danger, the Enemy, the wolf waiting to pounce on England if she were unwary or undefended. On land in the Low Countries and on the sea all over the world, Englishmen and Spaniards had fought and plundered, the vast invasion launched at this country had missed its mark only by a narrow margin, and many of the audience must have seen, and shared, their queen's act of thankfulness and devotion when she knelt on the stones in the sight of her people before the great West Door of St Paul's on the occasion of the official thanksgiving. And now, with the death of the King of Spain, the threat of war and burning and persecution must have seemed some degree more remote, and man could feel, albeit illogically, a sense of freedom and relief. That sense of unexpected, unhoped-for release from tension begets an impulse at once of gratitude and of humility, and a natural reaction is just that revulsion from any thought of self-congratulation. As it was after Agincourt and after the Armada, so it was after Mons and after Dunkirk—the very greatness of the peril made men feel that nothing but a miracle could have saved them, and their thanksgiving was made to express their indebtedness, not to congratulate their cause. Henry's attitude to his victory probably seemed the natural, almost the obvious one, to those who saw it in Elizabeth's reign.

The prologue to the last act shows how readily the play was to be accepted as the dramatic version of the book, since it opens with the straightforward phrase

> Vouchsafe to those that have not read the story
> That I may prompt them,

and goes on to describe a complete episode that is not represented on the stage, namely Henry's return to London before his courtship of Katharine of France. A topical allusion that helps to fix the date of the play is the comparison of his reception with that which would be given to Essex, 'the general of our gracious empress', if he were to return victorious from Ireland. (He came back in September unofficially and against orders, after receiving a letter from Elizabeth about his inefficiency that is a masterpiece of scarifying criticism, so that the passage in question must have become highly inappropriate in a very short time.) Then we are shown Pistol's discomfiture at the hands of Fluellen and the courtship of Henry and Katharine in broken English and worse French, giving a last chance to the main comedians and the French-speaking boy actor in turn, and finally comes the happy ending with the Treaty of Troyes. The oration that introduces it seems disproportionate and not entirely relevant in the eyes of modern critics of the play, but we may conjecture that in its own day, with the Spanish danger apparently withdrawing into the background, there was a ready welcome for a speech about the blessings of peace and the gradual reconstruction of a land worn out by war.

VII

The Playhouse comes into Fashion

WHEN SHAKESPEARE and his fellows changed their old citizen-audience of Finsbury for a less familiar one on Bankside, a change was coming over London itself. The Court was settling permanently at Westminster and for the first time it was worth while for the Elizabethan nobleman to have a house of his own in or near the metropolis. Little by little the open country between the two cities of London and Westminster gave place to houses, streets and gardens, and for the first time London possessed at once a purely residential quarter and a leisured, non-commercial play-going public. The polite audience, hitherto associated with special occasions and 'command performances' in banqueting-halls, was prepared to go more regularly to the ordinary play-house for its entertainment if it found anything worth going to, and playwrights had before them the increasingly complicated task of devising drama to suit all tastes without an undue amount of conspicuous incongruity. Persons of Quality had come to the theatre in the past, but they had been visitors from without. Now the playgoing courtier was becoming a regular member of the London public, and was worth considering when plays were being written and performances arranged, so the texts and con-struction of the plays themselves are henceforth our most helpful indication—if we look at them aright—of the types of mind to which they were intended to appeal.

Both comedy and tragedy are associated closely enough with this period to suggest how Shakespeare tackled the problem. The journal of a German visitor named Platter records that in September 1599 he saw a play about Julius Caesar at a 'straw-roofed house' upon the South Bank—presumably Shakespeare's

Julius Caesar at the Globe—and a date near enough to this in time is usually assigned, upon internal evidence, to *As You Like It.* Both plays show a change in treatment from previous ventures in their kind, in that they devote more attention to the people of the story and less to the story itself. Shakespeare's strong individual interest in human nature could now be given free rein, with the advent of these new spectators who were so readily inclined to share it. Earlier historical plays had been concerned with events, contentions and the overthrow of kings, but in *Julius Caesar* the main interest is not the murder of Caesar but the minds and temperaments of the people who murdered him—what they were like, why they decided to do such a thing at all, how they put their ideas into practice and what happened to them afterwards. We are invited to watch them not for what they do but for what they are.

For *Julius Caesar* is the first of its kind. It is a play about a murderer, not primarily about a murder. Brutus is the forerunner of Shakespeare's three great tragic figures, each of whom is driven on, Brutus-like, to commit a homicide that he does not quite believe in, only to find at the end that it has availed him nothing. Hamlet knows that the ghost (and quite possibly the world as well) expects him to avenge his father. Macbeth knows that his wife expects him to 'catch the nearest way' and establish himself upon the Scottish throne. Othello, on the threshold of murder, has to keep reminding himself that there is a reason for his action, that he *must* destroy the beloved creature who has betrayed him, and who might otherwise live on to betray more men. None of them goes about his business with the enthusiasm of a Richard of Gloucester, or the stern efficiency of a Boling-broke, none of them really has his heart in the work and in consequence none of them carries it out successfully to the end.

But their ill-success and their wrong-headed determination are themselves of supreme interest because they are essentially human qualifications. The man who plans and carries out a successful assassination and thrives on it is an object of fascinated interest, it is true, because he is someone outside our normal experience and imagination, but the man who has justified such a thing in theory only to find himself hampered in practice by all kinds of unexpected factors, his own nature among them, is an object of sympathy and understanding, because we suspect that in similar circumstances we might make no better work of it ourselves. The play is written for an audience that has come to the theatre not so much to be excited as to be interested, for it depicts a fairly small field of human action but an infinitely greater proportion of human nature. The author does not waste time trying to create local colour from vague memories of his schooldays or from the free use of his imagination; there is not much demand for local colour in this kind of play at all. It could be left to Ben Jonson to enrich his classical tragedies with a positive bibliography of footnotes explaining all his sources; the important thing about Brutus was his nature, not his nationality.

Caesar himself was rather different. He was a familiar figure to schoolboys even in those days, and to the schoolboy student of the *Commentaries* he appears as rather a pompous old party with an irritating habit of referring to himself in the third person. It was generally known or supposed, also, that he said, 'Caesar shall go forth', when he left home for the meeting at which he was murdered. The Duke of Guise had used those very words not many years before when setting out for the Court at Blois on the morning of his own murder, and still more recently that murder, and Guise's quotation of Caesar, had been presented on the stage by Henslowe when he put on Marlowe's *Massacre at Paris*. Shakespeare's Caesar is a character built up of the accepted sentiments, attitudes and catchwords. He comes far short of the Julius Caesar of history, and even the Julius Caesar of Plutarch, but he is the Julius Caesar of the average Elizabethan Londoner, and that was what really mattered in the context.

The opening of the play is a short, crisp scene with an effective piece of declamation in it, warranted to catch the attention of all the different types of playgoer that made up the audience at the Globe. Then comes a procession, containing most of the really important characters, and with pretty clear indications which is which. The soothsayer utters his warning to Caesar and the procession moves on to the games, leaving behind two men who address each other at once as Brutus and Cassius. We have no need to know more about them than their names, all the rest will be revealed to us in a few minutes' conversation, and remarkably illuminating it is.

Cassius has a long and critical account of Caesar to deliver, and in an earlier play, acted before a Moorfields audience, we may imagine it would have conveyed a great deal of direct information that such an audience would require to know. Now, on the other hand, it has a completely different function. The facts it relates are trivial and irrelevant, at the end of it we have learnt nothing really significant about Caesar, but the speaker has told us in the process a very great deal about Cassius, and something about the Brutus whom he is trying to persuade to his design, and this principle determines the general construction of the play. By overhearing, as it were, a series of intimate conversations we are made more and more deeply conscious of the emotions governing the various friends and enemies of the Dictator, and the whole situation is gradually built up for us in the round. The author apparently expects the new audience to be more readily interested in people and their humours than in historical events, and it may be said accordingly that nothing at all really happens in the play until the murder of Caesar just half-way through. All that has led up to this is not so much a series of events as a gradual revelation of the position as it appears to the persons concerned, so that the author allows us to see it from a variety of available viewpoints.

He does not, apparently, take sides. Brutus, Cassius and Antony are given every chance to appear to advantage. Antony is described in Plutarch as 'a wicked man', and in a recent production he has aroused comment and approval by being played so, but so far as the text goes, none of the characters is expressly labelled as hero or villain; each of them is acting rightly according to his own lights, and the tragedy comes when Brutus allows himself to follow Cassius' ideas of right rather than his own. All this would be of interest to the well-read, deep-thinking courtier who had some experience of litigation (the delight of so many Elizabethans) and some background of logic, philosophy and the study of humankind. In fact, Shakespeare was now writing for minds like those that took pleasure, nearly two and a half centuries later, in the complexities of human motives and reflections illustrated in the monologues of Robert Browning, and the important thing is not so much that the poet could write in such a vein, as that the public could enjoy it. Brutus, in particular, is a character conceived essentially in Browning's manner. We see it as soon as Caesar's procession has left him in privacy with Cassius, while his self-communing by night before the visit of his fellow-conspirators has all the characteristics, bar their inordinate length, of the later poet's 'Dramatic Lyrics'. What Sir Edmund Gosse, when writing of Browning, called 'an impassioned curiosity as to the conditions and movements of the soul in other people' was one of the chief interests of the thoughtfully-minded man of 1600 or thereabouts, and we may justifiably assume that this feeling was more widespread in Shakespeare's time than it was in Browning's. There is evidence to show that *Julius Caesar* and *As You Like It* were both popular with the public of their day, whereas Browning's reflective poems found a cold and scanty welcome, and had to wait for twenty years for a public that shared their author's particular curiosity for humankind.

The last part of the play suffers from the influence of too much historical fact. Most of the material throughout comes from Plutarch, in the standard English translation by Thomas North. As in the plays based on Hall's Chronicle, what the audience had read in the book had to be included in the play likewise, and the battle-incidents did not mix well with the character-studies that had gone before. It does not help our good opinion of Brutus when we see him lose the battle of Philippi through two major errors of judgement, or of Cassius when we see him kill himself prematurely because of a misunderstanding about what is happening to Titinius. And Titinius himself is someone whom we know so slightly that it seems almost an intrusion when he comes on and kills himself in his turn upon the body of his master. There is a smack of Pyramus and Thisby about the cross-purposes and suicides of this scene, and we have to wait for another Roman play to see how the maturer Shakespeare could handle a chain of deaths through misunderstanding or through loyalty and keep the tension at the highest pitch throughout. The death of Titinius has an abruptness verging upon absurdity, but in the sequel to this play a similar episode, very differently handled, attains real tragedy with the deaths of Eros and of Antony.

It is just the same with *As You Like It*. Instead of a history-book the poet has taken a popular novel and adapted it for the stage, but he has paid less attention to the story than to the characters. The source-book, Lodge's *Rosalynde*, was admittedly fiction, so the events of his story could be varied and adapted with greater freedom than could those of Plutarch or of Hall. We have passed from the study of events to that of people and problems. In a way, Shakespeare is doing again what he did with *The Merchant of Venice* and with *Much Ado About Nothing*, but it is not the same way. With each of those he took a popular story and made it 'come alive' as a serious commercial or social problem. Now, it is true, he is doing the same thing, but it is the characters that come alive, and as they do so the story goes by the board. The public is not breathless with anxiety to know what will happen, in the old cinema-serial way. Rosalind is certainly banished on pain of death by her usurping uncle, but we do not imagine those early playgoers as apprehensively following her fortunes as they did those of that other wandering heroine who went from Verona to Milan in doublet and hose. They do not give any particular attention to the fortunes of the Banished Duke, or spend much time wondering if, and how, he will be reinstated in his dukedom in the last act. The author has not expected this audience to be interested in anything of the sort, and has scamped the matter unmercifully in consequence by means of a 'messenger's speech' reporting not that the usurper has been killed in a righteous revolution, or even struck dead by a thunderbolt, but that he has been suddenly converted by an 'old religious man' whom nobody has mentioned before.

In fact, there are no strongly dramatic scenes in the play at all. The tyrant duke and the tyrant brother exercise their tyranny too early to create real tension; their harsh treatment of Rosalind and Orlando comes by way of introduction or prologue, leading those who know the novel to look forward with interest to greater things. Each of these two unpleasant people, one would expect, must have a strong scene at the climax of the play, when after various incidents he is confronted with the brother he has wronged. Be the result reconciliation or defiance, that meeting is something that the audience can quite legitimately anticipate in imagination. An earlier or a later audience would not have been disappointed. Rival had confronted rival already in *The Two Gentlemen of Verona*, brother was to confront usurping brother, many years later, in *The Tempest*, but in *As You Like It* the meeting between Orlando and Oliver takes place behind the scenes, and the final conflict between Duke Frederick and his brother never takes place at all, because the usurper suddenly goes into a hermitage—off stage, of course—so that the play can hurry comfortably to an end.

What is the reason for this sudden shuffling of the plot into the background as something unimportant and almost irrelevant? Recollections of *Much Ado About Nothing* may suggest an explanation. In that play, it would seem, the balance had been upset because the two light-comedy conversationalists had run away with the interest. There was in the audience an increasing proportion of people who found the cross-talk of Beatrice and Benedick more interesting than the actual plot, Hero's predicament and Don John's machinations. Accordingly, next time the author wrote a comedy for such an audience he let the Beatrice-and-Benedick spirit prevail unchecked. If the spectators liked characters and dialogue better than plot, then characters and dialogue they should have, and the plot should be kept in due subjection, to be ignored or introduced as seemed desirable from time to time. There was enough of it to give each principal a background and a set of circumstances to move in; after that, there was little need for anything more, and the characters and their conversations were enough to provide the necessary entertainment.

The play is full of brilliant, fascinating talk, such as the Elizabethan gentleman enjoyed. It is not necessarily the smart, ingenious, literary word-fencing of *Love's Labour's Lost*, the characters are not uniformly trying to be clever, as in the earlier play. Cleverness and brilliance they have, indeed, but these qualities are represented as springing from their nature, not from a deliberate cultivation of wit to the point of virtuosity. They are designed for an audience of intelligent, sophisticated, artistically-appreciative people, rather than for any special gathering of professed wits. Here the parallel is less with Browning than with 'Saki', E. F. Benson or A. A. Milne in the days between the accession of King Edward VII and the outbreak of war in 1914. They depicted, and Lewis Baumer independently drew, a genial, leisured society, not too intensely intellectual or too aggressively witty, but well skilled in the art of pleasantly inane conversation that had too much variety to become boring.

That is the kind of society that was now growing up with this new residential London that was coming into being. It was the society of the old country-house parties, but in the process of becoming urbanized and seeking entertainment from some other source than the hunting-field. What it liked in 1600 or 1911 was conversation that was smart enough to be amusing and yet not so clever as to be above its head. It could enjoy the situations of a popular novel, it could welcome the sight of a wrestling-match in which the hero vanquished a local champion, it could lend appreciative ears and applauding hands to the wit of Rosalind and at the same time take a briefly satirical attitude—if it felt superior and cynical—with the melancholy Jaques.

Once again, as he did in *The Merchant of Venice*, Shakespeare has written a play with something in it for everyone, and has practically said so in his title. We may take it as we like it, either as a romantic story if we concentrate on Rosalind, her lover and her father, or as a satire on the Simple Life, if we feel that the simple emotions and admirations are childish and unreal; we may take Corin and Silvius as true figures of the countryside and William and Audrey as caricatures, or *vice versa*, we may laugh cheerfully at the superior attitude of Jaques, or we may take our stand with him and smile tolerantly at everybody else.

The one natural man who walks impartially amid the cynics and romantics alike is the eminently practical-minded Touchstone, who is neither hero, cynic, philosopher nor clod, but is always ready to provide an antidote to any excess of temperament on the part of the other characters. He is our old friend the Clown, who seems to have had rather a poor time in the last play as Casca, but has been given his head in this one. His technique in the last few plays has always been the display of a strongly materialistic attitude to romantic situations. In *The Merchant of Venice* he had regarded the conversion of the Jew's daughter as a circumstance that might send up the price of pork by increasing the demand; in *Henry IV* he had treated the audience to his unromantic views on honour in the one play and on the death of his sovereign in the other; in *Julius Caesar* he had given a caustic and very funny description of Caesar's rejection of the crown, as it appeared to one who was not particularly impressed by it, and now we see him, with both feet firmly planted on the earth, refusing to be carried away by Le Beau's description of a sporting event, by Rosalind's weariness in Arden or by the idyllic simplicity of a shepherd's life. Like Sam Weller, he is consistently practical and usually disrespectful, and like him, also, he unhesitatingly follows his employer into adversity. Nor is he unduly carried away by the change that is coming over the audiences before him. He is too much himself for that; he is the natural, universal man, and is perhaps the one character who is transferred unaltered from the old type of comedy to the new.

Rather different tastes were served by a theatre of another type, in another quarter of London, when Richard Burbage revived a project started by his father some years before, and established a small indoor theatre in Blackfriars. Since the friars themselves had been ejected earlier in the century their premises had been put to various uses, and as far back as 1576 a hall in the precincts had been rented to the combined choirs of St Paul's and the Chapels Royal, who gave private performances to a select but paying audience. Lyly the Euphuist had been their principal playwright, but in 1589 he and the boy-players had got into trouble by throwing themselves too enthusiastically into the notorious 'Mar-prelate' controversy, which raged round a series of lively and scurrilous pamphlets attacking the bishops of the Established Church, and the playhouse was suppressed by the authorities. Eight years later, James Burbage had become lessee of the old dining-hall of the friars, and had fitted it up as a private theatre, but the neighbours objected and put up a petition to the Council. Accordingly, he was prohibited from going on with the scheme, and was left with the theatre on his hands, and when Richard inherited it from him not long afterwards, it was something of a liability.

But in 1599 the boys' companies began to revive again under distinguished patronage, when the Earl of Derby enabled choir-boys of St Paul's to re-form a theatrical company, which played in a rehearsal-room in the Whitefriars district. The place and the performers were at once nearer to the taste of polite society than were the common players in their rather low neighbourhood on Bankside, and the enterprise flourished, somewhat at the expense of the old-fashioned theatres. This time the boys' play-wright-in-ordinary was one John Marston, a well-to-do young man who had taken his degree at Oxford, come to London to study the Law and been tempted aside from his legal studies by the delights of literature. He had published one or two volumes of scornful and extravagant satires, and was now writing plays for the comparatively refined and intellectual public that had taken to attending the performances of the 'Paul's boys'. He was in fact a gentleman-amateur writing for his own kind, and doing it with more talent than technique, for in his first two plays, *Antonio and Mellida* and *Antonio's Revenge*, he shows himself unexpectedly old-fashioned in style. The second play in particular is con-tinually reminiscent of *The Spanish Tragedy*, with a strong seasoning of *Richard III*.

This is worth more than a moment's notice, as there is a strong suggestion that this new fashionable audience in the indoor playhouses had tastes that were strongly conservative, not to say reactionary, and players and playwrights had to cater for these tastes accordingly if they were to attract this audience into their theatres at all. As late as 1614 we find Ben Jonson writing satirically in his introduction to *Bartholomew Fair* of such men as 'hee that will sweare, *Ieronimo*, or *Andronicus* are the best playes', and whose judgement 'is constant, and hath stood still, these five and twentie, or thirtie yeares'. What had happened was that with the advent of the Court to the neighbourhood more or less as a permanency, a large influential and mature community had taken to regular theatre-going rather late in life, and had brought to this new pastime the memories and expectations of nearly a generation before. The men who were coming to the Blackfriars now as distinguished patrons had been young and impressionable in the days when Alleyn was first playing *The Spanish Tragedy* on the South Bank. One distinguished old gentleman—Lord Buckhurst, Her Majesty's Lord Treasurer, no less—had actually started the whole process by writing England's first blank-verse tragedy in collaboration with a friend, in his unregenerate days as a law student, a year or two before William Shakespeare was born. His *Gorboduc* had set a fashion in entertainment, and it is not surprising that he and his contemporaries should look instinctively for the 'good old stories' that had delighted their youth, or that theatrical managers should appreciate this want, and make their own arrangements to meet it.

Burbage and the Chamberlain's Men at last had a use for the small indoor theatre that had been on their hands for so long, but it may well have seemed to them worth while, likewise, to attract some of these new playgoers to the Globe by resuscitating one of the old dramas that they had enjoyed in the past, completely rewritten in the newest style by the member of the company best qualified to do it. The Admiral's Men had had that popular money-maker *The Spanish Tragedy* brought up to date by commissioning someone—probably Jonson—to write in

Figure of a king, from Holinshed's Chronicle, 1577.
The fantastic armour and short-sleeved tunic indicate
a stage or pageant costume, and suggest how the
Ghost in *Hamlet* may have been originally dressed.

certain additions. The Chamberlain's Men were more drastic.
Years before, in the course of a brief experimental co-operation
with the Admiral's company at Newington Butts, they had put on
a play called *Hamlet*, written, it seems, by Kyd and containing a
ghost in a mask, that cried 'Hamlet, revenge!' so lugubriously
that a disrespectful critic compared it to an oyster-wife. Now they
presented a new work by Shakespeare, treating the old and bloodthirsty story in a fresh and poetical way. The old-fashioned playgoer would find all the ingredients of the tragedy as he had known
it of old, complete with a usurper, a kingly ghost crying for
vengeance and a fine assortment of dead bodies at the end. For the
fashionably melancholy young man there was a character-study of
human doubt and disillusion that has not been surpassed in three
and a half centuries. The comfortable middle-brow Londoner, if
he still came to the modern theatre among the Quality, found an
exciting story of strange, tormented people in high life in a foreign
country, with one level-headed man of no particular birth or
fortune—Horatio the scholar—moving among them all and

serving as the normal being, the Touchstone without the comedy, who sets off the obsessions and extravagances of the rest.

It is almost certainly the practice of 'doubling' some of the parts that has brought Horatio, in some texts, into Ophelia's mad scene, where he has no business. Take him from this (as at least one eighteenth-century editor had the intelligence to do) and he becomes a recognizable human being like ourselves, not moving in Court circles as a matter of course, and never seen, indeed, in conversation with any of the nobility of Denmark except the Prince. His friends are Marcellus and Bernardo, who bring him to the guard-post to confirm that they have seen a ghost, and it is only the ominous appearance of this ghost that induces him to call upon his old acquaintanceship with Hamlet. In his turn, Hamlet brings him to the play to confirm that he has found a murderer. He is always the outside observer, the unprejudiced opinion, the normal, natural, well-informed man, and for those of the audience who did not affect any particular humour he represented the element of sanity in a crazy world.

To the psychologist or 'humorous' man—and there were many such in the literary London of 1600 or so—his very level-headedness would appear to be evidence of a watery or phlegmatic humour. Such a spectator would notice with approval that the three other young men on whom the play turned were likewise typical of the remaining humours or temperaments that made up human nature. Fortinbras is of the air, sanguine, and Laertes of a fiery or choleric humour, leaving to Hamlet the most popular of all, the melancholic humour engendered of earth; and the four would be observed throughout the play exercising, or exercised by, the humours that differentiated them. Their very attire would serve to mark the difference, Hamlet's suit of mourning being contrasted with the armour or half-armour of Fortinbras, the courtly fashions of Laertes fresh from the court of France, and the plainness, near to seediness, of Horatio in that familiar garment, the cassock-like gown of the scholar, still commemorated in the blue coat and leather girdle worn by the schoolboys of Christ's Hospital. The sanguine temperament of

Fortinbras leads him to a throne, the angry Laertes and the melancholy Hamlet are led to plan and execute murder and gain nothing by it, and the phlegmatic Horatio is at the end as he was at the beginning, undistinguished but still preserving his life and his reason in the midst of all, partly because he has never been greatly concerned about either. The play is sternly logical when regarded as a study of comparative humours from the Elizabethan standpoint, and would appeal, on that score, to the amateur philosopher of the time.

But the dramatist has not lost sight of the old audience in catering for the new. Philosophy apart, the story is an exciting one, told in an exciting way. We have lost something, it is to be feared, by its very familiarity, and by our own tendency to look on it as literature, and to learn what we can about it because it is 'Shakespeare'. To take one small instance, we have been told more than once about the drunken habits of the Danes and their practice of accompanying State toasts with flourishes and cannon, so that we look on Shakespeare's drums, trumpets and peals of ordnance as an ingenious piece of local colour on his part and not as an integral factor in the play. The Elizabethan playgoer who saw *Hamlet* for the first time would regard these flourishes rather differently. They have been fully explained twice over—once by the king himself, in a general command, and once by Hamlet to Horatio, when the sound reminds them of the king's feast in progress in another part of the castle. Finally, the matter is explained yet a third time in the last scene of all, and is shown to be playing its part in an ingenious plan of murder.

The audience knows—it has heard the king telling Laertes—that a poisoned cup is to be prepared for Hamlet in the course of his last fencing-match. It sees the match begin, it hears the king announce his intention of drinking Hamlet's health if he makes an early hit, and when he does so, the king's drink is accompanied with the utmost possible publicity. There can be nothing wrong with the cup, the king has been seen to drink from it, with full band and artillery accompaniment, before the whole company. And then, before passing it to Hamlet, he drops in a pearl, quite openly, and announces that he has done so and only the audience can see the subtlety of the crime. He has put something into the cup so publicly, after drinking from it himself, that nobody would ever think it was poison at all. The kettledrums and trumpets have contributed to one of the most exciting moments of a play about successful and unsuccessful murder, and it is only because we ourselves have been beguiled into considering it as great literature and into letting our minds wander into contemplation of its undoubted but irrelevant beauties of thought, phrase and feeling, that we miss as often as not some of the simpler emotions that the author would have considered 'necessary questions of the play'. We have looked too deeply below the surface, where our forefathers saw the picture on the surface itself, as they were meant to do.

There are other passages of all sorts, to suit all tastes, before we get to the climax. Polonius' little scene with Reynaldo is another character-study in the Browning vein—how Browning would have enjoyed writing 'your bait of falsehood takes this carp of truth' if Shakespeare had not thought of it first—and the arrival of the Players gives Hamlet and his friends a chance to make some topical remarks about current theatre conditions. Chief among these, of course, is a complaint of the extent to which the new 'private houses', with their boy-companies, are driving the older managements out of business. They are represented as crying down the professional theatres and making it unfashionable or even unsafe to patronize them without being ridiculed, and Rosencrantz implies, furthermore, that nobody will pay an author money for a plot unless it contains a telling attack on some literary figure, with personal allusions, recriminations and possibly fisticuffs.

Any playgoer at the Blackfriars would know all about this. Jonson and Marston had been assailing each other in just such a way for some time, attacking each other's style, parodying each other's diction and bringing each other on to the stage, thinly disguised under a classical name, to undergo humiliating criticism and sometimes unseemly punishment. The Chamberlain's Men themselves became involved, and eventually got Dekker to write *Satiromastix*, which contains a highly insulting and very funny caricature of Jonson, together with a group of character parts that might almost have come straight out of *The Merry Wives of Windsor*, and were probably played by the people who had taken the corresponding parts in that play. There is a doddering old party like Justice Shallow, a comic Welshman like Sir Hugh Evans, a foolish young man like a blend of Slender and Jonson's own Stephano and Matheo, a truculent captain named Tucca, who talks like the Host of the Garter and is taken name and all from *The Poetaster* (but Dekker explains that Jonson in his turn had based him on a real contemporary captain called Hannam) and, perhaps the most interesting of all, a genial, slightly consequential person who has a shrewd wit which everyone admires and a bald head which everyone laughs at. His name is Prickshaft, and there is a strong likelihood that he may have been intended as a dis-respectful but good-humoured portrait of Shakespeare himself. This is the 'stage war' to which the conversation of Hamlet and Rosencrantz refers, and such a general allusion to the troubles of the ordinary public company would be natural, appropriate and by no means unwelcome to the interested playgoer.

Polonius ushers in the actors, reading aloud what sounds like an advertisement from one of their own handbills, and soon Hamlet is asking for a speech from a play that had recently been unappreciated by its audience. He speaks of it with kindness and regret, as of something that might have had a better fate, and we may find on considering certain points in another play that he or his author had a particular reason for doing so. The declamation over, Hamlet entrusts the actors to the care of Polonius, in words that would come to the audience not only as part of the dialogue but as a just and modest plea for the regular theatre, which was going through a hard time and facing the unwonted difficulty of holding its own against semi-amateur competition. The whole scene is topical, but is so well set into the body of the play that, quite apart from topicality, it has a dramatic function to fulfil.

The Advice to the Players, on the contrary, is so well known, and so often cited out of its context, that we have overlooked its dramatic purpose and are inclined to accept it as an expression of Shakespeare's views on acting in general. It may be questioned whether we are entirely right in doing so. The lines are spoken, after all, by a character who is himself supposed to be an author, and the views expressed are not necessarily meant to be Shakespeare's, but Hamlet's. The Elizabethan gentleman at the play had no reason to be interested in Shakespeare's opinions on acting or anything else, but he had every reason to be interested in the actions and anxieties of the people in the story. Hamlet has announced his intention of watching the king's face when confronted with a play suggesting his own crime. The players have agreed to insert a speech written by Hamlet, which ought to make the murderer 'unkennel' his guilt. Now, just before the play, Hamlet is not an amateur lecturing professionals on the way to do their own work, but an author anxious to see, above all things, that his lines carry their full weight, and do not misfire through mouthing, insipidity, incongruous gesture or ill-timed 'gagging' by the comic man. Once again there are a few side-strokes at the ranting style associated with Alleyn, but Hamlet's main desire is to make sure that his all-important lines are not 'lost', and that there is nothing to distract the king at the significant moment. Viewed in this light, the little scene serves to heighten the anticipations of the audience, very much as Oscar Wilde's heroine does when she gives her instructions to the butler, almost on the same subject, in the first act of *Lady Windermere's Fan*. Much, for Hamlet, is to turn on the play and the original spectator could see it from his anxious approach to the players about their speech. Now, paradoxically enough, the author and the passage are so famous that we listen to it as an abstract and independent discourse 'though in the meantime some necessary question of the play be then to be considered'. We have elbowed Hamlet out of the way, for the moment, in favour of an unwilling and resentful Shakespeare, who wanted nothing of the sort and has been at some pains to say so.

When the Court comes in to the play, Polonius is induced to

tell how he played Julius Caesar at the University. In the usual stock division of parts, Shakespeare's Caesar used to be allotted to the 'first old man', whose part in *Hamlet* was naturally Polonius, so that there was an extra subtlety in his statement, when made before a house that had quite possibly seen him 'enact Julius Caesar' a few nights before.

Hamlet follows the statement with a couple of bad puns and a disrespectful remark before he settles down at Ophelia's feet. The madness he simulates now and then is not the needle-sharp cunning of the satirist—which would make him an object of suspicion at once—but the childish simplicity of the village idiot, which enables him to say a number of quite outrageous things to various people without restraint, and without the disagreeable impression created by a man who obviously knows what he is saying. But at one point in his explanation of the plot to Ophelia the king realizes that Hamlet has somehow got hold of the truth, or part of it. He rises, calls for lights and hurries from the hall. There is no suggestion that he is terrified of the dark, though modern producers have more than once made effective use of the idea. Julius Caesar, in Beaumont and Fletcher's *The False One*, calls for lights in the same way when he rises to leave the masque at Ptolemy's banquet. In a house lit entirely by lamps, torches and candles, a man who left one room for another would need to take some light with him. For a State theatrical performance all the available torches would have been brought to light the stage as a matter of course, and the other apartments would be empty and dark. The custom of escorting Royalty with lights to and from the play was one that survived for centuries; Sheridan did it when the Royal Family visited Drury Lane, the ineffable Alfred Bunn was depicted by Thackeray, in his *National Standard* days, posturing complacently with a candlestick in each hand to receive Queen Adelaide at the Opera, and only just before the late war an escort of torchbearers, in accordance with ancient custom, escorted King George VI across Little Dean's Yard on his way to the Westminster Play. To call for lights in the middle of a performance would suggest not fear of the dark so much as ordinary boredom or distaste, though Hamlet suggests another interpretation when he makes the polite but insulting enquiry whether the king had felt 'distempered' with drink? The episode has taken on a new character before audiences no longer familiar with indoor theatrical conditions in Shakespeare's day.

To an Elizabethan audience, also, this point would mark a double climax in the play. Hamlet's experiment has shown him at last that he is justified in believing the ghost, that it is not a kind of infernal *agent provocateur* like the lying spirit that encouraged King Ahab to go up to his doom at Ramoth-Gilead. He can take the ghost's word, as he says, and can take action accordingly. The idea that Hamlet had delayed unnecessarily, from some weakness in his own nature, is a comparatively recent one, born of an age that was beginning to pride itself on its scepticism, and of minds that no longer entertained the thought of the ghost's being an evil spirit sent to tempt Hamlet to his ruin. Hamlet's own comments on his delay are hardly relevant. One of them occurs when he has only just found a way to put matters to the test and wonders why he never did anything about it earlier, and the other is a natural cry of frustration when he sees himself unsuccessful and contrasted in his ill-success with the enterprising and energetic Fortinbras. Paradox has reappeared again, for the generations that had outgrown their belief in ghosts were the first to blame Hamlet for not believing more whole-heartedly in this one.

As soon as he—and the audience—can see that the ghost is to be trusted, he goes into action. For the first time in the play we see him with a chance to kill the king, but he refrains for reasons that are sensible enough in logic and still more so in drama, both for Hamlet and for Shakespeare. It is an unsatisfactory sort of revenge, to kill one's enemy at prayer, as Richard did Henry VI, so that he has the best possible chance of repenting his sins *in articulo mortis* and eventually getting into Heaven after all. Correspondingly, to let one's hero kill the villain from behind, during an act of devotion, would be highly irregular, as it would revolt the religious and the sporting instincts of the spectators.

Marston had made that mistake a year or two before, in *Antonio's Revenge*, where the wronged Antonio loses our sympathy—if he has retained it thus far—by his murder of his enemy's little son. A quick stab at an eavesdropper behind the arras is a very different thing, and it is Hamlet's instinct here to strike first and investigate afterwards, only to discover that he has stabbed the wrong man.

An act-interval has been inserted here in later editions, but it is in the wrong place. The older text is here a safer guide, as it shows us at once the events of the night hurrying on, the king coming in, on his guard, to compare notes with the queen, and the decision that Hamlet had better be sent out of the country as soon as possible. This, we may justifiably assume, was how the original audience saw them, taking a final remark of the king's about England as a reminder that the story is not an allusion to anything contemporary but is set in the days of the Anglo-Danish struggles that preceded the Norman Conquest.

It would be particularly worth remembering in the fourth act, where Laertes comes home unexpectedly from France and finds himself at the head of a populace prepared to make him king in the place of Claudius. It was only a matter of months since Essex had come suddenly home from Ireland, deserting his post and neither asking nor waiting for leave, in a frantic attempt at self-justification before his sovereign. In February 1600/1 came that ill-fated production of *Richard II* that ushered in his attempt to rouse the people in his support against the Throne. There were to be no awkward allusions here; the loyal spectator must be assured that this was a play about very early times (not that there is anything else, before or afterward, to suggest it) and may be imagined enthusiastically applauding when even the villain shows a kingly dignity in the face of danger and utters the unimpeachable sentiment:

> There's such divinity doth hedge a king
> That treason can but peep to what it would,
> Acts little of his will.

After these excitements, and this passage of particular tension of audiences of late Elizabethan London, comes relief in the form of a scene of cross-talk between our old friends the Clown and Pantaloon, in the process of digging Ophelia's grave. Londoners were by no means unfamiliar with the grisly practice of digging up long-dead skeletons and bundling them into a charnel-house to make way for new tenants in the burial-ground itself. Indeed, even the semi-sanctity of the charnel-house was sometimes more than they could obtain, and there were tales of bones taken away by the cartload and used for road-ballast or the like. Yorick's skull might well be disturbed to make room for Ophelia's body, even as the dried head of Jonson, in 1849, came rolling down into a grave in Westminster, newly dug near the spot where his skeleton still rests bolt upright in the earth. We may guess that the conversation of the gravediggers, both with each other and with the unrecognized wayfarer who stops to watch and comment on their work, reflects with reasonable accuracy the British Workman of their day.

Hamlet and Laertes meet, struggle and are separated, and the story moves rapidly on to its end. It is a different end from the one in the old Belleforest tale, but the author has paid lip-service enough to the old-fashioned playgoers before him, and is giving them their old story still, but finished in a new way. King Claudius makes what every Englishman in the audience would regard as a gesture of particular friendliness and favour to his stepson in organizing a sporting event with a handicap, and publicly backing Hamlet to win it at the odds. The fight takes place, and the stage-direction of 'foils and gauntlets' in the old texts indicates that it is to be fought with 'single rapiers', the other hand of each combatant being protected by a duelling-glove of mail or thick leather. Rapier and dagger play is mentioned by Osric as Laertes' particular speciality, and rapiers and daggers form part of the king's stake, but it is in single-rapier fencing that the change of weapons can occur in the course of ordinary play (see illustration below). Sixteenth-century books on fencing tell us how a fighter can gain a momentary advantage by catching his opponent's weapon and

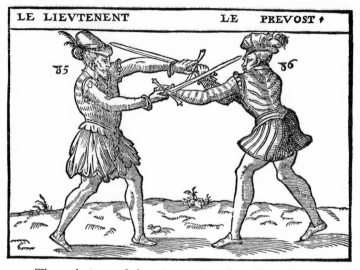

The technique of changing rapiers, from Saint-Didier's
treatise on fencing.

twisting it out of his hand. The only retaliation is for the opponent
to do the same, practically at the same moment, on which each
man falls back, having possessed himself of his adversary's sword
and at the same time relinquished his own.

That is what is done here. Each combatant in turn wounds the
other with the 'unbated' weapon, and from the king's point of
view this is the best thing that could possibly happen. The secret
will be safe with himself alone, any suspicion of foul play can be
laid at the door of the dead Laertes, and all will be well. The
uncalculated factor, however, is the queen. In all kindliness and
good faith she has drunk to the success of her son, her sudden
collapse brings the fencing-match to an end, and though the
king quickly tries to explain it away she has yet strength to contradict him and with her last breath to warn Hamlet against the
drink that has poisoned her. With his usual cleverness, Shakespeare has brought her into a sympathetic relation with the
audience at the last moment, and allowed her intervention to
round off the trouble that her frailty originally began. Such a

conclusion would appeal to the symmetrically-minded and academic spectator, while the student of humours would relish the sight of the four contrasted young men at long last on the stage at once. The sanguine Fortinbras comes to inherit the kingdom, the phlegmatic Horatio promises to explain the whole tangled story, and the two combatants, the choleric Laertes and the melancholic Hamlet, lie dead at their feet.

VIII

Three Kinds of Comedy

~~~~~~~~~~~~~~~

THERE IS no direct evidence in Shakespeare's plays to show that he took any active part in that 'war of the theatres' in which Marston, Jonson and Dekker were so strenuously embroiled. The allusions in Hamlet's talk with Rosencrantz are no more than passing comments on a matter of public interest, and we should have no reason to think that Shakespeare involved himself any further were it not for an anonymous play called *The Return from Parnassus*, which quite categorically says that he did, and that he gave Jonson 'a purge that made him bewray his credit'. It is natural to wonder what this 'purge' was, and if we consider the situation we may perhaps allow ourselves to guess.

As a serious dramatist, Jonson was deservedly admired. As a satirist, he was welcomed and applauded, since (when he was not too heavily overloaded with airs and graces) he could be up-roariously funny about other people. The trouble about him was the extent to which he gave himself airs. Not content with intro-ducing Dekker, Marston, Munday and the like into his plays and covering them with ridicule, he must needs put himself in as well, for the express purpose of patting himself on the back in public and explaining to all beholders how philosophically magnanimous he was, and how vastly superior to his petty-minded rivals and detractors. Under the guise of Crites, Asper, Macilente or Horace he stands aloof in a kind of easy disdain, unshaken by the vices and follies that he ridicules, treating the other characters with contempt and the audience with a kind of patronizing tolerance, reminding us that a year or two before it had been said of him that he 'now lives upon one Townsend and scorns the world'. When Shakespeare put Jaques into *As You Like It*, he may or may not have been laughing at Jonson; he was certainly laughing at the kind of solemn self-conceit which Jonson occasionally affected and for which Rosalind had so little use. It could be left to Dekker to invent a lively portrait of Jonson in the throes of composition, writing some of the lines that had just appeared in his own *Poetaster*. Shakespeare was concerned, not with the personality of his friend and colleague, but with some of the failings that occasionally made him seem rather absurd.

The joyous comedy of *Twelfth Night, or What You Will* gives his audience an opportunity of laughing at the rivalry of the two literary contestants, rather than at the contestants themselves. Feste the clown often breaks out into the polysyllabic mock-solemnity that was characteristic of Marston and was mercilessly ridiculed by Jonson. He is in desperate straits when we first meet him; he has been away from duty for some days and is out of favour for his truancy, he has been warned by Maria that he may lose his place, and he utters a passionate prayer that he may be inspired 'into good fooling'! A rattle of mock-learning earns him leave to make a jest at his lady's expense, if he can. He does so, and with just enough truth in it to win him grace again. Olivia has the wit and judgement to appreciate his hint that she is overdoing her mourning for her brother. She turns to her steward Malvolio to see whether he does not think the 'dry fool' is improving, and his agreement, though couched in terms of the greatest respect to her, is crushingly disdainful of the fool's talent. In fact, in his very first speech Malvolio is seen to be making a joke. 'Yes,' he says, 'and shall do till the pangs of death shake him: infirmity, that decays the wise, doth ever make the better fool.'

It is not a very good joke, it is superior, disagreeable and in the circumstances particularly ill-natured, but this does not prevent it from being the kind of remark that might come from the lips of that idealized Jonson who acts as chorus and interpreter to so many of Jonson's own plays. It is, in short, an eminently Jonsonian joke, and is intended to annihilate his adversary, but something goes wrong. The clown is quicker in the uptake and returns the insult politely but effectively in a way that makes Olivia laugh. Malvolio's reaction is to stand at once upon his dignity and decry, not the fool's profession but his proficiency in it. He is not a Puritan deploring fools in general, but a Superior Person criticizing this fool in particular, and including the audience in his condemnation if they are childish enough to find him amusing.

Olivia's answer to this might well be Shakespeare's answer to Jonson in his solemn-censorious mood. Both Jonson and Malvolio are at times 'sick of self-love', and 'taste with a distempered appetite', and the only treatment for such a sickness is to laugh the patient out of it. Even in the laughter comes a tribute to Malvolio's worth and integrity, and a caution to the clown, reminding him that there is 'no railing in a known discreet man, though he do nothing but reprove'. Indeed, as soon as Malvolio is momentarily out of earshot, Olivia takes his part. To oversee and, when necessary, to reprove is Malvolio's business, and it is the clown's business to give satisfaction to the household in general, not to take refuge in his lady's favour. A great lady has smoothed over the beginning of an undignified little squabble between two of her servants, and has contrived to say an appreciative word to each of them in the presence of the other.

Like many of its fellows, the play was written for a general as well as a particular audience, and therein lies its immortality. It was not enough for Shakespeare, as it was for so many others, to write a play full of shrewd wit and subtlety that depended on the audience's knowledge of current literary affairs. There is much in it to amuse the playgoer who had just seen one or more of the satirical plays of Jonson. Sir Andrew's ignorance of the formal courtesy of 'accosting' has a side-glance at several jokes about it in the long and almost intolerable *Cynthia's Revels*, and Viola's first sentences to Olivia ring very like those of the boy-players in more than one Jonsonian prologue, with their alterations between set speech and personal interjection. For those who know, there is a generous amount of witty allusion and ingenious parody and imitation—Jonson's elegant conversationalists Clove and Orange, in *Every Man Out of his Humour*, strongly suggest where Feste's

Pigrogromitus and the Vapians came from—but the important point is that, satire apart, the piece is a fascinating comedy for the ordinary public, who might know little of Jonson beyond his name and a vague rumour of the offences for which he had been in jail.

The lovelorn Viola bearing messages to her rival was a figure to appeal to the sound and sentimental London public that had applauded so many of the plays hitherto, including the same situation in *The Two Gentlemen of Verona*. Orsino, be he Count or Duke (he is called either indiscriminately, and in the same scene) is unquestionably the sovereign prince of his country, watched in his moody humours by a somewhat apprehensive household. Modern productions are inclined to make him languid and effeminate. Shakespeare's contemporaries knew better, and with good reason, as one may see by studying the careers of Sidney, Ralegh, Essex and other men of action who could turn themselves into philosophers or passionate amorists as occasion served. Ralegh and Essex had periods of suggesting, or actually professing, a hopeless adoration for the queen (they were both married men, but that signified little in the circumstances), Sidney is remembered by his death from a wound received in action and by his notorious love-affair with someone else's wife. The type is not peculiar to Shakespeare's age; our mistake perhaps has been to think it peculiar to our own, and to deny to an Elizabethan hero of romance that combination of poetry and piracy that inspired so many Elizabethan heroes of history.

The other comedians, though one would hesitate to say that they had their exact parallels in modern life, are found to be surviving unaltered, and jovially unrepentant, in modern fiction. We still like to be diverted by the fortunes of an imaginary 'great house' and those who dwell in it, and there is still a public to welcome the bibulous, peppery old aristocrat, the vacuous young man with more money than sense, the attendant sprites from the stables and the servants' hall, and the paragon of rectitude and efficiency whose very infallibility has made him both inhuman and insufferable. The Aldwych farces in which Ralph

Lynn and Tom Walls got themselves into trouble and out of it, the complicated evolutions of Jack Hulbert and Cicily Court-neidge in the course of some elaborate piece of detection or deception, the various chronicles of Blandings Castle, in which Dr Wodehouse has achieved the rare feat of creating a modern-dress Malvolio in the person of the Efficient Baxter—all these appeal to a side of our nature which responds in the same way to Shakespeare's treatment of much the same characters and themes.

There is no need to be well versed in Jonson and his works to enjoy Malvolio's downfall. He is a self-righteous, self-conceited person whom it is a positive duty to deflate, if any means of pricking the bubble can be found. Also, it must be remembered, he can be dangerous as well as disagreeable. He is an important person in the household, he has the ear of Olivia and he may well be able to influence her in the matter of showing no more tolerance to her disorderly old relative and his drunken friends. The scene in which he comes down to disturb their midnight festivity is customarily played in the key of the broadest farce—an affair of nightcap, nightshirt and possibly bed-socks—but there is nothing in the text to justify this interpretation, and a good deal, both textually and dramatically, that argues against it. Malvolio comes to the revellers straight from the Lady Olivia's presence, the accredited mouthpiece of the Lady Olivia's anger, and he gains weight and stature if he shows inflexible orderliness in the face of their disorder. He is not put out of countenance by their inter-jections, he is respectful but firm with Sir Toby, has a sharp rebuke for Maria's action in supplying him with liquor at all, and ignores the other two completely. In fact, he is the master of the situation, and we may be pretty sure that Maria's 'Go shake your ears' is not uttered until the steward is out of earshot.

Once he is out of the way Sir Toby and Maria recover from their fright and are instantly angry with the cause of it. Thus the conspiracy is born, to make him ridiculous and to spoil his unlimited, unforgivable self-possession, with Sir Andrew bleating applause at intervals. When the matter is put into practice, the two knights are supported, not by the clown (who is away singing in Orsino's palace) but by one Fabian, whom we have not met before, but who would seem to hold some office in the regions of the stable yard, since his grudge against Malvolio has something to do with an unauthorized bear-baiting on the premises. The letter is laid in place to bait the trap, but *before* he sees or opens it Malvolio has already shown us which way his ambitions are turning. His offence is not that of being in love with his mistress, but of gloating on the petty tyrannies he can exercise if it turns out that she is in love with *him*, and we welcome the arrangements for his discomfiture all the more heartily because we have seen how much he deserves to be discomfited. He muses on, in stately and somewhat pedantic phrases, and to those who had seen *Every Man Out of his Humour* there might well occur memories of Jonson's Puntarvolo seeing his wife's maid above at a window. 'Stay, mine eye hath, on the instant, through the bounty of the window, received the form of a nymph. I will step forward three paces; of the which, I will barely retire one; and, after some little flexure of the knee, with an erected grace salute her; one, two, and three. Sweet lady, God save you!' The cadence has a familiar ring. What is more, the earlier play had been produced (unsuccessfully) by the Chamberlain's Men before its author started writing for the boys' companies, so that Malvolio's part could be assigned to the actor who had originally played Puntarvolo, doubtless under Jonson's instruction.

It is probably by something a little closer than mere coincidence that the practical joke takes a form laid down in *Cynthia's Revels*. Here, one of the accepted ways of making a fool of someone (or 'giving him the dor', to use Jonson's tediously-iterated phrase) is to induce him, by means of a feigned message from his mistress, to appear with his dress or accessories of an unacceptable colour. There is no need to lay much emphasis on the parallel, but to a company that knew its Jonson as well as the Chamberlain's Men did, and to an audience that had recently seen his satirical comedies performed by his company or by the boy-players, there would be many points of resemblance. In short, Malvolio first appears to us with a piece of scornful criticism in the spirit of Jonson. When he indulges in slightly absurd soliloquy, his speech has the ring of Jonson, and he is persuaded to make an exhibition of himself by means of a device explained by Jonson in a recent play. This, it would seem, may well be Shakespeare's 'purge' for his conceit.

Unlike Jonson, however, Shakespeare laughs without bitterness, savagery or triumph. The farce goes on, Malvolio appears in unpleasing stockings and unfashionable garters and behaves in such a surprising way to Olivia that she charitably assumes he has gone out of his mind. In accordance with the accepted practice in such cases he is shut up in a darkened room to be catechized by a clergyman. Substitute a psycho-analyst, and the situation is one that can be used in farce to-day, and sometimes is. His responses are considered unsatisfactory in the highest degree, and here of all places we are shown Malvolio exhibiting the qualities of his defects. Stubborn he may be, but he is unquestionably sincere, and it is with surprise and some admiration that we hear him proclaim his faith in the nobility of the soul rather than buy his freedom by an easy apostasy to Pythagoras.

There is perhaps a similar hint of salvation in his very last line. Olivia has indicated to him how little 'face' he has lost. She promises him that he shall be 'both the plaintiff and the judge' of his cause when the matter is investigated, and that itself is a sign of her reliance on him. For his own part, he has every chance to be understanding, magnanimous and once more quite unforgivably superior (like a critical commentator in a Jonson play) as he sees himself restored to favour while Sir Toby has merely had his head broken and got himself married to Maria. Mercifully, the author lets him show himself a human being at last. Instead of smiling and forgiving, and being ever afterwards intolerable, he loses his temper, shouts a childish and impolite threat to the company in general, and rushes away. 'Pursue him, and entreat him to a peace', says the Duke when he has finished laughing, and for the first time we feel he may be worth it. Orsino has chosen his word well, for on his lips it has not yet gained its modern sense of imploring, and savours still of international diplomacy and solemn treaty and negotiation between Great Powers.

Altogether, the play is beautifully balanced and adapted to the interests of either a sophisticated audience or a gathering of simple pleasure-seekers. If people care to look for literary satire and allusion, there is a good deal of imitation Marston, a good deal more of imitation Jonson and a supercilious Jonsonian figure who is made satisfactorily ridiculous in the last act. If not, there is still a charming and romantic comedy of events in and about a Great House (much more true to life than old Capulet's pantomime-palace organization in *Romeo and Juliet*). There is a new clown, Robert Armin, with a pleasant singing voice, who makes his effects by being very witty, as a change from Kempe's technique of deliberately appearing very stupid, and there is a great deal of music, just as if one were at a performance in one of the new and exclusive 'private houses'. A play can hardly be satire and romance at one and the same time, and this one does not present itself un-compromisingly in either capacity, but proclaims its adaptability in its festive title—*Twelfth Night, or, What You Will*.

It has every sign (*pace* Dr Leslie Hotson's contention) of having been written with a view to production in a public theatre, before the usual sort of audience. *Troilus and Cressida*, on the other hand, seems to have been a private-theatre piece, and an unsuccessful one at that. Pagination in the First Folio suggests that it was very nearly left out, and was only put in between the Histories and Tragedies while the book was going to press. When published as a separate quarto it had been supposed to be a comedy, as it is so described in an introductory passage which is really an early example of the publisher's 'blurb', the advertising paragraph or Puff Preliminary that occupies a position on the dust-jacket of a modern book. Even a failure can be used to advertise a book or play; the publishers in 1609 made a point of the fact that this one was 'never staled with the stage, never clapper-clawed with the palms of the vulgar', just as they might nowadays proclaim a similar failure as 'The Play the West End was Never Allowed to See'. When it attains the stage in present-day revivals, it is usually produced in a spirit of rather savage cynicism, as an indictment of the cruelty and futility of war in general—a modern interpretation that would probably have surprised Shakespeare, not to mention the professional and amateur soldiers who thronged the Court. The futility and waste of the Trojan War as distinct from other wars had been a matter for comment as far back as the days of Aeschylus, but this play is hailed by its preface as a comedy, so we may assume that satirical comedy was what the author was trying to write, and make a guess at the type of playgoer for whom he wrote it.

The play is full of highly-born people and expensive armour, which was the Elizabethan equivalent, from the general social and economic point of view, of an expensive car. The characters are less readily acceptable for our friends and fellows than we have been led to accept of late. They are displayed more deliberately upon a stage for somewhat critical inspection, and the onlookers are not invited to sympathize with Troilus at the outset, but to regard his love-sick extravagances with the slightly ironical amusement of a Rosalind.*

The audience was obviously expected to be smart, cynical and sophisticated, accepting as a rule of nature that young men were fools, the heroes of Greece a gathering of boors, dolts and bores with only sufficient ingenuity to be dishonest, and that it would be folly to expect a young woman to stay faithful to one lover when she found herself the guest (and the toast) of the Officers' Mess. That was the way, no doubt, that people talked, and that some of them behaved, possibly in court circles and more certainly in the pleasure-haunts of Bankside. That was the attitude for which Shakespeare would be well advised to cater if he wanted to write a really smart, fashionable, witty modern comedy as a change from his painfully middle-class novelettes with happy endings. A successful play must be full of witty conceits, fearless

---

* But Shakespeare forgets himself before very long, when he turns him into a living, suffering human being, so that our laughter becomes uneasy and we end by seeing nothing to laugh at in the situation at all. What started as a quizzical reflection on the absurdities of love and war has come a little too forcibly to life, and it is not easy nowadays for the reader or spectator to look tolerantly on from a position of Olympian detachment.

invective and scorn of conventional sentiment, and must give countless opportunities to the actors to let the artistic world see how well they could fight, how fine they could look, and how beautifully they could speak poetry. Also, as the play would be performed indoors at a private theatre, it might be as well to have one scene at least with a special 'torchlight effect'. Marston was rather good at this sort of thing, and it usually seemed to be successful, so it would be worth the dramatist's while to bear it in mind.

That is the kind of counsel that is periodically given to playwrights, and it is quite on the cards that some such counsel was given in its day to Shakespeare. It would be about as useful as urging Dr Wodehouse to write something more in the style of Mr Somerset Maugham. Shakespeare could do most things, but he could not make a success of this mood of mockery and spiritual disillusionment. Somewhere at the back of his text, throughout the play, rings the defiant cry of Malvolio in his extremity, 'I think nobly of the soul, and in no way approve his opinion.'

He tries his best. The play is full of magnificent passages of poetry and poetic imagery which hold the attention so often and so long that they prevent everybody from getting on with the story. Almost every one of the finest and most memorable speeches can be cut right out without upsetting the play, and that in itself is not a usual thing in Shakespeare's dramatic construction. Nor, for that matter, is it usually considered a sign of a particularly good play. Such a form of construction is only tolerable when the audience has come with the intention of enjoying the technique of the performers rather than the general effect or merits of the work they perform. The Cabinet Meetings over which Agamemnon and Priam preside are almost Shavian in the opportunities they give to character after character to get up and deliver fine speeches that have much in them to admire and yet little relevance to the action. The performance of the Archbishop of Canterbury in *Henry V* was an exercise in rhetoric with a strict bearing on the matter in hand, but it would be difficult to say as much here. From time to time the minor characters bring the situation somewhere near to normal. Aeneas among the Trojans and Diomed among the Greeks are exactly the right people to act as seconds to Hector and Ajax in their single combat, and it is interesting to see how well the author has built up his effect here, quite unobtrusively, so that an ordinary English audience, particularly the Court-and-County element, can accept them at once in that capacity. They are the only men we have seen on either side who could be trusted to officiate both honestly and efficiently in a sporting event, Hector being already engaged and the kings ruled out by their position.

The fight between Hector and Ajax would appear to have been one of the great effects of the play. The text indicates that the stage was more or less cleared for it. Only the two seconds are in speaking distance of the combatants; Agamemnon and his colleagues on the one side, and Troilus and the Trojans on the other, seem to be looking on from the gallery over the stage and speaking their lines from there. Some time has to be allowed them, when the fight is over, to come down into the lists for conversation with the visiting team. From what they say, it seems likely that the champions are in armour, or at least the half-armour sometimes adopted for foot combats, especially at the 'barriers', in which the contestants fought on foot, separated by a waist-high partition, and consequently had no need of leg-armour.

The action of the play has given each champion plenty of time to put on his gear, and a stage fight can be more effective and exciting when both combatants are wearing helmets and breast-plates that can be hit without the risk of undue damage to the wearer's person or the management's property. An audience that was used to seeing contests at tilt or barriers in the Tilt-yard, with real armour, could not be put off with a vastly inferior stage substitute. Nowadays we have nothing to set the standard, and are content if the fight can be got through without ineptitude, but the courtier of 1601 had probably seen the Earl of Cumberland ride his courses as the Queen's Champion, wearing the gold-chased armour that was fashioned in the royal workshops at Greenwich and is still to be seen in New York, or the Earl of

Sussex fighting at the barriers in the half-armour and fantastic crest shown in his portrait in the Tower (illustrated opposite p. 138). Like the fencing-match in *Hamlet*, this is an exhibition bout between experts, in which the display of style is important, and as such it is very different from the combats in Shakespearean battle-scenes, in this same play or in the many others wherein they occur.

After the contest, the visitors are feasted by the besieging army. Troilus tries to get a sight of Cressida, but Diomed is before him, and he looks on from the shadows while the Greek overcomes the woman's half-hearted resistance and takes away Troilus' own love-gift as a token. The first line of Ulysses, 'Stand where the torch may not discover us', is at least a suggestion that the author has chosen this episode for a darkness-and-torchlight scene of the kind possible, and popular, in a covered theatre like that at Blackfriars. The audience is meant, presumably, to watch the whole episode with cynical amusement or a refined version of the emotions expressed by Thersites from his corner of the stage, but it looks as if Shakespeare had misjudged his courtiers here. Troilus is a good deal too realistic, his grief and resentment are uncomfortably human, and a smart, sophisticated audience does not like to be made uncomfortable—not, at least, by a play supposed to be a satirical comedy.

The last act is meant to be a whirlwind of action. Achilles has had a letter from a girl in Troy, and declines to fight. Ajax has not recovered from his success of the day before, and is too proud to fight. Troilus, on the other hand, is rabid for battle and vengeance, particularly on Diomed. Hector has gone out to battle against the wishes of his father and wife and the prophetic warnings of Cassandra. Agamemnon, Nestor and Ulysses in rapid succession describe the course of the action in language that recalls the ring of Alleyn declaiming Marlowe at the Rose in the old days, and as a culmination comes the news that Ajax and Achilles are arming after all. It is a scene emphatically in the old manner, designed to satisfy those who had been thrilled in their youth with the 'high astounding terms' of Tamburlaine the Great.

Alleyn himself (or Pistol, for that matter) would enjoy a mouth-filling passage like that about Margarelon, who

> Hath Doreus prisoner
> And stands colossus-wise, waving his beam
> Upon the pashed corses of the kings

and the whole scene leads up to a sight the audience has not hitherto been permitted to see—the magnificent Achilles in armour and prepared for war. There must have been an unusual amount of good armour available on this particular occasion, for it is much more significant here than it is in the ordinary historical plays. The very Prologue is armed when he comes before the audience to introduce the piece, and a particularly fine harness is required to bring about Hector's end.

Even here, in this unsuccessful play, there is evidence of the author's common-sense in handling practical problems of the stage. Hector, of course, must be able to act and fence, as a leading actor should. Ajax *must* be able to fence, but it does not matter if he is a thoroughly stupid actor. Achilles must have a fine presence and look resplendent when at last he appears in arms, but he has not much to do or to say, and is not a very significant character, so it is not so important that he should be able to do much else. He undergoes no emotional changes on the stage, his sentiments are simple and obvious, and the part may be safely given to a fine-looking man who can neither act nor fence. Hector and Ajax have given the audience their exhibition bout already; Hector and Achilles meet in battle in their turn, but Shakespeare arranges both their meetings so that Achilles never has to do any actual fighting. On the first occasion he is apparently at a disadvantage. He is out of breath, or out of practice, and Hector courteously pauses to let him recover. Achilles ungraciously disdains the courtesy, but takes advantage of it nevertheless, and goes away excusing himself and saying that Hector shall hear of him later on.

Their last meeting is at the end of the battle. Hector has finished his fighting for the day, and is engaged in stripping a dead Greek whom he has fought and killed for the sake of his splendid armour. On the stage he may well have taken off his own cuirass preparatory to putting on that of his enemy, as indeed, in the seventeenth book of the *Iliad*, he put on the arms of the dead Patroclus. Thus unprepared and unarmed, he is surrounded and killed by the Myrmidons under the command of Achilles, and the play ends with the young Troilus rallying the remnants of his army with a cry of hope and revenge, rather than despair. A rapid and improbable entry by Pandarus, with a characteristic piece of sniggering indelicacy, tries to recall the play to its proper function as a piece of smart cynicism for the sophisticated, but it is no use. For all its splendours it is very long, very diffuse and, in too many places, very tedious.

The foreword to the 1609 quarto not only says that it was never applauded by the vulgar, it mentions some 'grand possessors' as persons who owned the text and were in no mind to have it printed. This, too, sounds as if it had been a particularly un-successful venture at a fashionable private theatre, hushed up afterwards and suppressed so that its very memory might be forgotten. The author, however, may have had a kindlier feeling for it. Perhaps, among those who first saw *Hamlet*, there were some who had a wry smile for the allusions to a play that 'was never acted, or if it was, not above once.' Hamlet has a great deal to say about that play, and by no means all of it is relevant to his current purpose, but he goes in some detail into the verdict passed upon it by the beholders. In a few moments we learn that it contained a speech of Aeneas to Dido describing the fall of Troy (much as it is described in Marlowe's *Dido, Queen of Carthage*) and we are given extracts from the play itself.

The language of the extracts is reminiscent of Marlowe, but it is still more closely reminiscent of the really purple passages in *Troilus and Cressida*, not only in its sound but in its whole mood of passionate outcry against the heavens. As a final touch, one of the more extravagant remarks of Troilus to Hector is exag-gerated still further by the alteration of a word or two and put into the speech of the First Player. The 'whiff and wind of his fell sword' that upsets Priam is surely an echo of Troilus' 'Ev'n in the fan and wind of your fair sword', which is supposed to have a similar effect on the 'captive Grecian'. Perhaps this rather absurd line aroused a laugh at the performance, or comment after it, and Shakespeare made it a little more absurd and put it into the other play in consequence. He does the same in *Twelfth Night*, where a remark originally made by the villain in *Titus Andronicus* when confronted by a nurse and baby, and quoted satirically by Jonson in *Every Man in His Humour*, is put into the mouth of Maria when she hurries in to break up Sir Toby's drinking-party. Shakespeare was not above writing an extravagant line, and perhaps it was just as well for him to recognize its extravagance and join in the laughter before Jonson could get hold of it, as he might take a great deal longer to live it down. As it was, he had tried to write a fashionable ironic comedy and it had fallen flat, so it was best that it should lie safely dead and buried, with Hamlet himself to speak its epitaph.

There is one other Falstaff play which may have been a court comedy, and ought to be considered here, and that is *The Merry Wives of Windsor*. The principal character has been decried by critics as a pale, unworthy travesty of the real Falstaff, a mere hulk without his wit or his resourcefulness. Indeed, he differs considerably from the Falstaff of the other plays, but an examination of his part may suggest a reason for this, and a reason depending on the audience for which it was written. In the first place, let us see wherein this difference lies, and whether the author has indeed 'lost the knack', as some commentators have maintained. If it were so, we should expect to find at least an unsuccessful attempt to present Sir John in the usual way, winning our attention willy-nilly by one or two of those conversations in which he takes us into his disgraceful confidence, and coming up smiling and unsubdued in the face of accusation, however fully it be justified. Nothing of the sort, however, is to be found in *The Merry Wives of Windsor*. The play itself is against it, for its story denies Falstaff his resourcefulness and its construction denies us the spectacle of his ruminations and his wit. When he speaks, it is to the other characters, when he lays down the law, he is doing so in the story, and not stepping out of the action to give us his views on things in general.

The author has not abandoned the practice of writing those intimate little scenes with the audience, but in this play he has given them to someone else. The first person to come forward and claim a sympathetic hearing from the spectators is the joyous Mrs Page, chuckling with delight at the absurdity of getting a love-letter in respectable middle-age, and still more at the out-rageous impertinence of the letter itself. We have had a first act of brisk and bustling conversation, now we are given, and invited to share, a single character's view of the whole business, and the viewpoint on this occasion is that of the cheerful, sensible, middle-aged woman, who looks with amused tolerance on the follies of men in general and of fat old lady-killers in particular. For the first time we have a play with lines that seem to be directed at the women in the audience as if they were there not discreetly and on sufferance, with appropriate male escort, but boldly in their own right, ready to applaud anyone's effort to keep men in their proper place. Three centuries before the serious campaign for Women's Suffrage, Shakespeare is making an English housewife cry 'Why, I'll exhibit a bill in the parlia-ment for the putting down of men,' and claim that it would be easier to find twenty lascivious turtle-doves than one chaste man. And Falstaff is not the only man in the play to be held up to ridicule. The jealousy of Ford, the credulity of the Host, the pedantry and fussiness of Sir Hugh Evans and Doctor Caius and the glorious fatuity of Slender are all exhibited for us, with Pistol, Nym, Bardolph and Shallow as an equally ridiculous background, and at last the reasonable, even-tempered Master Page in his turn is shown to have been a little too sure of himself. We have had glimpses of this attitude in the earlier comedies, when noble ladies talked with their gentlewomen about their various suitors, but here the merriment of Portia flows through the whole comedy and needs no Nerissa, for it claims all the audience for confidant. In short, it is a play for women, to give them occasion to unite in laughing at all sorts and conditions of men.

Tradition says that it was written at the Queen's command and by her direction, and it seems that tradition is considerably borne out by various internal and external factors. Elizabeth seems to have developed a kindly interest in the theatre in her later years; it was as a result of direct intervention on her part that the Privy Council authorized the construction of the Globe and the Fortune. Official support and even toleration is not too easily secured for a theatrical enterprise unless personal influence can be brought to bear, but this time the players had found a useful champion. They 'had done her acceptable service and she was therefore graciously moved towards them', and the present play, whether or not it was specifically commissioned by her, has every sign of being constructed to suit her tastes. It is the respectable middle-aged woman, not the reprehensible old man, who establishes contact with the 'front of the house', taking the spectators for granted as kindred spirits. Our sympathy must lie with the Merry Wives, not with their persistent wooer. Mr J. B. Priestley has long ago pointed out that Falstaff is not a character whom women really consider funny in himself, however much they may laugh at the antics of the man who plays him, and it may very well be that we have here a Falstaff designed to show what the Crowned Virginity of England wanted to see—a bad old man making advances to respectable women and getting his deserts.

Some of our old friends in the cast have changed their nature to suit this rather different kind of audience. Mistress Quickly is no longer managing a tavern, but acting as cook-housekeeper to a comic French doctor, and is apparently a complete stranger to Falstaff, with no memories of any proposal of marriage in her dolphin chamber upon Wednesday in Wheeson-week. Pistol is noisy as ever, but several shades more respectable than he was. He is an obvious imitation of Alleyn in tragedy, but no longer a really libellous one. His first remark is an echo of the last cry of Doctor Faustus as it would sound if pronounced in a stage voice hoarse with doom, thereafter we see him ranting and strutting, but not fighting tavern-ladies and getting thrown downstairs or even getting cudgelled into eating a leek upon his knees. The ladies of this new audience, and the Royal Lady who was the chief of them, could recognize pompous acting when they saw it, and could laugh at an imitation of it, but their experience could not be expected to extend to the camp-and-tavern background against which Pistol had been seen before. He and his companions, therefore, do less and say rather more than they did in the strictly historical plays. Nym still talks of humours in the Jonsonian fashion, and Page's dismissal of him as a 'drawling, affecting rogue' indicates how his lines were to be spoken. Shallow stands upon his dignity and recounts his past prowess (like old Capulet, he goes back to the days of the long-sword), Bardolph accepts employment at the Garter, but they are amusing only by their personal conduct, not for any light they throw on general subjects like the recruiting and behaviour of soldiers, as they did in *Henry IV* and *Henry V*. Once again, this particular audience would not understand or appreciate the joke.

There are some new characters, however, who would be acceptable and amusing because they seemed to have come out of other plays and what is more, out of plays by other people. The recent success of the Chamberlain's Men with *Every Man in his Humour* had made it worth while to transplant two of the stock characters in which members of the company had distinguished themselves. The foolish gentleman and the nervously jealous husband are practically Stephano and Thorello—or Master Stephen and Kitely, as they are called in the better-known revision—out of Jonson's play, while the Host of the Garter sounds very like a spirited imitation of Alleyn playing a famous comic part. His exuberant good spirits and whirlwind burst of high-flown language are irrelevant to the story and tedious to those spectators who have no special reason to find him amusing. The real joke comes with an audience who can appreciate him as a skilful parody of the leading player in *The Shoemaker's Holiday*, which the Admiral's Men had had written for them by Thomas Dekker in 1599. Probably the part of Simon Eyre the jovial shoemaker was played by Alleyn, the star performer of that company. If so, we may imagine the rival organization delighting the Court with *two* imitation Alleyns, one depicting his way with solemn tragedy, the other his noisy life-and-soul-of-the-party manner for lighter plays. It is a small but corroborative point that Mistress Quickly, in her first scene, comes out with the catch-phrase 'but let that pass', which in *The Shoemaker's Holiday* falls so often and so suggestively from the lips of Mistress Margery the shoemaker's wife.

Sir Hugh Evans is another chance for somebody who had a line in Welsh character parts. Fluellen was presumably written for him, and quite possibly Owen Glendower. The comic Welshman and the comic clergyman can generally count on a welcome if they are not allowed to become boring, and when they are combined in one, and designed by a writer of Shakespeare's skill in the choice of words, they make a pleasant combination, particularly as the feeling it arouses is one of mirth without undue mockery. Mockery is reserved for the French doctor, who is so fierce with his rapier and so erratic with his English, and so full of his important business at Court, and the illustrious patients whom he can recommend, if he chooses, to the Garter Inn. His style of conversation would be very familiar to a courtier's ear, for it bears a strong resemblance to that of the famous fencing-master Vincenzo Saviolo, who had had a *salle d'armes* in London and had dedicated a treatise on fencing to the Earl of Essex in the days before the Earl had won a reputation at Cadiz and lost it in the swamps of Ireland.

Saviolo's individual brand of broken English, with his repeated use of the phrase 'one-two-three-four' in moments of excitement, has been preserved for us in the pages of George Silver's *Paradoxes of Defence*. Here, incidentally, is a story of a brawl at Wells involving Saviolo, an English fencing-master and a blackjack of beer, that reads like a scene out of an Elizabethan comedy, and Saviolo's language, especially in the reconciliation that followed the scuffle, has a closer resemblance to that of Doctor Caius than either of them has to the usual stage foreigner. The idiosyncrasies of a fencing-master are always welcomed, imitated and applauded among his pupils, and Saviolo's pupils had included most of the fashionable world of Elizabeth's court. When Silver's book came out in 1599, however, Saviolo had recently died, and it may be for this reason that the Italian swordsman has been transformed, somewhat unplausibly, into a French physician. By such a modification one could induce the audience to smile at the mannerisms without any thought of their having been lately rendered out-of-date.

Apart from these individual allusions and personalities, there are various general matters which would arouse a quicker response from a court audience (and a Windsor audience at that) than from the average Londoner. Dame Quickly's tribute to Falstaff's charm is a case in point. When she describes its effect on Mrs Ford, she says explicitly that 'the best courtier of them all, when the court lay at Windsor, could never have brought her to such a canary', and goes on at once with an account of the extent to which the nobility and gentry were accustomed to assail the lady with advances as unsuccessful as they were improper. This sidelight on the activities of the Court when at Windsor would go down at its best with an audience of courtiers and Windsor notabilities, each of whom would be ready to applaud a hit at the supposed habits of his fellows, and once again the spectator who could laugh most freely at the outrageous allegations would be the First Lady in the Land herself, as the one person of distinction who remained untouched by it. The Royal foundation of Eton, just across the river, might well be held to call for a topical allusion in a play written for a Windsor function. We need not be surprised, then, when we find Mrs Page taking her small boy to school, and Sir Hugh Evans asking him questions out of his Latin grammar. A schoolboy-and-schoolmaster scene would have enough local significance to be good for a laugh at the Castle.

Falstaff himself, when praising Mrs Ford to her face, utters a few technical terms which sound like the names of ultra-fashionable styles of hairdressing, and follows them a few lines later with a disrespectful description of elegant young gentlemen, while in one of his few speeches addressed directly to the audience—

when he has got home to his inn after being cudgelled in the guise of the Fat Woman of Brentford—he speaks apprehensively of what would happen 'if it should come to the ear of the court, how I have been transformed'. We can imagine the effect of this line if it was spoken not to a miscellaneous London audience, but to the glittering, laughing court itself, with the old Queen chuckling in the midst. In the same scene comes one of those passages about the Host's horses and their confiscation by some bogus Germans that have puzzled scholars into devising ingenious explanations. These may satisfy many of the demands of logic, but could never be made clear in the bustle of the play. It looks as if there were allusions to some episode, or some joke, which was either topical in 1599, so that it needed no explaining, or a jest of such age and familiarity that it could be recognized and laughed at on the slightest allusion. If, as has been suggested, there is a specific reference to the visit of Count Mümpelgart in 1592, the joke is once again a Windsor one, and of little interest elsewhere.

Court plays usually had the elements of the masque in them. The conclusion of *A Midsummer Night's Dream* is one example, and this play, somewhat unexpectedly, is another. Slapstick farce gives way to music, dancing and a deliberate attempt at beauty, accompanied by ingenious and artificial compliments to Windsor Castle and its Queen. Pistol, Sir Hugh and the egregious Quickly abandon their individual characters and their peculiarities of diction; the action of the play goes on, but with the formality of ballet, till the fairies are suddenly scattered by the sound of horns, Evans comes back to his Welsh accent, and character after character is disillusioned and made ridiculous in the last few minutes. Mrs Page has had her own plans thwarted in respect of her daughter's marriage, but she promptly accepts the fact, wishes her new son-in-law well and calls on the others to go home and enjoy the joke by the fireside.

The play is over, for good or ill. It is like no other play of Shakespeare's, but the very differences have a significance of their own. Instead of courtiers and kings paraded for the admiration of the citizen, we have seen citizens and their wives bustling around for the amusement of the court, while the music and thunder of poetry have yielded place to the brisk rattle of highly conversational prose. And above all, in place of a tavern philosopher, whose comments on life sought and stirred the lower instincts of our nature like deep calling to disreputable deep, a middle-aged housewife with a practical no-nonsense mind has engaged our interest and admiration. The Merry Wife has not exhibited her bill in Parliament, but it would seem that a Merry Old Maid of Windsor, by her 'direction and command' to a popular playwright, has exhibited a play in her palace 'for the putting down of men'.

IX

Tragedy at Court

THE YEAR 1601 had been a hard one for playgoers and players alike. There had been trouble and anxiety for many months; the revolt and execution of Essex and his fellows had left men's minds uneasy, and as time went by there were various rumours to make the Privy Council apprehensive. At the back of all, was the knowledge that the old Queen could not last much longer. For more than forty years she had governed England, she had outlived the courtiers and the ministers who had known her as a young princess of twenty-five, she had outlived her brother-in-law, suitor and enemy Philip II of Spain, she had seen king after king succeed one another upon the throne of France, but now she was paying the price of her longevity in the loneliness of her old age. Men's minds were reaching instinctively forward to see what would happen next. Nothing official had been announced about the succession; it was quite uncertain what Elizabeth herself thought of it, if she thought of it at all, or what anyone planned to do about it if she did not. Uncertainty breeds curiosity, and only too often curiosity breeds impatience. The court was full of factions and rumours and petty jealousies, whispering just too low to catch the ear of the old, ailing woman who still sat in the midst and resolutely refused to die.

It was in this uneasy, suspicious time, apparently, that Shakespeare wrote *Othello*—a strange play, but not unsuited to the period that gave it birth. We have no specific record of a performance earlier than 1604, but extracts from the play had found their way into a corrupt edition of *Hamlet* published the year before, so it would seem to have been an established favourite by the time it was played before King James, and may well have been performed—perhaps even written—for the diversion of Elizabeth and her courtiers in those last uncertain months of the Queen's life.*

For what sort of theatre was it written, and for what sort of audience? It has hardly the look of a play written for the Globe. There is comparatively little ranting in it, and next to no comedy. Its effects are intimate and subtle, a matter almost of whispers and implications, and there is little enough that an actor can throw off his chest in the open air to satisfy three tiers of galleries and a crowd standing in the pit. Moreover, it is a play of darkness. Twice in the first act, and once again in the last, we are confronted with scenes where men hurry about half-recognized by torchlight. The dialogue does not suggest the lighting to the spectators and leave the rest to their imagination, as in the last scene of *The Merchant of Venice*, but seems rather to underline and implement some effect already visible on the stage.

The very opening is a conversation, and a conversation which is full of meaning without resonance. The more care Roderigo and Iago take to let their lines come ringing out across the theatre, the less we remember to listen to their meaning, and to grasp what they are talking about. We must be close to them, easily in ear-shot, and 'overhear their conference' if we are to see them for what they are. Comparison of this conversation with the talk of Horatio and Marcellus on their guard-post at Elsinore will show how great a difference lies between a play written for a small audience, in a private theatre or even a large room without an echo, and one designed for declamation to a heterogeneous

---

* The well-known line 'But our new heraldry is hands, not hearts' was cited by Warburton as referring deliberately to a heraldic innovation of 1611, but it comes at a moment of emotional and dramatic tension where it would be most undesirable to divert the audience's attention by a smart allusion to the latest thing in contemporary heraldry. In a comic scene the author might have done it, but in that moment of drama between Othello and Desdemona contemporary witticisms have no place. It is safer to assume that the line was written in all simplicity in Elizabeth's reign and that the Jacobean introduction of baronetcies with their 'red hand' badge gave it a *double entendre* which the author had never intended.

London crowd. Even when Roderigo and Iago deliberately raise a clamour outside the house of Brabantio, their words have about them no ringing quality like those with which Macduff arouses the sleeping household at Inverness. Here, still, the sense and implications are of first importance, and the actual sound is almost irrelevant. Iago is even more obviously a blackguard than his first speeches have indicated to us, and Roderigo, on the other hand, comes out as no Aguecheek, but a well-mannered young man who treats Brabantio with a continued patience and respect that earn their reward at the end of the scene. The two men's natures are made clear to us if we can overhear them in conversation, but if once they raise their voices to the unnatural pitch of poetic oratory all traces of individual character are blown away upon the wind. Poetic oratory will come, but not in this scene, or upon these lips.

We are in a very different world from that of the public-theatre plays, or even that of *Troilus and Cressida*. The Duke's hurried session of the Senate by night is worlds apart from the stately eloquence at the council-boards of Priam or Agamemnon. It is not like poetry in a playhouse, but like emergency meetings of almost any responsible body, from Ward or Guild gatherings to Elizabeth's own Privy Council. The chairman and councillors have heard varying rumours, the figures in the different reports do not tally, the very direction of the main enemy movement is uncertain till a messenger with first-hand news is able to settle the anomaly. The name of an officer is suggested, but he is not available; while they are still arranging to send for him, Othello enters and is instantly warned for service against the 'general enemy Ottoman'. Hard on this comes Brabantio's charge that he has beguiled Desdemona by sorcery to elope with him, and Othello's explanation, with his story of the courtship, is one of the most famous and beautiful passages in the play.

Incidentally it is interesting to notice that Brabantio expresses no objection to Othello's race. It is the elopement that has aroused his anger. Various allusions in the text, and theatrical tradition as late as the first half of the nineteenth century, indicate that Othello was to be played as an African negro in European clothing. The word 'Moor' was used in Elizabethan English to denote a black man (as did its Greek and Latin originals), and in its intensified form 'blackamoor' it still does so. Peacham's drawing of the scene in *Titus Andronicus* represents Aaron the Moor as an unmistakable negro, and travel books of the sixteenth and seventeenth centuries make it abundantly clear that the term was no more confined to the inhabitants of Morocco than the name 'Indian' was, or is, to the inhabitants of India or Pakistan. The negro was not yet associated in the public mind with slavery or any sort of racial or social problem. To the average audience an African, be he Christian or pagan, was more acceptable than a turbaned Moslem, who stood for piracy, slavery and the galleys— all the things, be it noted, against which Othello is called to defend the Venetian state. The late F. M. Kelly, in his *Shakespearean Costume*, cited the interesting example of the King of Congo's Ambassador to the Holy See, one Antonio Manoel de Vunth, whose death at Rome was commemorated by a print showing the contrast between his African features and his European dress, and it is significant that the only person who sees anything unnatural in Desdemona's choice of a negro husband is Iago, when making some of his more unpleasant suggestions in a later act.

What would strike the Elizabethans as unusual and not entirely admirable is Desdemona's conduct of the courtship and wedding. Like Juliet, she is almost disconcertingly frank in the readiness with which she makes her arrangements. Whereas Juliet proposed marriage to Romeo from her balcony, Desdemona has given Othello the broadest possible hint, instead of demurely waiting for her father to choose a bridegroom for her in his own good time. Her impulse may be childlike and innocent, but it has made her do something that any playgoer of the time would recognize as undutiful and the gradual sequence of deceit and misunderstanding would move all the more easily by remembrance of that first evasion. The Duke does all he can, with consideration and sententiousness, to smooth over the awkward business, but

Brabantio will not be placated, and the last thing he says before he turns his back on her for ever is an ominous line of warning to Othello, 'She has deceiv'd her father, and may thee.' Othello may pledge his life upon her faith in answer, but the main body of the remark is unforgettable and unanswerable, because Othello and the audience alike know it is true.

What everybody said and believed about the young women of Venice was that they were ingenious and accomplished courtesans. (It is by no accident that Bassanio's Portia lives at Belmont on the mainland, and not in Venice itself.) Iago is no sooner alone with Roderigo than he says quite frankly that the marriage will not last, and that before long the 'super-subtle Venetian' will tire of her Moor and look round for someone younger. It is an unchivalrous attitude, but to the courtier of 1601 or thereabouts by no means an entirely unreasonable one.

There is a good deal more character-drawing in the next act, when the Venetian officers arrive in Cyprus. Cassio is given his one chance to display himself as Othello's immediate subordinate and possible successor. He is greeted with friendship and some deference, and he speaks in gallant and poetic language, not without a reminiscence of Marlowe in its command of sounding phrase. In a few moments Desdemona comes before us in her turn, and we get our first glimpse of Emilia. While they are waiting for the news of the next arrivals, they try to lighten their anxiety by deliberately witty conversation, challenging Iago to summarize different types of female character, beginning with Desdemona's own. His answers are cast in the form of 'sentences' —epigrammatic rhymed couplets not unlike the 'proverbial philosophy' with which the Duke had tried to relieve the tension caused by Brabantio's outburst in the council-chamber. The quotation or improvisation of such couplets would be considered one of the social accomplishments of a person of fashion or a professed cynic, like the epigrams with which the noblemen and gentlemen of Wilde and Pinero amused the stalls of the St James's Theatre in the days of Sir George Alexander's management. The author is catering now for an audience much more like that of the St James's than he was when he was writing for the Curtain or the Globe. As with the *Midsummer Night's Dream*, the public theatres could have it afterwards, but here again, surely, is a play constructed with a private, fashionable audience in view.

These epigrammatic couplets or quatrains have always been popular. The Middle Ages had a game by which characters, appropriate or otherwise, were picked out at random by players from a roll with tags attached to the different paragraphs; the Elizabethans had their fruit-trenchers—small wooden discs like table-mats—painted with cheerful, disrespectful verses. Cutlers put less ribald specimens on knife-handles, and jewellers on rings, and they have come down to us, not greatly altered, on the Valentine, the Christmas-card and the rhymed motto that until recent years was a regular feature of the Christmas cracker, though as pieces of impromptu composition they have been superseded, perhaps, by the limerick or the clerihew. Iago's impromptu couplets are blunt and cynical, and Desdemona has a poor opinion of them, but the last one of all is something more elaborate. It takes the form of a long character-sketch, in rhymed couplets, of a virtuous woman, the kind of wife and mistress of a household that Desdemona might well desire to be. She and Emilia—and quite possibly the audience—are waiting to hear what Iago thinks of this paragon, what word of praise he is to utter at last, to atone for his earlier censure, and out it comes—that all she is fit for is the life of the nursery and the stillroom and the household books 'to suckle fools and chronicle small beer'. Iago has no use for the domestic virtues, and is none too ready to admit that they are really to be found, all in one person. If they are, he sneers, they are not worth the finding.

The whole attitude is a familiar one. It is that of the person who thinks it smart and modern to affect an air of scornful disillusionment, who has and proclaims no nobler aim than his own advancement, and who looks with amused disdain on anyone who thinks otherwise. It is altogether a cheap, shoddy, third-rate attitude, and the author cannot be blamed for heartily disliking it. Iago is a villain, but that is not all; he is quite obviously a villain without splendour, not even the corrupt splendour of some of the very unpleasant people whom the audience were soon to see in the plays of Tourneur, Massinger and Ford. There were many who were beginning to think that sort of thing fashionable, but Shakespeare was not prepared to do them lip-service. He showed them, in this play and later in *All's Well that Ends Well*, what such people were like in reality, and what other people thought of them. Cassio's excuse for Iago is that 'you may relish him more in the soldier than in the scholar', and in so many words it indicates that he falls short of that combination of scholar and soldier that was the true standard of the Elizabethan gentleman. Later scholars and playgoers have occasionally elevated him to the status of a kind of fallen Lucifer, a figure of awe-inspiring wickedness, but the scholar-soldiers of Elizabeth's court would be more likely to see in him not merely a villain but an ill-bred and ill-behaved one to boot.

In scene after scene, as the play moves on, we find how needful it is to be near at hand, to watch the faces and eyes of the characters, to hear every inflexion of their voices in conversation rather than in rhetoric. Iago's main technique is that of saying the most outrageous things in a quiet, matter-of-fact way that gives them an undeserved conviction by the very ease with which their acceptance is taken for granted. The closer we are to him, the less need has he to raise his voice unnaturally loud, or speak at a pace unnaturally slow, to give his utterance time to carry across the theatre. When Cassio is waylaid in the street, and Iago is seen coming 'in his shirt, with light and weapons', an interior performance has opportunities for giving an impression of darkness, a darkness in which Lodovico and Gratiano speak to him unrecognized until they are face to face in the torchlight, and in which he can the more easily put an end to Roderigo as he lies in the shadow. However great its appeal upon the wider public stages, there are many grounds for reasoning that it was fashioned for a small one, and for an audience that had a lively appreciation of subtlety for good or evil, but little interest in broad comedy or the clown.

The name-part itself carries a certain amount of corroborative evidence with it as well. It was not ordinarily Shakespeare's habit to write what is practically a two-star play. Brutus, Cassius and Antony have been considered already as parts to suit three different types of actor normally to be found together in the same company, but Othello and Iago are two leading parts, each of which calls for an actor of an ability and importance not usually duplicated under one management. There are differences between them, but they are not the differences to be expected between two fellow-players so much as between two independent leading actors, each accustomed to play unrivalled in his own style. Indeed, they are more like the differences to be found between the Chamberlain's Men at the Globe and the Admiral's Men at the Fortune.

Richard Burbage is known to have played Othello in his time, and to have been highly praised for it, but it may be questioned whether his original part was not that of Iago. A man who had won renown in playing energetic intellectual figures, be they sympathetic like Hamlet or objectionable like Richard III, was hardly likely to welcome a play in which he was denied the opportunity of giving the public a chance of seeing him in some of his most effective manifestations. Very often Iago displays the irony, the hypocrisy or the blunt, brutal cynicism of Richard of Gloucester. His first scene with his master, in which he laments his lack of iniquity to do himself service, calls up memories of Richard's regretful self-reproach, 'I am too childish-foolish for this world', and he talks to Roderigo about the 'removing' of Cassio precisely in the tones of Gloucester telling Buckingham how to deal with Hastings. He has all Richard's valour and wickedness without his remorse, and his very name has an enemy sound about it, for Italian though he may once claim to be, Iago's is not an Italian name. It is the name of the tutelary saint of Spain, and we may be sure the audience knew it. There were those at Court who had heard it shouted as a war-cry, men for whom the very sound of it suggested battle and resistance against the pride and tyranny that had threatened their country for close on fifty years. It is an ominous, villainous name, particularly well suited for an actor already successful as a sardonic villain, and the great specialist in sardonic villainy and valour was the man for whom Richard's part had almost certainly been written, and who was inseparably identified with it in the theatre of his day.

Who, then, can have played Othello? The matter is not one beyond all conjecture, though conjecture is all that we may claim. The part does not seem, at first, to call for a physically energetic interpreter. All through the first act, Othello is not engaging in action, but refraining from it. He does not allow himself to be drawn into an altercation with Brabantio, either in the street or before the Senate. He is calm and resolute, with a commanding presence, and in contrast to the other characters he speaks poetry and music in almost every line. His speeches have just that quality of beauty, in their sheer musical sound, which we have noticed as absent from the conversation of his fellows. His rebuke to the quarrellers in the street—his own men as well as Brabantio's—his defence of his courtship and marriage, and his ecstatic reunion with Desdemona when he arrives in Cyprus, call for a high degree of technique and, if possible, a voice of natural beauty and resonance. He has no need for violent physical action, he lays hands once or twice upon Iago, and he murders his wife in the obscurity of the bed-curtains, but that is all. In verbal violence, however, he is tremendous. When his peace of mind has been irredeemably disturbed he lets loose a fury of emotion that turns him from the great captain of Venice to a roaring, suffering savage of unimagined strength. He questions his wife about her lost handkerchief in a way that scares her into the terrified, defensive falsehood of a child. He uses language of a splendour and an extravagance that recall the utterances of Ancient Pistol or, to go further back, the old days of *The Spanish Tragedy* and the grief-maddened Jeronimo. The stage history of the play has shown that Iago's is the part for the character actor and Othello's for the 'straight' speaker of magnificent poetry or prose. Irving and Edwin Booth were hailed as great Iagos and rather unsatisfactory Othellos. Each of them in turn, as Iago, played the other one's Othello practically off the stage. But years before, Booth's father had played Iago to the Othello of Edmund Kean. So, before that, had Charles Mayne Young—but only once—and so, afterwards, did Macready. Each time the result was the same. For half the play the driving energy and ingenuity of Iago dominated the action until the great burst of pathos, almost exactly half-way through it, that is Othello's farewell to arms. Then, at the change of thought that breaks out in 'Villain, be sure', Kean suddenly overwhelmed his adversary in a whirlwind of rage, and swept on unconquerable to the end.

An actor may be old, or stiff, or intemperate, or all three, but if he can still command the power to speak fine lines or fustian with volume and magnificence, he can go on playing Othello till he drops—as indeed Kean did, collapsing on the stage into Iago's arms. This being so, we may perhaps make a guess about the original casting. A play written for performance indoors, perhaps at Court on some special occasion, might be required to suit *all* the available talent, not merely the resources of the Chamberlain's Men. The Earl of Nottingham, Elizabeth's cousin and her Lord High Admiral, was still a distinguished figure at court, and he likewise had a company of players of his own. The Admiral's Men had moved from their old headquarters at the Rose to a new playhouse, the Fortune, in Golden Lane, and Edward Alleyn, who had retired from the stage some years before and settled down as manager of the Bear-garden, had been called back to the boards again at the old Queen's wish. It may be that we have here a further example of her tastes in the shape of an indoor play, passionately exciting in the old Kyd-and-Marlowe style, with a subsidiary moral for the attention of undutiful young women, particularly those who married without permission (a step which Elizabeth abominated), and two star parts in it written for the two great rival tragedians. The ageing court, with its pleasant memories of old days and old plays, might for a while revive some of the ancient enjoyment by seeing in one performance the villainy of Richard matched against the barbaric splendour of Tamburlaine and the torment of Jeronimo, depicted for them by the two actors who had each made one or the other style his own.

Court-considerations of a different sort may be conjectured to have affected our only text of the tragedy of *Macbeth*, which was written early in the next reign. Two or three scenes and speeches look as if they had been put in by another writer; the shortness of the play as we have it, and certain compressions and inconsistencies here and there, give ground for believing that a good deal has been cut out. Once again consideration for the audience may be the reason, for it has been suggested—and there is a strong likelihood, but no positive proof—that the play was performed in the summer of 1606, when the King of Denmark was on a visit at the court of England. Some such occasion would explain the introduction of a dumb-show of eight kings illustrating King James's descent from the house of Banquo, and the completely irrelevant passage about Edward the Confessor's gift of healing sufferers from scrofula. It was something inconvenient but unusual, and of undoubted antiquity, so it could well be paraded before a royal visitor from abroad, who could make no such claim to semi-miraculous powers.

The occasion would also account for certain omissions at the beginning of the play. The present text contains an explanatory scene with two very turgid speeches in it describing Macbeth's prowess in two successive battles, the first against a rebellious Macdonald, and the second against an invading army of Norsemen assisted by a traitorous Scottish nobleman, the Thane of Cawdor. In three lines, King Duncan decrees Cawdor's death and the investiture of Macbeth with his former title, but at his next appearance he is seen waiting anxiously for news of the traitor's execution. His son Malcolm describes it to him in terms that might well have been used to tell of the bearing of Essex on the scaffold in 1601—the last such execution that Londoners had known—and Duncan speaks of the dead thane with sad reminiscence before turning to embrace the kinsman who is to become traitor and murderer in his turn. This seems almost a disproportionate amount of interest taken in someone who has never

Tamerlane, from Knolles's *History of the Turks*. The
dress, wig and features suggest that the picture is in fact
a portrait of Alleyn in his stage costume as Marlowe's
Tamburlaine the Great.

appeared at all. Just possibly we were meant originally to see
rather more of the two men, the loyal Macbeth and the disloyal
Cawdor, and to appreciate Macbeth's chances of being nominated

161

as Duncan's heir. Some such preparation, with a sight of Cawdor himself, would heighten the interest of the opening scenes in various ways, all of them Shakespearean. It would show Duncan's 'absolute trust' betrayed by Cawdor and all the more firmly established in Macbeth, like Claudio's in Don Pedro after his first doubts in *Much Ado About Nothing*. It would prepare the audience, but not Macbeth, for the second title by which the Weird Sisters salute him. (As it is, the appointment has been explained to us merely by a rhymed couplet at the end of a con-fused and un-Shakespearean scene, and unless we have been duly primed beforehand Cawdor means little more to us, when the witches name it, than Glamis, whom no one has ever mentioned before.) It would prepare the audience and Macbeth alike for the possibility of Macbeth's being declared successor to Duncan on the throne of Scotland, and build up the effect of shock and dis-appointment when Malcolm is nominated instead. It would give weight and point, likewise, to the scene after Cawdor's execution, when the king's interest, and Malcolm's famous phrase 'nothing in his life became him like the leaving it', are the less effective because they are concerned with someone whom we have not been allowed to see, and in whom, accordingly, it is difficult to be really interested.

On the other hand, all this might be highly undesirable when the audience included kings. Just as the scene of the deposition of Richard II was omitted from texts of the play about him published in Elizabeth's lifetime, so these scenes of conspiracy against a king would have to come out on the occasion of a Royal visit. It is proverbially inadvisable to talk about rope in the house of the hanged, and a Renaissance court would have little desire to look on, or to be seen looking on, at a representation of rebellion or conspiracy against a lawful monarch. Macbeth's own treachery was rather different; the witches could be held responsible for that, but Cawdor's treason was a little too like the things that might happen in ordinary life, so it was better suppressed, or hurried over as quickly as might be.

The feeling is not peculiar to that day alone. The play of

Sir Thomas More, parts of which are tentatively ascribed to Shakespeare, is known to have been censored in very much the same way, by having its rebellion scene cut out and merely alluded to, instead of being represented on the stage, while in our own time, when a production of *Julius Caesar* was given before a reigning potentate in the Middle East, the producer received instructions beforehand that the actual assassination of Caesar was not to be depicted in the royal presence. The stage lighting was extinguished at the appropriate cue, and that central episode of the play was veiled in darkness, as being too terrible for normal representation in such company.

The excisions necessary to suit a royal audience in 1606 would entail a certain amount of patching and rewriting in the explanatory passages at the beginning, and sure enough, the confused and doubtful scenes come just where in the circumstances we might expect to find them. It is significant that in the Folio the lines of verse are jumbled and often so irregularly printed that the metre is entirely concealed. Dr Harrison maintains that this is a deliberate indication of the rhythm in which the more emotional scenes were written, while Dr Flatter, in *Shakespeare's Producing Hand*, goes even further, claiming that the short lines and half-lines indicate pauses for movement, gesture or stage 'business'. On the other hand, no such arguments can very easily be applied to the folio texts of certain plays of Beaumont and Fletcher (e.g., *A King and No King*) where much of the verse is uncompromisingly printed as prose. We may perhaps more safely interpret it as a hurried compositor's effort to set up a play from a confused manuscript, full of cuts, amendments, interlineations and odd passages written into the prompt-book at the last moment and not always clearly decipherable some years afterwards.

The principals may not have been very much affected. The chief sufferer is apparently Lennox, whose part has become almost incoherent by being augmented with lines and speeches written originally for other people. He has only a line and a half in his first scene, yet the cadence of the words reproduces the slow, measured speech of an old man. When he comes to Macbeth's castle with Macduff, however, he is obviously a young one, and says so in the course of his conversation with Macbeth about the weather. At the banquet he seems to have some seniority, and goes back to the earlier mode of speech. In his scene with an unnamed lord, he speaks with age and authority, and is sternly critical of Macbeth, but after the scene with the apparitions it is he who appears in some subordinate capacity in answer to Macbeth's call, and gives him word of Macduff's flight to England.

Last of all we see him among the revolted Scottish thanes who gather to welcome Malcolm and his invading army. Here, too, we may be allowed to suspect that something has been cut out, and for very much the same reason. It can be accepted as a common-place of theatre and history alike that wicked kings are in the end betrayed and deserted by their own followers, but even so, a tactful management will avoid dwelling too long on the process of betrayal and desertion when the piece is to be presented before a royal audience. Originally this desertion of Macbeth by his nobles appears to have dominated the last act of the tragedy. His own part in those final scenes in Dunsinane is full of allusions to it. The speech beginning 'Bring me no more reports' is his reply to the news of yet another departure, and the whole scene in which it comes reveals him as thinking continually of this dwindling allegiance. Now he is defiant, now despondent, now sternly practical with his measures for crushing possible waverers. It is a scene of reaction to a state of things which we are no longer allowed to observe in any detail. In the same way, the invaders, both Malcolm and old Siward, go out of their way to mention the help they have had from Macbeth's own men, and the 'noble thanes' of Siward's speech are obviously the Scottish rebels who have allied themselves with Malcolm against the usurper. As at the beginning, so at the end, our text is the one prepared for a special audience, and is disjointed and inconsequent because the really important matters were deemed unsuitable for that audience, and had to be cut out.

Certain other scenes, being quite unexceptionable, were re-tained unmutilated and appear disproportionate by comparison.

One such is the interview between Macduff and the exiled Malcolm. Practically all of it is to be found in Holinshed, and it has been put into the play *in toto* because it was considered important. Nowadays it is apt to suffer because of a tendency to underplay Malcolm, whose part may be assumed to have lost a certain amount of text and a great deal of character in the process of cutting the play to the form in which we have it. Malcolm is the young and heroic figure (possibly represented in the person of the actor who had played Claudio and Henry V) who distinguishes himself at the same time as Macbeth and whose nomination as the official successor to Duncan gives Macbeth the final impetus that starts him in the direction of usurpation and murder. He is the rightful heir, the champion of the oppressed and terrorized Scottish nation, the figure who walks in light where Macbeth plods through an ever-thickening bloody mist, and it is he who is to stand at the end as the herald of happier days to come. Audiences must have been meant to feel more interest in him than we do now, and quite possibly the lost Cawdor scenes gave them the chance. As it is, we never really take in the fact that the Bleeding Sergeant at the beginning has just saved him from being taken prisoner, and in his long scene with Macduff in the fourth act he is apt to seem callous and rather priggish, largely because we are making no effort to regard the scene from Malcolm's own viewpoint.

If we think of him as the 'heroic youth' of a historical play, the interest and tension begin much earlier in the scene. Macduff is urging him to come back to Scotland in arms and lead her people against the tyrant. Malcolm has no means of knowing whether his visitor is a genuine patriot, an agent of Macbeth sent to tempt him to his destruction, or an independent adventurer, ready to follow any pretender, however undesirable, so long as he himself can make a profit out of the business. When Sir John Gielgud revived the play in 1942 this scene stood out as quite unexpectedly dramatic, simply because we were instinctively in tune with the situation. The refugee, appealing for immediate assistance against an oppressor, was a familiar figure, and correspondingly familiar was the necessity for verifying every point of his story that could be tested, in case he was an enemy agent urging us to open a second front at a time when we should be going blindly into a trap if we were to do so. For a brief while Malcolm's problems and suspicions were real to us because they were our own. In the turbulent sixteenth century they were real enough for Holinshed to describe the interview at some length, and by Jacobean times it had become an integral part of the story, and was consequently put into the play almost as it stood. The drastic cutting of some parts of *Macbeth* tends to make the uncut portions appear unduly long, and as the interest of audiences is nowadays apt to be fixed on Macduff rather than Malcolm, we are eager to see him receive the tragic news about his wife and children, and correspondingly impatient with the long scene that goes before.

We have a contemporary spectator's account of this play in the journal of Dr Simon Forman, who saw it at the Globe in 1611, but he cannot be accepted as representing the general public, for it is difficult to persuade oneself that the average Jacobean play-goer came away with such a scrappy and inaccurate impression of a performance. Dr Forman was a practitioner of bad reputation and unpleasant habits, and it is quite possible that when he went to the theatre on the twentieth of April in that year he was in no state to take in exactly what was happening on the stage, or to record it intelligently afterwards. His account says that when Macbeth and Banquo were riding through a wood, there stood before them '3 women feiries or Nimphes'. Nothing in the play as we have it suggests the presence of horses or trees, and there is nothing of the nymph or fairy about the appearance of the witches as described by Macbeth and Banquo themselves. Forman at this point is telling the story rather than describing the performance, for his account differs from the scene in Shakespeare but tallies with the illustration of it in the first edition of Holinshed, published more than thirty years earlier (see opposite). There are the horses, there is the wood—at least, one widely-spreading tree and a couple of plants behind a boulder—and the Weird Sisters are nothing like the conventional witch, as represented elsewhere

Macbeth and the Weird Sisters. From Holinshed.

in the volume, but wear elaborate dresses of the type associated with unspecified antiquity, Orientals or supernatural beings. Here, then, and not on the stage of the Globe, are the 'feiries' of the doctor's notes.

His mention of a scene in which Macbeth and his lady found the stain of Duncan's blood impossible to wash off may just possibly be, as Dr Harrison has suggested, an indication of something that has now dropped out, but it may be no more than a drunken or inattentive man's hazy recollection of the last part of the murder scene. For all we know, he may have fallen asleep in his seat and been roused by the knocking at the gate, to fix his attention on a lady and gentleman gesticulating at each other with red and reeking hands, and withdrawing before he can do more than grasp the fact that Macbeth, at any rate, does not think he will ever be able to wash himself really clean again. It is sad, but undeniable, that our only first-hand witness of a performance of *Macbeth* in its author's lifetime is so wildly inaccurate in matters that can be checked that we cannot put any trust in him over those for which he is the sole authority.

By the time Forman saw the play, its author was no longer a regular member of the company playing at the Globe. His name drops out of the acting-lists after 1607, and in 1611 he was back at Stratford, living in a house which he had bought and renovated a good many years before. He may even have sold his shares in the Globe and Blackfriars theatres by that time; at all events, he was in no position to object—perhaps not even to know—if the company chose to play *Macbeth* in the curtailed, distorted version that had once been prepared to suit a royal entertainment.

X

At the Globe

THE ACCESSION of James VI of Scotland as James I of England was the occasion of an advance in fortune for the Chamberlain's Men. They were taken under the new king's patronage, and henceforth called themselves the King's Men, their rivals from the Rose and the Fortune coming likewise under royal favour and reappearing in their turn as the servants of Henry, Prince of Wales. Performances at court were more frequent, and plays and players would adapt themselves increasingly to the tastes of a well-bred, well-educated audience hitherto associated only with isolated 'special occasions'. But all this time the Globe was still a going concern on Bankside. Plays were continually being given there, and the pleasure-seekers of the South Bank had their own tastes and requirements, which Shakespeare and his fellows must naturally attempt to satisfy.

Some indication of those tastes has been observed already in the *Second Part of King Henry IV*. We have seen that Bankside was not a particularly respectable neighbourhood in Elizabethan days, and it did not improve socially or aesthetically under King James. The incidence of a new reign and a new century seemed to encourage the growth of a rather raffish kind of smartness that prided itself on being up-to-date and progressive, chiefly on the strength of having discarded the restraints and conventions of the last generation.* Fynes Moryson noted that there was a change in

---

* The same convention was to be seen at the beginning of the eighteenth century, and with very few variations at the beginning of the nineteenth and the twentieth, the Stuarts, George III and Queen Victoria being successively spurned into the background with much the same gesture of progressive scorn.

the colours of fashionable clothes. Where black, white or a combination of the two had been *de rigeur*, there was now a change to red, yellow and green, and the Baron de Rosny, coming in state to bear the condolences of the King of France on the death of Elizabeth, had to be warned at the last moment not to put on the elaborate suits of mourning which he had provided, as a matter of course, for himself and his suite.* Times were changing, and manners were changing with them, and a suit of black at the court of King James was likely to cause as much irritation and offence as Hamlet's mourning did at the court of Denmark. All was to be pleasure, festivity and freedom. Elizabethan formality was dead and buried, and it was time for a gallant to show his daring and originality in his ordinary behaviour, lest he should be thought a moralist, and out of date.

Dekker's ribald pen made merry with this attitude of mind in *The Gull's Hornbook*, a burlesque manual of instruction for would-be fashionable young men. It is entertaining enough on its own merits as a piece of richly humorous writing, but it is of additional value for the light it throws upon current fashions of ill-bred behaviour. The reader is told how to conduct himself at the play, or when taking a meal at his 'ordinary', or eating-house, as well as in various other places and occupations popular among those who liked to spend time and energy, and even a certain amount of money, in showing to each other, and to all outsiders, how daring and smart they were. Shakespeare's technique is rather different. Instead of describing this way of life and urging his audience to join him in mocking its showiness and shoddiness, he depicts it unerringly and uncompromisingly yet almost without comment, while writing ostensibly about something else, and leaves the spectators to take what view of it they please.

Two of his comedies dating from this time bear every sign of having been written for such an audience. Their plots both turn upon the same joke, and a typical Bankside joke at that, namely the inability of the novice at love-making to tell one bedfellow

* Memoirs of Maximilien de Bethune, Duc de Sully, Book XIV, concluding paragraphs.

from another in the dark. *Measure for Measure* and *All's Well that Ends Well* are both of them well-known stories worked up in the author's characteristic manner into plays about disconcertingly human beings. The scene of *Measure for Measure* is ostensibly Vienna, the last outpost of civilization and Christianity on the savage fringes of Eastern Europe, and therefore a good non-committal site to choose for the murder of Gonzago or the curiously Mikado-like legislation of the present play. The characters, on the other hand, savour of the Thames rather than the Danube, and most of them might have been found at one time or another in the audience at the Globe. Isabella one must admit would hardly be likely to go there, but even the princely Angelo might at some time have spent an hour or two in the best seats with his Mariana, while the disguised Duke would have felt it incumbent on him to patronize the entertainment, much in the spirit in which Jonson's Justice Overdo went to Bartholomew Fair in search of 'enormity'. (Indeed, the episode and the name suggest that Jonson may very possibly be sneering at the continued popularity of the present play.) As for Froth, Lucio, Pompey, Mistress Overdone and their company, they were to be seen many times over in the appropriate parts of the house. It is a play for Bankside people, very largely about Bankside people, though it pretends not to be. In fact, the audience has come into its own.

Where Dekker and Jonson are mercilessly satirical, Shakespeare plays the calm, sympathetic, almost uncritical observer, depicting people as he knew them to be, and as the spectators could see them to be if they looked round about them. His characters are all allowed to speak in their own defence and to show themselves at their best, even when that best is nothing much to be proud of. The trouble is that once again, as in the past, he has made some of them too real, so that they begin to run away with the play. Angelo, the Duke's deputy set to administer the laws in his absence, is not so much Puritan as bureaucrat, trying to carry out the law without sentiment, partiality or emotion, like the Government official that he is. Unfortunately, the negation of these often involves the negation of common sense into the bargain. He is appointed to enforce all the laws in general, but he makes a bad error of judgement over one law in particular by condemning an offender whose breach of that law has been technical rather than flagrant. Claudio's offence is that of intimacy with someone whom he had intended, and still intended, to marry. Most people regarded this as vaguely reprehensible but not uncommon, while some saw nothing wrong in it at all, provided the parties got married at an early opportunity. It had happened to people in all walks of life; to the Earl of Southampton, for instance, to Sir Walter Ralegh and also, apparently, to Shakespeare. A Bankside audience at its most respectable would consider that Angelo had chosen a somewhat unsuitable case for making an example of a law directed rather against the habitual libertine than the incautious amateur.

There is no need to think of Claudio as a weakling. On the contrary, he is more effective when played as a simple, hearty, enthusiastic young man like Fielding's Tom Jones. In all conscience he cannot see why some people are taking his offence so seriously. There was never any question of his deserting his Juliet; indeed, they were bound 'upon a true contract', by which some people would count them as practically married already. His first reaction to Angelo's terms for his redemption is a natural indignation at anyone's making such a suggestion to his sister. Next comes an equally natural exasperation at her rejection of the terms and refusal to make what he considers a very trifling sacrifice, or at least to show some readiness to do so.

We must bear it in mind, as the Bankside audience would, that Claudio does not see anything very wrong in what Isabella has been asked to do. In fact, as he and his betrothed have yielded to temptation, it seems downright unneighbourly of his sister not to do the same in a good cause. As it is, he is in prison, condemned to death and horribly uncertain what will happen to him afterwards. He has never had occasion to think about his mortality before, and he would much rather not think about it now. As she has not offered to save him, and has not given him the chance of nobly rejecting her proposed self-sacrifice, he has to ask her himself, and she rounds on him with indignant scorn. The conventional way of playing the scene is one of passionate appeal on Claudio's part, but there is nothing in the lines to justify it. After that one blunt request, 'Sweet sister, let me live,' there is no cry for mercy, no appeal to the ties of kinship. What he asks, and asks again, is the usual request in many a brother-and-sister argument, namely that she should pause in her tirade and only listen to him! The Duke's intervention checks Isabella from saying more, and when Claudio speaks again his next words are 'Let me ask my sister pardon.' For all we know, that may be what he has been trying to say for the last five minutes, if she would only let him.

But we must not look at Isabella from her brother's point of view alone. An audience does not necessarily condemn a virtue that it does not itself possess. On the contrary, it is quite likely to applaud it in another, partly from genuine admiration, partly, perhaps, from the feeling that applauding a virtue is an adequate and labour-saving alternative to practising it. The character in the play who seems nearest to the original audience is the pleasant but disreputable Lucio. He represents most nearly, for the spectator of his own day, the natural man by whose measure the obsessions of the other characters are best to be reckoned. His counterpart, among the respectable characters, is probably the Provost, and both of them, the 'good fellow' and the good official alike, treat Isabella with sympathy and respect, so that the audience will instinctively follow their lead.

It may be assumed, likewise, that when the part was played by a boy, it was much easier to credit Isabella with the simplicity and innocence of someone not yet fully conscious of her womanhood. In their first conversation Lucio admits that he regards her not as a woman but as 'a thing en-skied and sainted', and she is presented to the audience from the beginning as a person set apart, with standards of conduct that may naturally be expected to be higher than the average. Audiences—particularly large and miscellaneous audiences—like a heroine to *be* a heroine, and not a mere portrait of the type of girl one might find anywhere. It is the old story of Portia and Bassanio over again, the audience likes to watch and admire the unfamiliar, and takes pleasure in contemplating actions, and listening to sentiments, that are unlikely to be encountered in the ordinary routine of life.

With the comic characters it is the other way about. The rowdy young gentlemen who patronize Mistress Overdone's establishment, the foolish Mr Froth, who never enters such a place without getting 'taken in', the constable who has never pretended to have the qualifications for his post but is always being engaged as a deputy by people who will not trouble to do the work themselves, are all figures who would have their counterparts in the contemporary world centred in the purlieus of the Clink and the Stews. More extravagant but equally entertaining are the hangman Abhorson, with his professional resentment at being saddled with an assistant out of a bawdy-house, and the assistant in question, the apologetic Pompey, who takes quite cheerfully to employment in the jail, and calls a criminal out to the scaffold as urbanely as if he were bringing him his boots and hot water at Mistress Overdone's—not to mention the criminal himself, who has not got over his last night's drinking and flatly refuses to come out and be hanged that day for anybody.

These people represent the reality of Bankside life, while the Duke and Isabella stand for its romance. For such an audience there is no incongruity in Isabella's abandonment of her sacred calling in the last moments of the play. No life of dedication can lift her higher than her own nature has done when, setting aside all resentment for her wrongs and the express discouragement of the Duke, she kneels at his feet to beg for the life of Angelo. She has become something more than human, and as such, may most properly find her reward in the call to share a ducal crown. The modern convention of dressing her as a nun makes the end more difficult to carry off successfully on the stage. The Folio, in one of its few stage-directions, specifies Francesca as 'a nun' when she and Isabella come in together, but this may be taken as a sign that she is wearing a religious habit and Isabella is not. Lucio's greeting to Isabella not many lines later claims to recognize her virginity from her cheeks. If she had been wearing the dress of an Order, one would have expected him to pay his compliment to that. Likewise, neither she, Angelo nor Claudio makes any reference to the specially heinous offence of violating a woman dedicated to religion. It is surely permissible to present her as a woman whose description 'in probation of a sisterhood' denotes that she contemplates taking the veil, indeed, but is still at liberty to change her mind if she sees fit. (The late William Poel, I think, actually did so present her when he produced the play.)

Angelo and the Duke are figures whose relative importance has been reversed in the course of time. The Restoration practice of introducing real actresses to play the women's parts is very largely accountable for the change. The precocious little boy, who could be beaten, if necessary, when he got above himself, had given place to the Leading Lady, and the whole presentation of the play had had to undergo a change in consequence. Instead of a virginal figure with a simple sense of values, who refuses compliance with Angelo not because it is degrading or distasteful but because it is wrong, and no amount of temptation or argument will make it otherwise, we are faced with a Leading Lady indignantly defending her virtue, and the gentleman against whom she defends it assumes a considerable increase in importance, to the exclusion of the Duke who has so little time upon the stage with either of them. The play seems to deliberate less about Sin and more about Sex as we watch the progress of the action, and the virtuous Duke is edged unobtrusively into the background.

He deserves a better fate. Much of his part in the story follows an anecdote told by Lipsius about Charles the Bold, Duke of Burgundy, and his treatment of a deputy who had proposed a similar bargain to the wife of an imprisoned citizen, only to confront her, after she had yielded to him, with the dead body of her husband. When the Duke heard of it, he compelled the deputy to marry her and to settle his estate upon her and her children, and then asked her if she were satisfied, to which she said she was. 'So am not I,' said the Duke, and told her to come next day to take home her husband from the prison. She did so, and once more found a dead body. The shock of the Duke's grim justice was too much for her, and she did not long survive her second widowhood.

The story is quite possibly true—it is certainly not ill-assorted with what we know of Charles the Bold—but in its original form it would hardly do for Shakespeare, and certainly not for players writing and performing under the patronage of James I. Out goes all trace of impetuous despotism, however well-meant, and the central part—the Burbage part, probably—becomes a wise, benevolent ruler watching in disguise over the frailties of his people. When Angelo, as a character, begins to develop too fully and become too interesting, he is discreetly shelved for the best part of two acts, and it is only by hearsay that we hear of his blackest act of treachery, when he decides after all that in spite of Isabella's sacrifice, Claudio must not live to bear witness against him. He has a very short scene at the end of the fourth act, when discussing the rumours of the Duke's return, but apart from that he is not seen from the time of his dishonourable suggestions in the second act to his unmasking in the fifth. This is not the stuff of which leading parts were made in Shakespeare's time, and in that time Angelo was no more than a supporting part, albeit a good one.

Shakespeare's Duke not only begins the play and ends it, he is intended to be the principal figure throughout, moving un-recognized among his subjects, watching them in wisdom, aiding them with counsel and appearing in majesty at the end, when all is unravelled before him, to deal out reward, punishment and pardon. The spectacle of a kind of Haroun-al-Raschid, a sub-limely wise, just and merciful prince, would be particularly welcome to King James, who thought he was one, so it is not surprising that the play was performed at court on Boxing Night in 1604. At the same time, the Duke's state entry in the last act would have reminded audiences of a recent public entertainment. Rumours of plague had necessitated the omission of the new king's state ride through London before his coronation, so the pageant was performed almost a year later, on the fifteenth of March 1604, and Shakespeare and his fellow-actors were in the procession as Grooms of the Chamber, and had four yards each of red cloth for their liveries.

The Duke's part calls for intelligent playing and very intelligent speaking. Some of the lines and sentiments echo those of Ulysses in *Troilus and Cressida*, and make one wonder if the resemblance is purely coincidental, or if the leading actor of the Chamberlain's Men did indeed play Ulysses in that ill-starred experiment. Here he has some of the finest lines to speak, and is the central figure in the most dramatic moment of the play. He is the embodiment of justice and majesty, Isabella the embodiment of that virtue which is more than the negation of vice, and the mating of these two ideal characters becomes a natural and desirable conclusion when we see how the two stand above, or at least apart from, the very human figures who make up the rest of the play.

Something of the same combination of idealism and reality can be seen in another Bankside comedy of about this time, *All's Well that Ends Well*. This time Shakespeare has taken a story out of Boccaccio, translated it into terms of ordinary life and almost upset its balance by making it too human. The theme, if not the actual plot, is one that has done duty in our own time both on the stage and on the motion-picture screen. In various contexts we have seen the heroine impelled to do some service to the hero, only to be dashed to disappointment when she realizes that she has merely made him horribly uncomfortable and resentful at being put under an obligation, sometimes a public one. Blended with it, in Shakespeare's version, is another theme not infrequently handled by him in North and South London alike, the theme of a likeable young man getting into bad company. We have seen already how it appeared in *Henry IV*, more recently we have seen Roderigo gulled, mocked, robbed and gradually corrupted by Iago, and this play shows us a still more realistic, everyday example in the admiration of Bertram for the flashy, vulgar, dishonest and cowardly Parolles. Here, even more than in Iago, the author has presented the shoddy cynicism of the new age. Parolles is a typical gull-catcher of the Bankside, a worthy epitome of the *Gull's Hornbook*, drawn with an accuracy worthy of Dickens, and all the more mercilessly for the lack of scorn or disapproval. To anybody but the inexperienced Bertram he is obvious for what he is, and his Dickensian equivalent is to be found, not in the rich absurdity of Jingle, but in the realism of Mr Smangle or Mr Montague Tigg. (Lucio is infinitely preferable as a companion; after all, he has the rare gift of suiting his conversation to his company, or trying to do so, even when talking to a clergyman.) Iago has valour, which Parolles has not, but otherwise they may be regarded as two studies in the same type of blackguardly cynicism, devised for court and Bankside audiences respectively.

Once again, the presence of women on the modern stage has affected the reception of the play. Helena, like Isabella, is a heroine of romance, and not a realistic figure like the Countess of Roussillon or the old widow of Florence. Bankside liked to see a paragon, and paradoxically enough, a Helena who was not played by a woman could achieve just that detachment from, or independence of, her sex that the part requires. She could make her request, and ask for a husband in true fairy-tale fashion, and yet keep the audience's sympathy without arousing any suggestion of the predatory female in pursuit of her chosen male. She is a heroine, and behaves as heroines should behave, with a proper combination of intelligence, modesty and an infinite patience. When she has healed the king and become a privileged figure at the court, her choice of a husband is awaited with eagerness by the unmarried courtiers. In her own eyes, she is at last in a position to pay Bertram the greatest compliment she can, and in the eyes of king and court alike she does so, passing by the eager claimants for her favour and submitting herself, in terms of the most moving humility, to the acceptance of the youngest, rawest newcomer, a young cub from the country only recently come to court as the king's ward.

But Bertram sees it differently. As in the old days, with Proteus and the Claudios, Shakespeare has drawn a character who is not a fairy-tale hero but a young man behaving reprehensibly but realistically in the way that some young men did, and do, behave. The spoilt young nobleman, newly come to court, is looking forward to romantic adventures in the fashionable world, with ladies like the daughter of Lord Lafeu (as he himself confesses in the hour of his repentance) and it is a grievous disappointment to him to find himself getting betrothed and married to his mother's waiting-gentlewoman, a doctor's daughter whom he knows quite well already, as she has been kept in the house more or less as a poor relation. When he recoils, Helena withdraws her suggestion at once, and it is the king who insists, indignant alike at Bertram's discourtesy and his attempted disobedience.

Like Roderigo, Bertram is a potentially pleasant young man in danger of being spoiled by the company he keeps. There were plenty of them at court and on Bankside alike, and the type would be recognized at Blackfriars or the Globe. When he goes away to the Italian wars we are given to understand that he acquits himself well, and he must have been played as a sufficiently attractive person for audiences to feel pity for the way in which he is being misguided by Parolles. His callow advances in Florence, with his blundering attempt on the virtue of Diana, would show them-selves not as the behaviour of a practised libertine but as the efforts of a boy who is young enough and ignorant enough to think that he ought to be one. With Bertram as the centre of interest, the stratagem of Helena's substitution for Diana becomes a welcome resolution of the tangle. The audience does not really want Bertram to commit himself to a piece of conventional debauchery, and is all the readier to take Helena's point when she prepares for him to come 'with wicked meaning in a lawful bed'. Intending to do wrong, he does right to his own wife, though it is without his knowledge and against his will.

It does not automatically reform him. When he finds himself confronted by Diana he breaks out into ungentlemanly recrimina-tion, doing everything he can to shift the blame. The supposed loss of Helena, and his knowledge how badly he has treated her, make the Florentine episode all the more unpalatable to remember, and it is very much the companion and pupil of Parolles who tries to justify himself by desperate evasions and falsehoods until overwhelmed by the evidence against him. A shamefaced line of confession, and he stands silent through the interrogation of Parolles and Diana. Then, on top of it all, comes the incredible revelation that the audience have been awaiting, the sight of Helena living, though she calls herself no more than the shadow of a wife, 'The name and not the thing'. This time he makes a swift, simple answer, 'Both, both, O, pardon!' and he is at her feet. He has surrendered unconditionally, and only then does he learn that Helena has in fact fulfilled his arrogant conditions, she has won his ring and is to bear his child. The court might not like to admit the existence of young men who thought, talked and behaved like that; Bankside, at any rate, knew all about them, and was prepared to watch the progress of one of them with sympathy and understanding, even while it made no pretence of approval.

The comic scenes for the most part revolve round Parolles. There is a clown at the castle of Roussillon, with the usual simpleton's wisdom and very obvious cunning, and his slight resemblance to Costard in *Love's Labour's Lost* is one of the arguments used by those who seek to date this play some ten years earlier than the period we have assigned to it. The frequent use of rhymed couplets is another, but rhymed couplets in Shakespeare are by no means evidence of an early date. The Duke in *Othello* has a good series of them when he is being sententious, and they are the natural medium for Iago's epigrams on womankind a few scenes later on. Moreover, one would not expect an Elizabethan audience to enjoy such characteristically Jacobean jokes. With the Maiden Queen safe in her grave at Westminster, and the new generation being tacitly encouraged to make a mock of what she stood for, Parolles might safely utter his observations about virginity wearing her cap out of fashion like an old courtier, and being of no more use to anyone than a withered pear, but it would hardly have been wise to utter those sentiments, or to applaud them, while Elizabeth was living. Likewise, the joke about the gentleman who had been an officer at Mile End 'to instruct for the doubling of files' is one more fitted to the South Bank than to the audience at the Theatre or the Curtain. North Bank Londoners, and the shopkeeping population generally, took their amateur drill with reasonable seriousness. They might laugh at its foibles, as John Leech did at those of the Volunteer Movement in Victorian days, but the mere mention of it was not sufficient to raise a laugh. The higher and lower social levels at the Globe, on the contrary, would be moved to merriment at the very idea. Once again, a jest with a mild local significance has served as a pointer to the place, and consequently to the date, of a Shakespeare play.

XI

Malcontents and Majesty

THE GENERAL uncertainty and apprehension of the early seventeenth century, followed by the breaking of so many links with the past on the death of Elizabeth, gave the writers of the time a marked impulse in the direction of what may be called defiant gloom. The melancholy Jaques was coming into his own, and in plenty of surviving plays a rich poetic fancy combines with extravagance of imagery and savage crudity of plot. Cyril Tourneur would seem to have written *The Atheist's Tragedy* in the opening years of the new reign, and *The Revenger's Tragedy*— if indeed this is his, and not a precociously early work of Massinger—a year or two before its publication in 1607. The former is a solemnly absurd melodrama presented in language that has been praised highly, to the point of extravagance, and is in many places of unquestionable beauty and interest, while the other, though still extravagant, is much better written, and is a story of hatred and revenge played out among a number of singularly unpleasant people with names indicating the different vices and follies that they typify.

Marston, of course, had made his contribution to this type of drama, as far back as *Antonio's Revenge*. He had made up his quarrel with Jonson, collaborated with him and Chapman in a comedy called *Eastward Ho* and just escaped going to prison with them when they were all prosecuted for a highly disrespectful allusion, in that play, to King James's practice of bestowing knighthoods at thirty pounds apiece. And in 1604 he had dedicated to Jonson his play of *The Malcontent*, which reflects most clearly the general bearing of the time. The Malcontent himself is somewhat of a Jonsonian character, a displaced duke who attaches himself in disguise to the court of his supplanter and affects a kind of Bernard Shaw bluntness by being very disrespectful to his master and very disagreeable to his fellow-courtiers until he is revealed and reinstated and pardons everybody in a superior manner in the last few lines of the play.

The type had been worked hard on the stage for several years but was still popular. Jaques with his melancholy, Hamlet with his combined melancholy and dissimulation, Iago making a parade of honesty and illustrating it by coarse, blunt cynicism, serve to show us that Shakespeare could handle the character with more variety than some of his contemporaries. Now, however, the general attitude seems to shift a little. The plays are not content with being plays about malcontents, they attempt, as far as in them lies, to give the impression of being plays by malcontents. One character may be melancholy and scornful as before, but it becomes more and more likely that all the others will be trivial, contemptible or corrupt. Jonson's *Volpone* shows how the same blight could fall on the characters of a comedy. The play lives by its wording and by its fierce, driving energy, and we enjoy it because of the intricacy of the plotting and the splendour of the language, not for any attractive qualities in the people portrayed.

Looking at the ingredients of *King Lear*, written in 1606, we find a good deal that seems devised to suit the taste of the time. Bloodshed and horror were becoming popular again in the old *Spanish Tragedy* fashion, if *The Revenger's Tragedy* were anything to go by, and here is a play on the good old theme of the persecuted patriarch—a kind of intellectual *Titus Andronicus* with a bluff, blunt cynic in disguise thrown in, an equally bluff, blunt, double-dealing villain and a sprinkling of other characters weak enough or wicked enough to absolve the author from the charge of being a soft-hearted old Elizabethan writing for citizens' wives in Shoreditch. And, of course, *not* a happy ending, even though there was one in the original story. The audience must go away feeling that life is hard and merciless, that virtue is helpless and vice not much better, and that the whole scheme of human fortune is a matter for educated persons to contemplate with savage amusement.

Like the doom of Titus, the doom of Lear and Cordelia comes from a moment of decision in the first scene, when the protagonist has two or more courses open to him, is given time to choose and then, in full sight of the audience, chooses wrong. If Titus had listened with sympathy to the pleading of Tamora he would never have become the victim of her vengeance, nor she of his. If Lear had had the sympathy and understanding to see what lay behind Cordelia's 'Nothing, my lord', he would never have found himself storm-driven on the heath. In each play we can actually see the point at which the movement originates that is to sweep away most of the characters like an avalanche.

Moralists may say that the original error is too slight to earn so terrible a retribution, and Shakespeare has been taken to task for paganism and pessimism on the strength of it. But the original audience is unlikely to have shared this view. The suffering would appear to them not as retribution for the error but the ultimate consequence of it, which is a very different thing. When Shakespeare's contemporaries went to the theatre it was not for the sake of hearing anyone 'justify the ways of God to men'. They had plenty of that at compulsory church on Sundays; at the playhouse and in the middle of the week they would not expect it or need it, and would not have wanted it if it had been given to them. The whole point of remarks like 'The gods are just, and of our pleasant vices make instruments to plague us' is that we have no need to put our misfortunes down to deliberate supernatural judgement, for as often as not they spring naturally from our own misdeeds. Lear is a dictatorial and self-conceited old person, fishing for compliments from his family and losing his temper if they are not forthcoming on the instant. His mental and physical sufferings are the natural consequence of this arrogance, not a heaven-imposed punishment for it. The disproportion of the suffering to the original error is displeasing to the present-day moralist who thinks of it in terms of retribution, but to Shakespeare and his fellows that disproportion gives the real point to the story and to the warning it conveys, like those posters that indicate to the unwary smoker how easily he may cause a conflagration.

Two minor features of the play are worth considering in the light of the events that were fresh in men's memories at the time of its production. For one thing, Lear seems over-ready to find, and to assume that everybody else will find, something of blasphemy or impropriety in the notion of any opposition to his royal will. He is not only angry but shocked and revolted by the possibility of such a thing, and it is apt to lose him a good deal of sympathy if he cannot prevail on the audience to regard matters from the same standpoint. Personal resentment at a slight is what one would naturally expect, parental indignation against undutiful daughters is something easily accepted as proper to an earlier, stricter age, but the old king's anger has something of amazement in it, as at a revelation too appalling to be believed. This is far past the calm confidence of Claudius in the divinity that doth hedge a king, and there is a danger that we may not be prepared to go so far with a monarch so continually and vociferously indignant in his own cause.

The other point is one of stagecraft. No less than three times in the course of the play is someone accused of treachery on the strength of an incriminating letter. First comes the forged letter which Edmund produces and shows to his father as evidence of Edgar's treason, then a few scenes later comes the genuine letter which Gloucester has received from an unnamed source, and which Edmund steals and shows to Cornwall, and finally we have the love-letter which Regan tries in vain to read, but which is found in Oswald's possession and reveals Edmund's intrigue with Goneril. Ordinarily, in a serious play, the production of one such letter is a matter for careful preparation if it is not to seem too obviously a contrived artifice. To have no less than three, one might imagine, would be to invite comment and criticism from all directions. It was bad enough, at the end of *Othello*, for Roderigo to have been conveniently carrying incriminatory letters in his pocket; at least they served merely to confirm what the audience knew and most of the people in the play had guessed. Now, however, the author really seems to be overdoing it, yet he appears completely unconscious of the fact. At all events, he takes no noticeable steps to prepare the audience for such a surprising piece of artificiality.

There was no need for him to do so. Internal evidence indicates that *King Lear* came out in the summer or autumn of 1606, and the events of the last year had been such that the audience had been primed already to accept the extravagance. The country had been profoundly shocked, in the previous November, by the last-minute discovery of the Gunpowder Plot. Attempts to assassinate Elizabeth had aroused alarm and indignation in their day, but this was something on a larger and more terrifying scale. Had it succeeded, it would have meant the simultaneous annihilation of the sovereign, the heir to the throne and practically all the government, so it is not unnatural that its discovery and prevention should beget a general feeling of passionate loyalty to the Crown, and of horror and resentment against any opposition to its authority. Guy Fawkes and his fellows had induced in the general public—and not improbably in the King's Men themselves—just that state of mind that could be most readily stirred to indignation at the affronts put upon King Lear.

In the second place, the way in which the conspiracy had been brought to light was the most obvious and theatrical imaginable. A conspirator who could not agree to wholesale destruction of the House of Lords had written an anonymous letter to a friend, advising him to keep away. (The letter is still in existence in the Public Record Office.) The discovery and interpretation of a letter had saved England from an unthinkable catastrophe and had led to the arrest and execution of a nest of traitors. If such a thing could happen in real life, the London audience could well accept, and might even look for, episodes of the same kind, even doubled or trebled, in realistic plays about treason and conspiracy. There must have been many original spectators of *King Lear* who had stood in the crowd a few months earlier to see Fawkes hanged, and to them, at any rate, Edmund's assortment

A group of malcontents. From a German leaflet on the
Gunpowder Plot.

of compromising correspondence would be no playwright's
extravagance but a natural feature to be expected in such cases, as
experience had lately shown.

There is not much room in this play for comedy. Kent has
some passages of satirical humour when he takes service in his
malcontent disguise (probably, in those days, a black cloak like
Hamlet and a black hat like Guy Fawkes) under the master who
has banished him. Lear's Fool is no Touchstone or Feste, but a
figure for pathos rather than laughter. It looks as if his part had
been doubled by the boy who played Cordelia. That, at any rate,
would explain the Fool's absence not only from the end of the
play but from its beginning. Such a scene as the partition of the
kingdom, with Cordelia's answer to her father and his reaction
to it, would normally be the very place for a shrewd critic
privileged by the motley on his back or in his brain, and one
would have expected Shakespeare to take full advantage of the
opportunity. Perhaps, when the scene was written, he had never

thought of giving Lear a Fool at all, and the possibilities of the character only came into being when he found he had packed his youngest boy-actor off to France as a bride and must perforce keep him there unprofitably for the next two or three acts unless an effective supporting part could be found for him to play meanwhile.

There is another malcontent in *Timon of Athens*, a play based on a character Shakespeare would have met in Plutarch's life of Antony, but there is little of ancient Greece about its treatment. Save for Timon, Alcibiades and Apemantus, who are all named by Plutarch, the names are not Greek but Roman, while the characters are essentially English. We are shown a great, genial, reckless figure, generous in friendship to the point of prodigality, and sublimely careless of his own dwindling fortune. When his steward tries to make him attend to his accounts, he has no leisure for such matters, being confident both that his resources will be equal to all possible demands and that in real need his friends will help him out with as much readiness as he has shown to them in his time. His confidence is unfounded in both respects, and in rapid succession he is faced with the two incredible, unimaginable facts that he has no money and that in consequence he has no friends. The double disillusionment drives him to something very near madness, and allows him to express himself by railing against humanity in the way audiences particularly liked at that time of progress, frustration and uneasiness.

There is little else in the tragedy for anyone to do. Timon is dissatisfied with humanity, and turns his back on it with curses. Alcibiades is dissatisfied with Athens, and turns his face and his army upon it to set it right by force. Apemantus is dissatisfied with everything in general, and jeers at it without trying to amend it. The early years of James I were full of bitterness and disappointment for a good many people; the old queen, the old century, the old Tudor dynasty itself, had had their day, and mankind was moving onward to a revised, up-to-date existence free from the old fetters that had hampered it. Such, at any rate, was the position in theory, but it did not seem to be working out like that in practice. Catholics hoped for sympathy and understanding from the son of Mary Queen of Scots. Protestants looked for uncompromising zeal from a king brought up in the strictest principles of the Reformed Church. Nobody—at least, no Londoner—could say that the new state of things was the glorious future that everyone had been expecting. The country was full of Scotsmen on the make, just as a hundred years before it had been full of Welshmen, and ninety or a hundred years later was to be full of Dutchmen. Vague disappointment and dissatisfaction lay at the back of a good many minds, so that a play about more violent disappointment and dissatisfaction was well devised to hit the public taste.

Its logic in the matter is rather thin. We have seen Timon leave Athens because of debts and disappointment. We have seen Alcibiades quarrel with the authorities about their sentence on one of his officers or friends. (It is not a revolt in the presence of the Senate, by the way; the present stage direction differs widely from that of the Folio, in which Alcibiades meets the judges unofficially as they leave the court after passing sentence.) At the end, however, we are shown Alcibiades marching on Athens as Timon's champion, indignant at wrongs done to him by certain unspecified Athenians and ingratitude for his former services (also unspecified) to his city in the past. Audiences do not always want to be told that life and human nature are wretched enough to bring about such misery without assistance. It is a more consoling thought to believe that somebody, somewhere, was to blame for it, and is to be duly punished. That gives Alcibiades a more exalted function as the defender of Timon, the healer of wounds and the bringer of peace and justice to a much-tried city, and it gives the audience a happier picture to go away with. If *King Lear* was written for the Quality in a private theatre—as it may well have been—this play was directed more definitely at the old-fashioned London audience that liked to see its evening of history or tragedy lighted at the end by a gleam of rising hope. Richmond, the Bastard of Faulconbridge, Prince Hal, Octavius, Fortinbras, possibly a wounded and repentant Cassio, take their turn in reminding us of youth and aspiration to make all things even. Now we have Alcibiades in the same role, preparing the way for Malcolm and Octavius Caesar in their turn—a new generation, young and heroic, going forward still to do better than the sins and follies of the old.

This is all the more important because the play is a realistic one. The friends who borrow Timon's money and are so regrettably embarrassed when asked to pay it back are no satiric exaggerations (though modern producers occasionally like to make them so) but ordinary people of some social position and considerable charm. The play is pointless when they are presented as a crew of epicene half-wits whom no Timon in his senses would have trusted with sixpence. His fault appears not as generosity but as plain imbecility, and we have no patience with him from the outset. Shakespeare's Timon finds his tragedy in disillusion, and the audience would need to be shown a plausible illusion first, if it was to have any respect at all for the chief character's intelligence. Timon's friends are close enough to him in social and financial status for him to assume that they are his equals likewise in generosity, and the tragic theme of the play is the unpalatable fact that one can never be sure of anything of the sort. People's ideas of gratitude, and obligation, and the force of circumstances, vary to an alarming degree, and it is always dangerous to seek too readily to disprove Polonius' dictum that 'loan oft loses both itself and friend'. It has a way of proving itself true in spite of all, and the experimenter may find himself resentfully faced with the knowledge that he has taken a goose for a swan and come off the worse for it.

The historic Timon was apparently a misanthrope continuing to live in Athens, but refusing to see anybody but Alcibiades, and behaving, on the whole, very much like the ordinary Jacobean malcontent. It is Shakespeare who has contrived for us the story of his hospitality and disillusion, and his flight from civilization to live like a hermit in the wilderness. Possibly the dramatic scene of Lear's flight into the storm had been sufficiently well received to be worth repeating in another play. Certainly the principal effects are the same, with the tragedian, furious and disappointed, turning from mankind and tearing off his clothes, to undergo the discipline of nature, be it by tempest or by the hard existence of primitive man, till Lear is driven to madness, Timon to savage melancholia.

Two other episodes, also inserted by Shakespeare and without any origin in Plutarch, might be warranted to go down well with a popular audience. Sophisticated cynicism might endorse Timon's opinion of the essential baseness of human nature, but the hard-living, sentimental public that patronized the Globe knew better. This public would appreciate and applaud the little scene where Timon's servants take leave of Flavius the steward and of each other. The household is broken up, the master gone, and the men must go out in their turn to seek employment as they may, but at this moment of leave-taking they find a common bond. Their hearts, as one of them says, yet wear Timon's livery, and they embrace and part, consoling themselves and each other with the memory of having served him. Certain indications here and there suggest that some of them at least were intended to be played as young pages and footboys, and this may well explain the dearth of female characters in the play. Two of the pages might make a brief reappearance later on as the mistresses of Alcibiades, but this tragedy is primarily one about a great man and his household of dependants. The faithful and devoted service of these minor figures helps to confirm to the spectator the nobility of the master whom they served, for if Timon is not noble, he is nothing.

Our recollections of the play are bound up with Timon's prodigality, his sudden poverty and his poetry, which lead us to neglect what is left of the plot. Earlier audiences were harder to please, and would not be content with the knowledge that the play was by William Shakespeare and was therefore Great Literature. What they wanted was to see something happen, and the author provided it for them, not out of Plutarch but out of Lucian. Timon is seen living in solitude, digging for roots to give him sustenance, and in so doing he finds a buried treasure.

He has no more use for gold and lets it lie with a curse, but when Alcibiades comes by with his troops and his mistresses, marching against Athens, Timon unexpectedly presses gold on warrior and women alike, with vehement and unflattering explanations of his reason for it.

Apemantus in turn comes to sneer at him and says roundly that if he had money again he would soon be back at his old ways, but he is put sharply in the wrong by the revelation of the gold for which Timon cares so little, and goes grumbling away to spread the news of the money and bring down on Timon the type of company he detests. It is a poor sort of way to work off a grudge, but it is the best Apemantus can do, and is the last we see of him.

Well suited to the Globe, too, is Timon's reception of a group of ex-soldiers turning to robbery for a livelihood. The men are scorned, lectured, brow-beaten, given gold by the handful and exhorted to go back to Athens and commit every kind of villainy they can, and the result is that they lose all desire to do anything of the sort. Crime, as a career, sounds quite distasteful as Timon describes it, and they make their way back to the city not to rob, but with some vague idea that Athens is in trouble and may need their service, for 'there is no time so miserable but a man may be true'. As in the scene of the servants' leave-taking, the Bankside public would welcome an episode disproving Timon's contention of the essential baseness of human nature. This scene and the next—the meeting and parting of Timon and his faithful steward —would hardly have done for the private-theatre cynics but might yet win sympathetic understanding from an audience that believed in human nature in real life and liked to see people believe in it on the stage.

But Timon's nobility does not affect all men alike. As a foil to these scenes, he is visited by the flattering poet and painter who courted him in his prosperity and reappear as soon as there is a rumour that he has money to spend. The result is a passage of broad comedy. They are welcomed with sardonic effusion, taken apart confidentially while each is solemnly warned against keeping company with the other, and finally overwhelmed with vituperation and a sound beating, probably with the property spade. It is a far cry from the encouraging phrase 'I like your work, and you shall find I like it', of the old leisured days when Timon could afford to be a patron of the arts.

The end is admittedly a muddle. Timon has left Athens for one reason, now we see him asked to come back and defend it against his friend Alcibiades as if his reason for leaving had been some injury or neglect on the part of the Senate. The trouble is that Shakespeare has gone back to Plutarch for the source of his next great speech, and the famous offer of facilities for suicide is appropriate to Timon the city malcontent rather than Timon the wild man of the woods. The opening line of the passage, 'I have a tree that grows here in my close', is a little surprising to us when we have had no suggestion that Timon has made, or wanted to make, any kind of private enclosure in the wilderness. In point of fact the remark comes out of the Plutarch story in which Timon had not left Athens at all, but had shut himself up unsociably in his own house and grounds.

Altogether it is an ill-balanced play in the form in which we have it—the First Folio text. There is no necessity, however, to think that Shakespeare wrote it quite like this in his lifetime, or to find emotional excuses for his doing so; what we have is what someone, be it actor, editor or management, had made of it seven years after he was dead. Quite possibly the Folio text represents the version used in one particular Jacobean pro-duction, with cuts, interpolations and alterations bringing it to the verge of incoherence. (Even so, it was nothing to what was done to it later on, to bring it into line with the requirements of audiences and actresses in the eighteenth century.) Heminge and Condell, in their dedication of the First Folio and in their Preface to the General Reader say expressly that *all* the plays in the volume had stood the test of performance, but it looks very much as if their only text for this play had had to be reconstructed like a Bad Quarto, from a combination of uncertain memory, a frag-mentary prompt copy and perhaps odd scraps of scenes and speeches which the author had drafted but decided not to use, like those similar fragments of Ibsen preserved and published in his *Efterladte Skrifter*. Whoever put it together, the Folio gives the credit to Shakespeare as the author of the original play, just as it does *not* include two plays in which he would seem to have added lines, speeches and sometimes whole acts of work originally begun by others. One of them, *The Two Noble Kinsmen*, was published among the collected works of Beaumont and Fletcher, the other, containing a greater and more coherent amount of his work, appeared as a separate quarto in 1608 and was included in the Shakespeare canon only in the late seventeenth century and after, under the name *Pericles, Prince of Tyre*.

It would seem to have been written originally by one George Wilkins, and its first two acts are confused, extravagant and depressingly bad. It seems to be one of those interminable romances, all plot and no character, that were coming into fashion with the progress of the century. Here and there in the opening acts occurs a line or two with the true Shakespearean ring, as if the script had been passed to him to do what he could to make it tolerable on the stage. First there are odd lines and phrases, then comes a scene between some comic fishermen with a welcome echo of the soldiers in *Henry V*, then at the beginning of Act III the adapter seems to have lost patience with his original and found it less trouble to abandon it entirely and write the rest of the play himself, fitting it with a good many effects that had been successful in his other recent productions. There is a storm as terrible as King Lear's, but on the high seas instead of the countryside. There is a king who turns misanthrope, lets his beard grow and refuses conversation with human beings, like Timon. There are some more rude studies of the staff and patrons of an establishment like Mistress Overdone's in *Measure for Measure*. There is a guilty tyrant with a scornful and unscrupulous wife, who look and sound rather like a minor Macbeth and his lady. And, in point of dramatic scenes, there is a wonderful passage of hesitant, half-timorous recognition between a father and daughter that sets out, by no means unsuccessfully, to recreate the conditions of King Lear's awakening in the tent of

Cordelia, leading on to another recognition-scene that restores to Pericles the wife whom he had prematurely buried at sea. Quite possibly the play is a piece of patchwork run together in a hurry because something was wanted as an improvement on unadulterated Wilkins, but when Shakespeare was the patcher, his patches had a quality of their own, and this play has given us short but memorable studies of good and bad women in an unusual number for a Bankside entertainment.

The present-day Shakespearean heroine has one great advantage over her Elizabethan counterpart, in that she can take so much longer to grow old. The youth and charm originally given her by nature can be prolonged, renewed or imitated by art or personality or acting technique, or by an indefinable combination of all three, as all must know who saw or heard even the last performances of Ellen Terry in her old age. Barrie in *Rosalind* wrote a play about this phenomenon; but Shakespeare's original Rosalind must have found old age creeping on him all too soon when his voice began to be less certain in the ring and his cheek to call for the attention of the razor. One milestone on the road to age may be seen, perhaps, in *Twelfth Night*, for there are many remarks that indicate Viola-Cesario to be a singer. But perhaps the production came just too late, the boy-actor's voice began to break instead of being all that Orsino still calls it, and Feste had to be fetched arbitrarily from one Great House to the other to sing 'Come away, come away, death'.

This need not mean the end, however. A breaking voice might be all the more eerily effective for the shrieking of Cassandra, while in the next great tragedy we find in Emilia someone who *must* be able to act but need not be so well dowered with womanly grace as a good many other Shakespearean ladies-in-waiting. Isabella, half-dedicated to the cloister, is a figure whose requirements might still fall within the range of a boy leaving boyhood behind, but when we get to *All's Well that Ends Well* we find the author has written an old woman's part that can go near, on occasion, to stealing the play. The public liked to see a popular favourite giving something of his known and admired quality, and it would be to the interest of the King's Men and their author to keep a talented and popular boy-actress in petticoats as long as suitable roles could be found to fit him. It is in the plays of this period, then, that we see those female characters who have power rather than girlish charm. Either of Lear's elder daughters can be played thus and contrasted with the ultra-femininity of her sister and rival. *Pericles* gives us the brief but powerful study of Dionyza tongue-lashing her reluctant husband into approval of her treachery, and soon after we have the same character brought out again, elaborated and enriched into the tremendous figure of Lady Macbeth. Here is no place for a 'small pipe . . . as the maiden's organ, shrill and sound', the part calls for a young man's strength, and with a bold stroke the author prepares the audience for it. Almost as soon as we see the passion of her ambition rising within her, the woman cries out to the listening spirits of evil, bidding them help her to renounce her woman-hood, and later on, when urging Macbeth to persevere in his design, she boasts of her denial of womanly tenderness. It is enough, the seed has been sown in the spectators' minds, and any harshness of voice or movement, any momentary unwomanliness or excess of violence, will be associated less with the short-comings of the player than with the requirements of the play.

Lady Macbeth, though dramatically of the first importance, is a comparatively small part. Even in the uncensored version which we have imagined in the preceding pages there cannot have been so very much more of it. Perhaps the author and the management were cautious about the way audiences would receive their ageing boy-heroine. If so, the experiment must have justified itself by its success, for about this time was written the great historical tragedy of a pair of lovers well past their youth, a tragedy in which the woman survived the man by a whole act, and was given a death-scene that is among the finest that Shakespeare ever wrote. Even more than Lady Macbeth, Cleopatra has the ground subtly prepared for her, so that the audience shall not look to her for qualities that she can no longer display. Her enslavement of

Antony is described to us in the opening lines, so convincingly indeed that we have accepted it, and take it for granted, before we have even seen her, and it is only with some effort that we call to mind the fact that these two great lovers rarely appear on the stage together, and that when they do, they are generally quarrelling. Shakespeare has done with Cleopatra's personal fascination what he did, years before, with the battle of Agincourt, and given us so clear a picture of the feelings it engenders in different minds, and the results of it on different destinies, that we fail to notice how little we have seen of the thing itself.

One of Cleopatra's characteristics is her practice of unflinchingly alluding to her age. At one moment she is 'wrinkled deep in time', at another she apostrophizes the dead Caesar with the recollection

> When thou wast here above the ground, I was
> A morsel for a monarch.

There is never a shadow of regret, no wistful looking back to catch the memory of a departed fragrance; on the contrary, she is able to contemplate her successes of the past because she is confident that with a suitable variation of technique she can still repeat them. It is no ordinary charmer who can give a new admirer her hand to kiss and with that very gesture recall having done the same thing to his employer's father, yet that is what she does to Thyreus, and she does it successfully enough to drive Antony roaring-mad with jealousy. Wit, majesty and an indomitable relish for life make up a character in which we never miss the lack of youth and beauty, and the part is ideally written for a young actor who had all the energy of youth but was perforce losing the graces of womanhood. For a few lines at a time he might recall them, as in the brief passage where Cleopatra gives Antony her blessing as he takes his leave for Rome, but he is never required to keep the illusion up too long. That is done for him by the author through the mouths of other members of the cast, notably Enobarbus, both in his disapproval of Antony's infatuation and his grudging but genuine admiration for the cause of it.

197

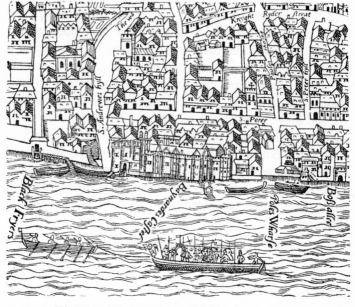

The Royal Barge. From Agas' map of London.

Consciously or unconsciously, another figure must have been fresh in the memory of author and spectators alike. In one scene of the play, Cleopatra speaks of the Messenger as one who 'hath seen some majesty, and should know', and though James of Scotland had been some years on the English throne, there were still many in that audience who at one time or another had seen Elizabeth. For such, there was a ready-made tradition of majesty and valiancy in a queen, coupled with all the incalculability of a woman. The famous passage in which Enobarbus describes Cleopatra's barge is based on Plutarch, it is true, but to those first spectators it would more readily recall the Royal Barge of England on its way up or down the Thames between Greenwich and Westminster or Richmond, its cabin-tilt decorated with the Royal Arms in the blue and gold circle of the Garter, the watermen and Gentlemen Pensioners in their coats of scarlet and gold, the beauty and bright colours of the ladies-in-waiting and, in the middle of it all, a glimpse of the pale face and red-gold hair of the indomitable, incalculable old Queen. By the same token, the scene in which Cleopatra questions the Messenger about Octavia, demanding precise information about her rival's height, colouring and personal appearance, has no parallel in Plutarch, from whom Shakespeare got most of his material for the play. It has a parallel, however, in the memoirs of Sir James Melvill of Hall-hill, who had himself undergone just such a catechism from Elizabeth of England on the subject of Mary Queen of Scots. Mary was his sovereign, Elizabeth was his hostess, and his answers had had to be worded accordingly with considerable tact.

The story is a good one, as he tells it, and the events it records were some forty years old by the time *Antony and Cleopatra* was written, but the memoirs themselves remained in manuscript for the greater part of a century, and were not printed until 1683, so we may assume that Shakespeare took the episode not from any published work but from gossip and tradition, because it was true. 'Age cannot wither her, nor custom stale her infinite variety', is Enobarbus' famous comment on Cleopatra, and to the Londoners of 1608 or thereabouts, that was the Elizabeth they remembered. They would have forgotten the last dragging months of age and sickness, and their own eagerness to see what a new reign would bring; the Elizabeth of their recollection would be the grimly humorous, bejewelled figure, relentlessly unwithered by the time her tirewomen had fitted her to appear in public, quelling men with her eye, scarifying them with her tongue, charming them with unexpected insight and graciousness and always, always keeping their interest alive by the sheer impossibility of foretelling what she would do next.

Their memories of majesty were well served again in another Roman play. A second Cleopatra was more than any boy-actor could hope for, but the more austere side of the old Queen made its impression in its day, and that impression, among other things, must have gone to the making of that redoubtable Roman matron Volumnia. As before, Shakespeare has taken his story from Plutarch and his characters from human nature, but in *Coriolanus* more than any other of his plays we miss the author's presence to answer queries that may well have been put to him at rehearsal and would have been promptly and easily answered by him on the spot, chiefly how far Coriolanus is supposed literally to mean what he is saying, and how many remarks are merely extravagances made when he has lost his temper. At present there is a tendency to treat him, on the stage or in the study, as a symbol of patrician arrogance as opposed to plebeian unruliness. The late Lord Norwich, in his otherwise delightful *Sergeant Shakespeare*, calls him 'a traitor to his country', and 'a man for whom I can feel nothing but disgust and loathing'. Dr Masefield, on the other hand, sees in him a combination of nobility and incomprehension that typifies aristocracy at odds with the world. What did Shakespeare himself see in the man, and what did he want his audience to see in him?

First, perhaps, the professional soldier, as distinct from the soldier-scholar who had been the Elizabethan gentleman's ideal. The Jacobean gentleman was somebody rather different, essentially a civilian, with political and diplomatic interests in an age of peace at any price. The warriors of the old Queen's day were all gone save two, and of those the Earl of Nottingham, the Admiral of Armada days, was old and disregarded, and Walter Ralegh lay captive in the Tower under a long-suspended sentence of death. In Coriolanus the spectator saw someone less like the romantic adventurer and more like the Continental commander of his own day, a man of inordinate valour, intemperate vocabulary and no knowledge or ideas outside the camp and the field.

Very often the essence of such a man as Coriolanus lies in the contrast between his language and his opportunities, let alone his inclinations. It is in matters where he has no jurisdiction, and knows it, that he speaks most extravagantly of what he would do if he had his way. He says roundly that it is a shocking waste of supplies to make a grant of corn to the plebeians, but he says so after the grant has been made, and when there is no possibility that his expression of opinion could stop it. He is a master in the fine art of objurgation, and a word or two from the author at rehearsal, or at the preliminary reading if there was one, would have made it clear to the player how many of the speeches were to be taken as expressions of the man's real thoughts and how many were to be flourishes on the part of a fire-eating general who was expected to behave as such.

His own men recognize his quality well enough. He may curse them roundly for pausing to loot when they should be capturing a city, but he is ready to forgo his share of the spoils after the victory so that there may be all the more for those who fought under him. He has but to call for volunteers, and every man who hears him steps forward for the enterprise. When they are beaten back from Corioli, he turns on them with a flow of abuse that would be repeated afterwards by the survivors with appreciative reminiscence, and calls them to follow him again to the assault. It is not the technique of Henry V at the breach of Harfleur, but it is a different way of getting the same result. He is shut in alone, but in a moment his men see that he is still alive and fighting, and on a word from Titus Lartius they make a fresh assault, succeeding, in the cause of their commanding officer, where they had failed when attacking in the name of Rome. Anyone who has served in the ranks under a warrant officer or field officer of real vituperative eloquence will know the admiration that it can inspire. It is received not as abuse or ill-temper but as a special performance by a virtuoso.

But this technique, admirable as it may be among soldiers in the field, does not go down well with free and independent electors—a very different class of person till comparatively modern times. Coriolanus has no particular wish to stand for the consulship, still less at the price of standing in the street in the *toga candida*, soliciting votes by being unctuous to civilians. In the days when the soldier and the politician were more strongly differentiated than they are now, there was matter for comedy in the sight of the one conscientiously and resentfully masquerading as the other. The hero of the battlefield can still be turned into a figure of genial absurdity now and then, and the Elizabethans would find a certain amount of matter for amusement in the sight of him being urged, coaxed or goaded, like a bull in a ballet-skirt, through the tricky dances of political canvassing.

His solicitation of the first four or five citizens is a passage of sheer comedy, then when he is momentarily alone he breaks out into indignant scorn of the whole process, but controls himself again, makes a dutiful answer to the next comers and is finally relieved by his friends, with the news that he has stood out his appointed time. So far he has shown us something not only to laugh at but to admire, since he has dutifully tackled a piece of uncongenial work and carried it through to success. Unfortunately he speaks his mind to his fellow-patricians with almost military freedom, roundly blaming them for allowing the plebeians to have tribunes at all, and this pleases nobody. He does not even find sympathy at home. His mother, to his surprise and disappointment, censures his outspokenness and tells him to go back and apologize. She has almost persuaded him when he rebels at the last moment and draws down on himself a sharp and scornful rebuke as if he were a boy again, culminating in a statement that must appear to him inaccurate and unfair,

> Thy valiantness was mine, thou suck'dst it from me,
> But owe thy pride thyself.

To the spectator it is a contest of giants, and the old lady is the older and more experienced fighter, so she comes off with the last word. Coriolanus capitulates, promises to behave himself and goes off to the market-place, where he conscientiously keeps himself in hand, agreeing, if necessary, to accept 'lawful censure' by the people's officers for anything they can prove against him. It requires a tremendous effort on his part, and the effort is nearly successful, but at last the demagogue Sicinius roundly calls him 'a traitor to the people', and the two words in conjunction act like a spark in a powder-barrel and blow all comedy to the winds. The angry soldier loses his temper, says something about the people that cannot be explained away by Menenius or anybody else, and gives the tribunes their excuse to denounce him to the mob as a public enemy, so that he is hooted out of Rome.

From this point the play is quite straightforward. He is a malcontent with a difference, and audiences ancient or modern can have nothing but admiration for his valour, tenderness and consideration as he takes leave of his friends and family at the gate, or for his patient endurance of rebuffs and insolence from the servants of Aufidius when he stands unrecognized at his enemy's hearth. They mock him for his poverty and try to turn him away, but even before learning who he is they are impressed by his quality and his quiet strength. There is excitement and appreciation in the servants' hall when it is known that their master is entertaining his famous rival and that the two are planning a joint assault on Rome. When in due course Aufidius begins to regret their partnership he gives at the same time a very shrewd summary of his partner's character and of the qualities that led to his sudden banishment, and it is a useful pointer of the way Shakespeare apparently meant our sympathies to lie.

Volumnia has appeared, so far, in various capacities, first as a grim old gargoyle of a mother-in-law, snubbing her son's wife and expatiating on his youthful virtues and on the way she brought him up, then reprimanding Coriolanus himself like a small boy who has been behaving impertinently in public, and next as his unflinching champion in adversity, ready to turn her fury on anyone who dares to criticize him and showing a fluency and ferocity of language that rivals his own. There is a reminiscence of Queen Margaret in her dismissal of Menenius' invitation to supper. 'Anger's my meat, I sup upon myself,' she says, and calling Virgilia to follow her she goes from them, leaving Menenius to mutter, 'Fie, fie, fie,' and inherit the laughter of the audience as the tension is relieved.

From a near-comic character she has become a heroic one, and she achieves the grandeur of tragedy when she leads the last deputation of Roman suppliants and bows her proud knee before her son. Her speech is almost exactly that given to her by Plutarch, but transformed as only Shakespeare could transform it, by infusing into it the sense of enormity at the need to make it at all. She never upbraids Coriolanus with being a traitor to his country; to her, as to everyone else in the play, to the seventeenth-century London playgoer at the Globe and to Plutarch in his original narrative, the professional soldier is fully entitled to take service with whatever employer he may. What does arouse her indignation is that her son should have so far forgotten himself as to disregard her wishes when expressed in public. He was upset, and very properly so, when she began to kneel to him on her arrival, and after her speech she turns that embarrassment to good advantage with the merciless line, 'Down, ladies, let us shame him with our knees.' If there is anything more bitterly scornful and contemptuous than that gesture of humiliation it is the sequel to it, when she rises to her feet again to go away unsatisfied, and that is more than Coriolanus can bear. He capitulates, knowing at the same time that his doing so means certain danger and almost certain death, even as Volumnia herself has known it. Small wonder, then, that when the news reaches Rome, and the citizens are hurrying through the gates like the incoming tide foaming through an arch—a familiar simile to those who had come to the play by being ferried over the river to Bankside with London Bridge in full view downstream—she has no word to say. The crowds are cheering, the trumpets are sounding, the pathway before her feet is strewn with flowers, and the three women in their black mourning veils walk across the stage in silence. Volumnia has spoken her last word, her interpreter has created his last leading woman's part, and will soon abandon petticoats for ever and continue in doublet and hose, playing insignificant young men until he grows old enough for principals, so that the Cleopatra of one season may dwindle into the Philo of the next.

XII

The Audience at a Distance

THERE ARE various documents in existence that show us
how Shakespeare invested the money he was making. As far back
as 1597 he had bought the large house known as New Place, and
at intervals thereafter he bought land and house property, and a
half-share of the parish tithes, in and about his native town of
Stratford-upon-Avon. In London his name appeared as one of
the lessees of the playhouse at Blackfriars in 1608, but when he
was called upon in 1612 to give evidence in a lawsuit in London
he did so as a gentleman of Stratford. He was no longer a London
actor and part-manager, he was a country gentleman living on his
property as a person of some consequence in his native town,
though we can see that he had not retired completely from the
world of the theatre. Still, he was no longer in close and continual touch with the people who spent some part of their lives,
be it for employment or entertainment, in the playhouse he had
served so long. When he wrote now, as he still did, he was
writing for an audience at a distance, whose reactions he could
not predict so easily. The old intimacy had gone, and in its place
was something else, admirable still but not the same.

It was a distant audience in another sense as well. The Children
of the Queen's Revels had got into trouble again, in the indoor
theatre in Blackfriars, with a play about the King of France
that made the French Ambassador complain. There was the usual
drastic action, and the ultimate result was that the boys' company
had to give up the theatre, and it came back into the hands of
Burbage and the King's Men, to become their winter headquarters
for the future, the Globe being kept only for the summer months,
when the weather was more suitable for open-air performances

and access to the building was pleasanter than in wet winter afternoons on Bankside.

This meant that they were established in the equivalent of a West End house at last, playing before something like a West End audience, and plays and production had new standards to conform to. Structurally, the stage lights and the proscenium arch remained the adjuncts of the semi-amateur indoor masque and had not been applied to public performances of ordinary plays, but the plays of this period had apparently gone some way to meet them none the less. A little study of them shows that they are deliberately contrived so that the situations and passions of the characters are watched, but not shared, by the audience. Perhaps the private-theatre habit of letting privileged spectators have stools upon the stage itself, on 'the very rushes whereon the comedy is to dance', had something to do with it. Whatever the cause, the new dramas allowed for little or none of the old exchange of sentiments and confidences between playgoers and players. The characters were often of high station, elegant bearing and unnaturally noble nature, but they kept themselves to themselves and did not seem to admit the existence of a theatreful of spectators.

We see marked evidence of the change when we consider *Cymbeline*, which is a specimen of the kind of play that was becoming increasingly popular as produced by Beaumont, Fletcher, Massinger and their contemporaries and successors. The essence of such a play is ingenuity coupled with effectiveness. So long as the characters can be displayed in a series of good theatrical situations, it matters little or nothing how they got into them and not much more how they are to get out of them. The sentiment or sensation of the moment is all that is required. They have no existence before the rise of the curtain, and need have had none. Three or four, indeed, of the characters in Shakespeare's play take their names from pre-Roman Britain as described by Holinshed, but there is no attempt to follow the story as told by the historian. Instead, the names come out of Holinshed, the story is partly out of Boccaccio and partly a version of Snow-

White and the Seven Dwarfs, and there are opportunities for a good deal of music, a certain amount of stage spectacle and that *sine qua non* of fashionable Jacobean drama, an interpolated masque.

For about an act and a half the author dutifully tries to write a suitable Ben Jonson-Beaumont-and-Fletcher play for polite society. Sardou himself could not have been more helpfully explanatory in his opening scene between a couple of nonentities. The First and Second Gentlemen are not moved by any human emotion like the tribunes in *Julius Caesar* inveighing against the holidaymaking crowds, or Philo explaining the infatuation of Antony. They tell each other of the state of things at court, the secret marriage of Imogen, and the relations between Cymbeline, his children and his stepson, but it is only for the information of the audience. Leonatus' wooing and wedding of his master's daughter are mentioned but not explained, they are circumstances necessary to create the opening situation, but they do not determine the course of the play.

One has only to compare this wooing with Othello's to see the difference. There, the very nature of Desdemona's elopement, involving her in an act of deception and disobedience to her father, has its influence on Othello's mind when he is led to think himself deceived in his turn. Here, on the other hand, the secret wedding serves merely as an excuse for the immediate parting of the lovers and for Posthumus' being packed off to Rome. The situations are ingenious and theatrical rather than dramatic. Now and then humanity breaks out for a few minutes, as in the scene in Rome where Posthumus quarrels with Iachimo and finds himself committed to a wager which he dislikes yet cannot in decency refuse, but it gives way once again to artificiality when Iachimo makes his attempt to win the favours of Imogen. The villain's advances and the heroine's virtuous rejection of them are full of poetry and effective dialogue, yet for some reason they are not particularly interesting, probably because they were written consciously for an audience that would take more interest in the players—and even, perhaps, in the words and artifices of their conversation—than in the characters of the play.

Mercifully this does not last. When Iachimo climbs out of his hiding-place and bends over the sleeping Imogen, he speaks with the true magic of Macbeth and Othello in turn, and when he comes back to Rome and confronts Posthumus and Philario with her stolen bracelet as the apparent token of his success, the scene among the three men is one of real drama, the poetry and expressiveness of its language being no more than contributory to its power. Once more, a change of attitude on the part of audiences in general has led to the weakening of one of its most important moments. Iachimo has made his claim to have prevailed over the virtue of Imogen, and has tormented Posthumus by giving him a momentary glimpse of the bracelet, but Philario puts in the sensible argument that it may have been lost or stolen, as in fact it was. Posthumus grasps eagerly at the suggestion, but is faced with the Italian's quiet asseveration, 'By Jupiter, I had it from her arm'. To us, the expletive suggests a euphemism to avoid profanity, and has a slightly frivolous ring about it, but it is meant to be a solemn oath, by the Father of the Gods himself, and that is how the orthodox Jacobean playgoer would regard it. Moreover, he would appreciate that Iachimo has not, in fact, forsworn himself. He had the bracelet from Imogen's arm indeed, though the audience had all seen that it was got by stealth while she lay sleeping, but the one statement that he has made on oath is unquestionably true. After that, Posthumus himself checks him from swearing any further oaths, so that having done all the necessary mischief he has yet succeeded in keeping clear of the technical offence of perjury.

At about this point Shakespeare seems to have given up the attempt to write in the new-fangled modern style. A rather unpleasant little soliloquy for Posthumus closes the act, quite after the manner of Fletcher, but with the next scene we are back at a piece of straight Shakespeare, and very welcome it is. The opening of Act III is almost as crisp, firm and explanatory as the opening line of *King John*—which it echoes almost word for word. The characters come alive all of a sudden, Cymbeline, Cloten and the Queen all speak like human beings, not literary abstractions, and Caius Lucius duly counters their patriotism with the urbanity of Rome. We are given a picture instead of a pattern, and can take a much livelier interest in consequence. Imogen's flight with Pisanio, her piteous disillusionment when she learns what her husband thinks of her, and her refuge with the young hunters in their guardian's cave may be episodes that belong to the world of romance rather than to that of reality, but wherever they belong, they take us with them, whereas the earlier scenes have never called us to turn our thoughts beyond the limits of the playhouse.

Within those same limits the private theatres had other features and resources which an audience there might legitimately expect to see employed, and might be allowed to have, without undue distortion of the play. One of these—perhaps the principal one—was music. With the boy players in their 'private house' an evening's entertainment customarily included a good deal of playing and singing, and consequently less dialogue in the actual play, so that when Marston's *Malcontent*, for instance, was played on the old-fashioned open stage of a public theatre, the management had to lengthen it out by the addition of a dramatic prologue, or the audience would have complained of short measure. Shakespeare has put an unusual amount of music into *Cymbeline* to suit this requirement on the part of his audience. Cloten's early morning concert for Imogen is introduced with a speech that shows it to have been in two parts. First is to come 'a very excellent good-conceited thing', presumably an instrumental ensemble of some sort, and afterwards 'a wonderful sweet air, with admirable rich words to it', though nowadays we forget the remarks about the musical introduction and concentrate on the lyric alone. When Imogen swallows the queen's drug and falls into a death-like trance, her body is impressively carried on to the stage to an accompaniment of 'solemn music', rather an unexpected feature in the mountain caves of Wales. As soon as the sound is heard, Belarius justifies it by referring to an 'ingenious instrument' which has not been played since his wife died. There is nothing like a complete explanation, the remark is just enough to reconcile us to the presence of a musical instrument in the wilderness, and the theatre orchestra may do the rest. The dirge over Imogen, on the other hand, is not to be sung. The author has taken care of that. It is spoken antiphonally by the two brothers, and is the more impressive for it, whereas the tension would have been hopelessly slackened if they had chosen this occasion to break into song.

The most elaborate musical feature in the play, and the one most closely in accord with the new fashion in such things, is the masque of ancestors in the last act. When Posthumus lies unrecognized in prison, happy in the thought that his death may serve in some degree as atonement for his treatment of Imogen (false to him though he still believes her), he is visited in a dream by the spirits of his father and mother and of two elder brothers 'with wounds as they died in the wars'. They enter to solemn music, 'circle Posthumus round as he lies sleeping', and plead for him to Jupiter in stanzas that look little better than doggerel, and would seem at first to have no place in the same play as the incomparable 'Fear no more the heat o' the sun'. Impassioned critics have denounced them as non-Shakespearean rubbish, practical-minded producers have usually cut them out, and the whole point of the prison scene with them. Read or spoken aloud, they are as laboured and fatuous as the earlier lament for Imogen is effective, but they take a very different character if they are set to music. The whole episode is a musical, almost an operatic, interlude in the culmination of the play, and the words, ridiculous enough from the point of view of ordinary diction, take on an unexpected dignity at the slightly slower pace associated with song. There is dignity and sonority, likewise, in the speech of Jupiter that follows. His eagle and thunderbolt are details possible with the scenic resources of an indoor theatre, and may perhaps be further concessions to the public desire for an increased amount of music and machinery. In any case, whatever the shortcomings of Jupiter's mechanical eagle, they are forgotten as soon as it is out of sight, since the awed words of Sicilius Leonatus to his companions create an image of the great bird rising through the infinite heights above them till the floors of Heaven open to receive it home.

In the last scene, Shakespeare has managed to supply a sufficiently complicated series of revelations to satisfy the needs of the Blackfriars playgoer without letting his characters lose their individuality. This is another play in which the use of a 'real live actress' has somewhat upset the balance by concentrating the interest more closely on her than was really intended. The principal character in the 'great unravelling' is not Imogen but Cymbeline himself, who learns, almost in the moment of his victory, that his queen is dead, that she never loved him, and that by her beguilement he has cruelly wronged his daughter Imogen. His kindly welcome of the latter in her disguise leads directly to the confession of Iachimo and the passionate self-revelation of Posthumus, and indirectly to the recognition of Imogen in her turn, but his emotions do not end there. He has praised and knighted the young mountaineers who rescued him in battle, but finds himself on the point of condemning the elder one to death as the self-confessed killer of Cloten, till he is given the culminating assurance that they are the sons he has mourned for twenty years as for ever lost to him. It is too good to be true, instinctively he puts forward an objection by naming a personal mark on the neck of the lost Guiderius which he cannot hope to find upon this stranger, but his doubts are needless, the gods are not deceiving him and the mark is there. He has his children once more about him, and it is the easier for him to smile upon Imogen's marriage now that her brothers are found again and she is no longer the heiress to the throne of Britain. In a final burst of generosity he liberates his Roman captives and agrees, in spite of his victory, to pay to Caesar the tribute he had formerly denied.

The audience has been regaled with an elaborate study in varied emotion. It is a *tour de force* for the actor, and nothing in Cymbeline's behaviour hitherto has prepared us for it, since he has not done anything, or said anything, in the first four acts that seriously affected the course of later events. Still, practically everyone else has had a chance of giving a solo performance of some sort, or at least taking part in a striking and effective scene, and Cymbeline's own turn comes last of all, so that he can dominate the stage at the conclusion of the play.

This somewhat artificial conception of a play as a series of loosely connected 'turns' by the various characters is common to a good many plays written for Jacobean audiences, and reflects the increasing tendency of those audiences to concentrate their attention on the rendering of individual scenes rather than the effect of the piece as a whole. In such a play, it is much easier for the fashionable spectator to conduct himself as laid down by Dekker in the appropriate chapter of the *Gull's Hornbook*, and to come in late, watch a certain amount of the action and then start yawning, smoking or playing cards with his neighbours, to prove that he was not so boorish as to be really interested in the show. It is in fact the opera-box technique of the eighteenth and nineteenth centuries, where indiscriminate admiration is unfashionable and the correct course is to applaud some individual scene, artist or 'number' and express the utmost boredom with all the rest.

But this was essentially private-theatre practice. The Globe was still in use by the King's Men in the spring and summer, and it was there that Doctor Forman saw *The Winter's Tale* in May 1611. His notebook shows that he took in much more of it than he had done of *Macbeth*, and that he was particularly impressed by Autolycus the comic pickpocket. The play ingeniously combines the main features of outdoor and indoor drama. Bankside was still a good deal simpler than Blackfriars in its tastes and still liked a good story with plenty of passionate declamation and something for the Clown and Pantaloon to do. At the same time, now that the players had achieved the distinction of regularly playing before the Quality in their 'private house', their old patrons at the Globe would be eager to see something of the special features associated with such productions, and in the fourth act the author has taken care to provide them. There is no instrumental concert, it is true, but there is a musical interlude at the shearing-feast, when Autolycus and two shepherdesses sing their merry ballad to the tune of 'Two maids wooing a man', and a dance of twelve satyrs to do duty for the fashionable entertainment of the masque. The audience on the South Bank could feel that it was enjoying the same fare that was served up in season to high society in Blackfriars.

The jokes in the main are South Bank rather than Blackfriars jokes. The clown on his way to market with his shopping-list, the rogue Autolycus with his discourse on the fine art of picking pockets in a crowd—most apposite in a place like the Globe, where there might well be somebody doing it at the moment—the country girls avid for sensational news in printed ballads and convinced that if it was in print it must be true—all these are primarily matter for mirth on their own level, and not quite the fare for a court or county audience that affected to look down on rusticity. Such audiences would laugh at them, and doubtless did so when the play was performed at Court later in the year, but it was not for them but for the cheerful stews-and-tavern playgoers on the other side of the Thames that the scenes were written. Bankside would not worry its head about the incongruous combination of Christian oaths, heathen oracles and a sixteenth-century Italian artist whose name was associated, in the mind of such a public, with the provision of appropriate illustrations to the notorious sonnets of Pietro Aretino. It would not cavil (as Jonson did, of course, and a good many others after him) at the author's getting the countries of his source-book wrong way round, and giving a sea-coast to Bohemia when it was Sicilia in the original story. What mattered was the story itself, with its jealous yet sympathetic tyrant, its much-wronged queen, its trial scene with the crowning blasphemy of Leontes' contradiction of the oracle, and the inimitable statue-scene at the end, that can move us to this day with its picture of recognition and reconciliation after so many years.

The conventions of the time would have served to intensify, at this point, the sense of wonder and compensation for what had seemed irremediable loss. Little Mamillius has been called 'the best child in Shakespeare', and we have seen enough of him to appreciate the crushing effect upon his father's spirit of his illness and death during the trial of the queen. At the end, therefore, we still miss him; Hermione returns from the shadows, but she returns alone, and there is no further miracle to make the end of Leontes' life, in Dr Masefield's phrase, 'as happy as the beginning if our dead could be given back to us'. It was not quite so, however, in 1611. The boy-actor's work was not done for the evening when he was hustled away from the company of his mother in the second act. There was another part to be played, a girl's part, not required until the next act but one, so that there was ample time for doublet and hose to give place to the habit of a flower-decked shepherdess, and for Mamillius to be transformed to Perdita. Mamillius, the boy, it is true, might never come again, but at least the spectators would see Leontes and Hermione, at the end of the play, welcoming a child grown into the very likeness of the one that they had lost.

In the last two plays we have considered, the main passions were those of jealousy and suspicion. Wronged wives had been vindicated, and jealous husbands brought to repentance and apology, but it was time for a change. The public must have other subjects to think about and wonder at, and one of those other subjects, at that time, was science. In the light of recent discoveries almost anything seemed possible. Galileo was Professor of Mathematics at Padua, Kepler was laying the foundations of modern astronomy in the Observatory at Prague, and the studies and discoveries of the age were filling the world of learned men with scientific text-books and the mouths of unlearned men with semiscientific jargon. Any serious study of mathematics was bound up with that of physics, chemistry and astrology, and any deeplyread man of science was expected to be well versed in the 'secrets of nature', the secrets which are natural, not supernatural, and have always had such a strong and long-lived fascination for the lay mind.

There was no saying what the trained scientist might not be able to accomplish, and audiences must have felt about such matters very much what their successors were to feel in relation to Jules Verne, H. G. Wells and the science-fiction of to-day. It is known vaguely that science can do marvels; the theatre-going public is not sure *what* marvels, but is already prepared, in the name of science, to accept a certain amount of marvel as natural and possible. Jonson despised this attitude and wrote *The Alchemist*; Shakespeare accepted it and wrote *The Tempest*. Jonson's scientist is a charlatan playing ingeniously, entertainingly and profitably on the combined covetousness and gullibility of his clients, Shakespeare's is a man of wide and deep learning who has at length attained some degree of control over the forces of nature, and whom we behold at the time when he has his one chance of turning them to account.

As often as not we first meet the play in our schooldays and regard it suspiciously in consequence. Quite fortuitously, it has many secondary qualities that make it a pedagogue's delight and a favourite piece for the classroom or the examination-syllabus. Its morals are unimpeachable, there are points about the date and circumstances of its production which are eminently suitable for examiners, it abounds with magnificent poetry and also with material for essay-questions—the characters of Ariel and Caliban, for instance—or short 'contexts and explanations' about flat meads thatched with stover, or the whereabouts of the still-vex'd Bermoothes. Small wonder, then, that there is a school of thought that regards *The Tempest* as an examination-piece and Prospero as a beard-and-bedgown bore with long, long speeches of explanation and a schoolmasterly impatience with other people. A tendency of the last twenty or thirty years has been to treat the play as frankly impossible, and to fantasticate it accordingly. As a result, Prospero becomes too heavy, and even more of a bore; when everything about him is whipped up into a light confection of unreality he remains solid and indigestible in the middle, like a sad, heavy cake, and lies as heavily on those who try to assimilate him.

It was otherwise with the original spectator, who could take him seriously. His wonder-working is that of the scientist, not the conjuror, and seen from this angle he passes from the domain of the fairylike-unreal to that of the might-be-possible. Most of his miracles are not far removed from what the Jacobean public regarded as science. Some of them, such as the disarming of Ferdinand or the gradual awakening to consciousness of the dazed Alonzo, could be repeated in a modern play and justified by being ascribed to hypnotism. The amenities he has provided for the island as a whole are not very different from those created in similar circumstances by human ingenuity in *The Admirable Crichton*, and Prospero becomes a much more easily endurable figure if he is regarded as a mortal man struggling successfully with Nature, instead of the omnipotent effortlessly performing the impossible.

Dispossessed dukes and princes were familiar figures in the playhouse. Shakespeare had already created one such, fleeting the time carelessly in Arden. Marston had given the stage another in Malevole the malcontent, in reality a banished duke of Genoa. Beaumont and Fletcher's Philaster, though not actually banished, was a dispossessed and slighted prince, as indeed was Hamlet of Denmark. But, as usual, Shakespeare had taken a stock character and made the audience take an interest in him as a human being with human qualities and shortcomings. Instead of being asked to accept the fact that a duke has been banished from his dukedom, and to go on from there, the audience is given an early account of his character and the reason for his banishment, and finds it easier to believe in him at once. It is awkward for Prospero to have to tell his fifteen-year-old daughter that he was not a very efficient duke of Milan, that he neglected his dukedom for his scientific studies, and was supplanted by his brother in consequence. This is the part of their conversation in which he is least at his ease, and almost pathetically anxious to make sure that she understands. Before this, in reassuring her about the storm, and after it, in the narration of specific events, he is firm and coherent and has no need to go over the ground again or ask if he has made himself clear.

By this explanation of his particular studies, we are suitably primed for the introduction of Ariel. A magician with a familiar spirit is not a very suitable character for the King's Men to introduce upon their stage when the King they serve has himself published a tract against such persons and their practices. Prospero the wizard, with a book of spells and an attendant fairy, would savour of dangerous dealings with the Devil. Prospero the scientist, on the contrary, with a book of alchemical formulae that have given him some degree of mastery over the elements, may quite properly be attended by a representative of those natural forces over which he has gained control. It is quite clear from the outset that Ariel's powers are limited. He can do a good deal with the winds, he can assume various shapes, or no shape at all, and play practical jokes on human beings, he can take his part in an entertainment or an illusion, but we never see him exercise any direct physical influence on things or persons as Puck did on Bully Bottom.

Therein, perhaps, lay the real interest of the play for its first audiences. It was a play about human ingenuity coping with natural difficulties. There was no taking for granted that Prospero could do whatever he chose or get whatever he wanted by the mere waving of a wand. The author has taken care to give an early explanation even of the clothes worn by him and by Miranda, and the general resources of their island home, by mentioning incidentally that Gonzalo's kindness had equipped their boat with 'rich garments, linen, stuffs and necessaries', just as in *The Winter's Tale* Perdita's first conversation with Florizel contrives to show us why she is dressed rather more decoratively than might be looked for in a shepherd's daughter. Not only is there to be no incongruity, there is to be no misapprehension either, and people who have begun to think Miranda rather improbably well dressed for one brought up on a desert island will be prevented at least from assuming that Prospero could make clothes for her by the omnipotence of his magic. That, at least, was the position when the audience was still obliged to listen to the words of the play to learn what it was about. We have got so thoroughly used since then to regarding it as a whole, and as a piece of literature, that our very familiarity with it is likely to come between us and its original freshness as a piece of dramatic entertainment.

Taking it from the standpoint of the Jacobean playgoer, we are given a brisk and sensational opening, with a rapid glimpse of various important people in an emergency. They pass rapidly before us and are gone, and in their place we behold the man who has called up the storm. The first two lines of the scene tell us so much, but in a few moments he takes off his enveloping robe for a quiet conversational scene with his daughter. To the believer in astrological science, the robe is not an adornment to make the wearer look impressive, or to indicate his status in the hierarchy; it has a specific function, to counteract or intensify certain planetary influences. A scientist on the modern stage can obtain much the same effect by taking off some such professional garment, be it the protective clothing of the radiologist or the plain white overall that calls up vague suggestions of the laboratory or the hospital ward. Once it is off, the man beneath it appears more human, more vulnerable, a being to be regarded with interest and even sympathy rather than uncomprehending awe. It is the best possible preparation for an account of Prospero's human relations and shortcomings in the past.

The story proceeds as that particular story always does proceed in whatever age it occurs. The wicked rich men are seen as castaways upon the shore; some of them are noble in mourning, others are plotting further wickedness, the quizzical old man contrives to be witty but is so likeable and even-tempered that he does not bore the audience, though it is obvious that his shipmates know and avoid his conversational resources. The young man is cast ashore by himself, meets and falls in love with the scientist's daughter and is somewhat gruffly snubbed by her father, who sets him to a task hitherto associated with an uncouth native servant. The comic men are cast ashore with a supply of liquor, and nearly cause serious trouble by giving drink to the native servant, who is not accustomed to it, and finally all parties are brought into unavailing conflict with the scientist, who

Pictish hunters, from Holinshed. The dress is quite an
accurate representation of that worn by the "Wild Irish"
of the sixteenth century.

triumphs not only by his technical resources but by his wisdom
and force of character, even as Stevenson and Osbourne's mis-
sionary dominates the beachcombers in *The Ebb-Tide*. Looked at
thus, we can see that the ingredients are all those of the usual
Island Romance, nowadays usually located in the South Seas.

In the course of it there are two or three incidents that remind
us of the audience's continual demand, by this time, for some of
the features of the masque. At one point the newcomers are
shown an illusory banquet, which vanishes 'with a quaint device'
when Ariel appears like a harpy and claps his wings over the
table. The trick table, which can appear bare or laden in an instant, is not extinct even now as a piece of stage carpentry.
Henslowe had one, as may be seen from the Dulwich property-
lists, for a play about a mythical personage called Bellenden or
Belin Dun, whose wonder-working table could spread itself and
serve up a banquet at will. Similarly, the wedding-masque of
Ferdinand and Miranda gives a pretext for using another familiar
piece of theatrical apparatus. The stage directions of the First
Folio indicate that while Iris and Ceres merely 'enter', Juno
'descends'. Not everybody shared Jonson's lofty contempt for

Romans and Britons, from Holinshed. The Britons are
here represented as feathered savages like the inhabitants of the New World.

plays and playhouses where a 'creaking throne comes down the
boys to please'. Jupiter had come down from the skies, and
ascended to them with great effect, in *Cymbeline*; the machinery
was there, and in working order, and there was every justification
for using it again in the new play.

One or two more of the *Cymbeline* ideas and effects are here
repeated or varied. Nobility in exile, outlined in the woodland
figure of Belarius, is perhaps intensified in the character of
Prospero, while the noble savages of the first play are replaced,
in the second, by the sub-human Caliban. The audience can be
given a child of nature once more, but one as far removed from
Cadwal and Polydore as William and Audrey were from Silvius
and Phebe in the forest of Arden. In *Cymbeline* we may imagine
the two young princes to have been played as dignified, long-
haired figures, perhaps dressed like the contemporary Irish
hunters, perhaps even feather-crowned like the Ancient Britons
who flee from the invading Romans in some of the illustrations to
Holinshed.* But the author does not make the mistake of repeat-

---

* It must be admitted that Holinshed used his illustrations quite irrespon-
sibly and got them second-hand as often as not, from books on other subjects, so his Romans in Britain may well have been meant for Spaniards
hunting Indians in the New World.

ing his effects too obviously. Next time he gives the audience a savage to look at, he takes some of the less pleasing qualities described in travellers' tales. The new savage is far from noble. His very name suggests Caribbean Cannibals, he is of unpleasing appearance and uncivil tongue, and he has 'a very ancient and fish-like smell'. At the same time he has some of the most beautiful lines in the play to speak, and his blunt animal-like simplicity makes him preferable to the debased and drunken Stephano whom he so readily serves.*

When the final situation is imminent, and Prospero's enemies are brought, all mystified and half-dazed, within the compass of his cabalistic circle, we see the visual effect of one more of the play's rare stage-directions. At the beginning of the act, Prospero has been noted as entering 'in his magic robes'. This is an important point, and worth the emphasis of a stage-direction, as it serves a double purpose. First, it shows the scientist in his professional capacity, about to conduct the last stage of a complicated but successful experiment. Then, at the moment of revelation, he uses the significant phrase

> I will *discase* me, and myself present
> As I was sometime Milan.

The gesture, and the effect, are those of the breaking of a chrysalis and the emergence of the gorgeous creature within. In his first scene, Prospero's robes had been removed to reveal the plain, everyday garments of the old hermit of the island, about to have an intimate conversation with his daughter. This time, however, the revelation is a very different one. Under the robes, he is fully dressed as the Italian nobleman he is, needing only the hat and rapier—fetched for him at once by Ariel—to stand before his

---

* Since these lines were written, Miss Lilian Harrison's production of the play for the Royal Academy of Dramatic Art has shown how much more effective Stephano is when played as a straightforward, reasonably bibulous Elizabethan seaman, who might well have sailed with Drake, and is almost, but not quite, competent to take charge of a force consisting of one timid subordinate and one unreliable native auxiliary.

visitors as one of themselves, and greater than them all. But the hat and rapier must be a hat and rapier, *not* a crown or cap of maintenance and a Sword of State for him to carry in the crook of his arm like Punch. They are the only accessories which could not be hidden under the robes, and they were the last articles assumed by the man of fashion when about to appear in company. The line reveals for us a Prospero we have not seen before; it is a request for inessential ornaments, on the part of one who has never been quite sure that he would ever have occasion for them again.

One trouble about Prospero's sublimity is that it gives him little to express in the way of human doubts and fears. After that first awkward admission to his daughter he finds it all plain sailing, or nearly so, to the very end. When he undergoes any mental conflict, or suffers any uncertainty, after that great scene, he keeps it almost entirely to himself, and only in one brief conversation with Ariel do we see any traces of a change of purpose. Audiences coming to *The Tempest* for the first time, however, without our present-day pre-knowledge of it as an English classic, might well have been looking for a grand climax of confrontation, revelation, reprimand and vengeance. The victory of Prospero's 'nobler reason' over his desire for revenge (and Jacobean audiences must have got to know quite a lot about revenge if they went at all regularly to the theatre) would come to them as a fresh and unexpected turn in the development of the play. By this time Prospero has raised himself above the main human emotions, and it is to Alonzo, accordingly, that the author gives the opportunities for expressing sorrow, despair, madness, penitence and the final half-incredulous wonder of reunion with his son.

There is no general outburst of penitence and pardon all round. Caliban makes unexpected submission and promise of amendment, but Antonio and Sebastian are Antonio and Sebastian still. There is no suggestion that they will go back to civilization any the better for their adventure, but they would be all the less well drawn if they did. Half the power and magic of this play is due to the author's skill in blending realism with its romance.

It is the same with *Henry VIII*. Instead of giving us another Romance of Science, he turns to the Romance of History, but handles it differently from the way he did in the old days. In *Henry VI* he had taken a number of impressive characters and effective episodes and slung them together without much attention to historical accuracy, in *Richard II* and its successors he had virtually dramatized Hall's Chronicle, with embellishments from Holinshed. This time we find him dealing with a historical subject in still another fashion. It is no longer something out of a book, it is something that happened in the time of the spectators' fathers and grandfathers. For the first time he is able to turn to the narratives of people who actually saw, or even took part in, some of the events described. Hall had written of the Wars of the Roses as a historian, but he wrote of the Field of Cloth-of-Gold as an eye-witness, because he was there. Wolsey's gentleman-usher George Cavendish had written a biography of his great master, and though it had not yet been printed as an independent work, John Stow had had access to the material and had incorporated much of it in his *Annals*, notably the story of King Henry's visit in masquerade to the cardinal's banquet in York Place. In the same way, Cranmer's secretary Morice had made his notes accessible to John Foxe the martyrologist, and the story of Gardiner's attempt against Cranmer, and its frustration by the personal intervention of the king, is to be found in the pages of the *Actes and Monuments*, even to the speeches of many of the people concerned. Audiences were disposed to take a detached attitude nowadays, and contemplate the actions and emotions of their stage kings, warriors and lovers without pretending to share them. The dramatist could turn this attitude to his own advantage by giving them a fine array of actions to contemplate, and speeches to listen to, that would have to be accepted without much question or contradiction because they were a reasonable echo of what was recorded as having been really done and said.

The verse, too, has the smooth-running cadence that was now

fashionable, and Victorian commentators on this account raised the idea that much of the play had been written by Fletcher and perhaps Massinger. But if so, we must assume that on this occasion, and on this occasion only, Fletcher and Massinger collaborated in using Shakespeare's sources in Shakespeare's way and with Shakespeare's attitude of mind. Perhaps it is a less extravagant assumption to suppose that the poet who could give his hearers such good imitation Greene or Marlowe at the beginning of his career could give them equally good imitation Fletcher at the end of it, to accompany the passing of a Wolsey or a Buckingham.

This is another play in which the abandonment of the boy-actress has thrown the piece out of balance. Like Isabella in *Measure for Measure*, Katharine of Aragon has become a part no longer for an intelligent boy but for a Leading Lady, and has given unintended prominence accordingly to her great antagonist. The interest of an audience naturally centres on her and on Wolsey, and automatically flags after her death at Kimbolton, so that producers are quite used to cutting most of the remaining scenes and hurrying as quickly as may be to the christening of the infant Elizabeth at the end. But to the original spectators, the ordeal of Katharine was only a part of the story. The Prologue of the play had told them of persons who had lived great and popular, and had fallen from mightiness to misery, and sure enough there passed before them the unwisely resentful Buckingham, the good Queen Katharine, and Wolsey himself, fallen 'like a bright exhalation in the evening' and leaving his pupil and protégé to make his rash attempt at tyranny over Archbishop Cranmer. It is not entirely a catalogue of decline and fall. Two figures are shown as rising to fortune, Anne Boleyn by her charm and innocence and Cranmer by his integrity, with no fore-shadowing of the scaffold and the stake that ultimately await them.

Comparing the text of the play with the narratives of Hall, Stow and Foxe, we can see how consistently and faithfully the playwright has used first-hand evidence whenever he could get it.

Details of ceremony or costume, when they are recorded by the authorities, go down into the stage-directions, and conflicting reports, when they occur, are duly transcribed for the spectators to hear, consider and use their own judgement. The matter of the king's divorce is a case in point. The chroniclers say that popular opinion held the cardinal and Anne Boleyn responsible, but that popular opinion was wrong, the king's conscience having been seriously troubled about the validity of his marriage before ever he met with Anne. Shakespeare puts the popular rumour into the mouths of his First and Second Gentlemen, and the Dukes of Norfolk and Suffolk, but he never shows or suggests any attempt on Wolsey's part to influence the king's mind in the matter, and he is careful, on the other hand, to include Wolsey's public appeal to Henry to say whether he had ever encouraged him to break with the queen, and the king's emphatic—and historical— testimony that he had done nothing of the sort. 'These are the facts,' the play seems to say. 'Study the evidence and draw your own conclusions.'

Before the rise of Queen Katharine's part, and the consequent aggrandisement of Wolsey's, the leading figure in the play was undoubtedly King Henry. Under Charles II it was Henry, not Wolsey, that Betterton played, and Lowin, before him, was said to have been coached in the part by Shakespeare himself. Like Cymbeline and Prospero the king is given little to do, considering how much he has to say, but the dramatist who is presenting a historical figure on the stage very often finds himself obliged to paint a portrait rather than tell a story, and the portrait here is a striking one when it is not obscured by the queen and the cardinal.

Henry's very first appearance is to be characteristic, he must come on, says the stage-direction, leaning on the cardinal's shoulder. That was how Henry liked to walk informally, with his arm flung across the shoulders of a familiar friend. He may have done it to Wolsey, he certainly did it to Thomas More, and there might be old men in the audience at the Globe whose fathers had seen him walk so, or who had even looked on from afar, as round-eyed boys, to see him come back triumphant from the capture of Boulogne. There must be a first glimpse of Henry's legendary affability, and the audience will be all the more able to relish the force of his legendary anger as it sweeps him off the stage at the end of the scene. Gracious to Queen Katharine, gallant to Anne in the half-dozen lines which are all we hear him speak to her, a terrible adversary to those who oppose him and a somewhat terrifying patron to those of whom he approves, the Henry of the play is very much the Henry of Elizabethan popular legend, which in its turn meant popular recollection, so that he is not too far removed from the Henry of history.

This care to reproduce the actual appearance and behaviour of historic personages was not merely incidental, but was made what we should now call a major feature of the production. The very title of the play, when it appeared at the Globe, was *All is True*. The Prologue and Epilogue were designed to lay particular emphasis on this adherence to truth, and it certainly drew comment from one member of the public who was not prepared to give it unqualified approval. Sir Henry Wotton, writing to a friend in 1613, mentions the spectacular production, with its Knights of the Garter in their insignia, and guards in their embroidered coats, as 'sufficient in truth within a while to make greatness very familiar, if not ridiculous'. We cannot tell whether Sir Henry's opinion would have been shared by the general public and had its effect on the success of the play, because when the signal-gun was let off to announce the arrival of the royal masquing-party at York Place for the cardinal's banquet, it started a fire that ultimately burned the theatre to the ground. No lives were lost. Wotton puts the damage at 'wood and straw, and a few forsaken cloaks', and mentions that one man had his breeches set on fire but put them out again with bottled beer.

But Wotton is thinking of spectators' losses alone. For the players, a great part of their stock must have gone up in smoke, including the contents of the wardrobe, the tiring-house and we cannot tell what in the way of manuscript parts and prompt-books. There may well have been other Shakespeare plays among them, of which we have no record, and can have none. Heminge and Condell ten years later published all they could lay their hands on, but by that time a new Globe had arisen on Bankside, with a public that applauded new plays by new men. For the public at Stratford there were four lines of doggerel on a gravestone, to guard the bones beneath from the fate of Yorick's, and the new monument of a local worthy, with his bust and coat of arms upon it, gazed out in respectable stolidity from the northern wall. After a professional career in rather varied urban and suburban society William Shakespeare, gentleman, had settled down at last among his own people.

The Original Publishers' Preface

to the first collected edition of Shakespeare's Plays, 1623
(The Famous First Folio)

To the Great Variety of Readers,

from the most able, to him that can but spell. There you are
numbered; we had rather you were weighed, especially when the
fate of all books depends upon your capacities, and not of your
heads alone, but of your purses. Well, it is now public, and you
will stand for your privileges, we know—to read and censure.
Do so, but buy it first. That doth best commend a book, the
stationer says. Then, how odd soever your brains be, or your
wisdoms, make your licence of the same, and spare not. Judge
your sixpenn'orth, your shillingsworth, your five-shillingsworth
at a time, or higher, so you rise to the just rates, and welcome, but
whatever you do, Buy. Censure will not drive a trade, or make the
jack go. And though you be a magistrate of wit, and sit on the
stage at Blackfriars or the Cockpit to arraign plays daily, know,
these plays have had their trial already and stood out all appeals,
and do now come forth quitted rather by a decree of Court than
any purchased letters of commendation.

It had been a thing, we confess, worthy to have been wished,
that the Author himself had lived to have set forth and overseen
his own writings. But since it hath been ordained otherwise, and
he by death departed from that right, we pray you do not envy
his friends the office of their care and pain, to have collected and
published them, and so to have published them as where before
you were abused with divers stolen and surreptitious copies,
maimed and deformed by the frauds and stealths of injurious

impostors that exposed them, even those are now offered to your view cured and perfect of their limbs, and all the rest absolute in their numbers as he conceived them who, as he was a happy imitator of nature, was a most gentle expresser of it. His mind and hand went together, and what he thought, he uttered with that earnestness, that we have scarce received from him a blot in his papers. But it is not our province, who only gather his works and give them you, to praise him; it is yours that read him. And there, we hope, to your divers capacities you will find enough both to draw and hold you, for his wit can no more lie hid than it could be lost. Read him, therefore, and again, and again, and if then you do not like him, surely you are in some manifest danger not to understand him. And so we leave you to other of his friends, whom if you need, can be your guides; if you need them not, you can lead yourselves and others. And such readers we wish him.

JOHN HEMINGE

HENRY CONDELL

Publishers' Preface

to the quarto edition of Troilus and Cressida, 1609

A Never Writer to an Ever Reader. News.

Eternal reader, you have here a new play, never staled with the stage, never clapper-clawed with the palms of the vulgar, and yet passing full of the palm comical; for it is a birth of your brain that never undertook anything comical vainly, and were but the vain names of comedies changed for the titles of commodities, or of plays for pleas, you should see all those grand censors that now style them such vanities flock to them for the main grace of their gravities; especially this author's comedies, that are so framed to the life that they serve for the most common commentaries of all the actions of our lives, showing such a dexterity and power of wit that the most displeased with plays are pleased with his comedies. And all such dull and heavy-witted worldlings as were never capable of the wit of a comedy, coming by report of them to his representations, have found that wit there that they never found in themselves, and have parted better-witted than they came, feeling an edge of wit set upon them more than ever they dreamed they had brains to grind it on. So much and such-savoured salt of wit is in his comedies, that they seem (for their height of pleasure) to be born in that sea that brought forth Venus. Amongst all there is none more witty than this, and had I time I would comment upon it, though I know it needs not (for so much as will think your testern well bestowed) but for so much worth as even poor I know to be stuffed in it. It deserves such a labour as well as the best comedy in Terence or Plautus. And believe this, that when he is gone, and his comedies out of sale, you will scramble for them, and set up a new English Inquisition.

Take this for a warning, and at the peril of your pleasure's loss, and judgments, refuse not, nor like this the less for not being sullied with the smoky breath of the multitude, but thank fortune for the 'scape it hath made amongst you, since by the grand possessors' wills I believe you should have prayed for them rather than been prayed. And so I leave all such to be prayed for (for the state of their wit's healths) that will not praise it.

VALE

Index

233